Children's Influence on Family Dynamics

The Neglected Side of Family Relationships

Children's Influence on Family Dynamics

The Neglected Side of Family Relationships

Edited by

Ann C. Crouter
Alan Booth
The Pennsylvania State University

LAWRENCE ERLBAUM ASSOCIATES, PUBLISHERS
2003   Mahwah, New Jersey   London

Camera ready copy for this book was provided by the editors.

Lawrence Erlbaum Associates, Inc., Publishers
10 Industrial Avenue
Mahwah, NJ 07430

Cover design by Kathryn Houghtaling Lacey

Library of Congress Cataloging-in-Publication Data

Children's influences on family dynamics: the neglected side
of family relationships / edited by Ann C. Crouter,
    Alan Booth.
        p. cm.

Includes bibliographical references and index.
ISBN 0-8058-4271-3 (h : alk. paper)
1. Family. 2. Children. 3. Parent and child. 4. Child rearing.
    I. Crouter, Ann C. II. Booth, Alan, 1935–

HQ518 .C535   2003
306.85–dc21

                                        2002192791
                                               CIP

Books published by Lawrence Erlbaum Associates are printed
on acid-free paper, and their bindings are chosen for strength
and durability.

Printed in the United States of America
10 9 8 7 6 5 4 3 2 1

Contents

Preface

Any parent who has raised more than one child is likely to be keenly aware of subtle or even striking differences among their offspring. Although siblings raised together in the same family often differ markedly in terms of gender, temperament, abilities, interests, personality, choices of friends and activities, and so on, all too often family researchers have ignored individual differences in children. The central premise of this volume is that children bring personal qualities to their relationships with other family members that help shape family interaction, family relationships, and even family processes that family researchers have called "parenting". The chapters collected in this volume address how children's personal qualities make their mark on families in ways that may in turn influence childrens' subsequent development.

The chapters in this volume are based on the presentations and discussions from a national symposium on "Children's influence on family dynamics: The neglected side of family relationships" held at the Pennsylvania State University, December 6-7, 2001, as the ninth in a series of annual interdisciplinary symposia focused on family issues. The book is divided into four sections, each dealing with a different aspect of the topic. The first section sets the stage by focusing on the features of children that make a difference, as well as the kinds of research designs that are likely to shed light on the role of child influences. David Reiss, a psychiatrist whose research weds family systems theory and behavior genetics questions, provides a provocative overview, using data from an ambitious longitudinal study of the role of the nonshared family environment in adolescents' lives. Thoughtful commentary is provided by Kathleen McCartney, a developmental psychologist, Xiaojia Ge, a family sociologist, and J. Richard Udry, a demographer with wide-ranging interests. In distinct ways, their chapters underscore the importance of leaving behind questions about the relative importance of nature vs. nurture and emphasizing instead the mechanisms that link family processes and the individual characteristics that children and adolescents bring to their family interactions and relationships.

The second section of the volume focuses on early childhood, particularly the role of infant temperament and other individual differences in very young children in shaping their parents' behaviors, reactions in turn that feedback and influence the developing child. The lead paper is provided by Susan Crockenberg and Esther Leerkes, developmental psychologists with a keen sense for the nuances of family interaction in the early years. The discussants' chapters emphasize different aspects of this complex topic. Cynthia A. Stifter draws attention to physical issues such as infant colic. James P. McHale, Kathryn C. Kavanaugh, and Julia M. Berkman, and Pamela M. Cole, in different ways, integrate insights derived from clinically-informed research.

Attention in the third section moves to adolescence, a time when young people are able to exert more choice in how they spend their time and who they spend time with. Lead speakers Margaret Kerr and Håkan Stattin, using a longitudinal data set on Swedish youth, take a provocative stance in which they argue that by adolescence children exert considerable influence over so-called parenting behaviors such as parental monitoring. They develop an elegant and intricate picture of how the child influences parenting and parenting in turn influences the developing adolescent. Not all of the discussants agree with Kerr and Stattin's argument, however, and each in different ways underscores the importance of learning more about the extrafamilial context, including the culture in which families are embedded. Elizabeth G. Menaghan, a family sociologist, encourages researchers to think about extrafamilial influences such as parents' work lives. Gene H. Brody, a developmentalist working with a unique sample of rural African-American families, provides research findings that are somewhat at odds with the Kerr and Stattin argument. Deborah M. Capaldi's remarks pull from the remarkable legacy of research on parenting conducting by her research group at the Oregon Social Learning Center. Kerr and Stattin have the last word in a short chapter in which they respond to their discussants.

In the final section of the volume, Eleanor E. Maccoby steps back and looks at the big picture, bringing a wealth of experience to the task. Indeed, her insights and observations extend back over 50 years and show that psychologists have recognized child influences for a long time, even though they have not always found their way into analytic models. The importance of gender as a characteristic that children bring to their family environments weaves its way through her chapter. Susan M. McHale and Ann C. Crouter use examples from their family studies to show that children's gender functions as a fundamental building block of the family context. They argue that the gender constellation of sibship provides opportunities and constraints for parents and leads to different patterns of family dynamics. Håkan Stattin and Margaret Kerr caution that in spite of the scholarly focus on viewing parent-child relationships as a reciprocal process unfolding over time, this emphasis has not yet found its way into advice given to parents. They also describe temporal and conceptual features that need to to be taken into account in studying parent-child relationships as dyads.

Finally, Nicki R. Crick, a developmental psychologist, responds to Maccoby's points with illustrations from her own research on relational aggression, a gendered quality that children bring to their relationships with family members and peers. The volume ends with an integrative commentary provided by Lilly Shanahan and Juliana M. Sobolewski that pulls the themes of the volume together and points the way for future research.

I

What Features of Children Shape Family Relationships and How?

1

Child Effects on Family Systems: Behavioral Genetic Strategies

David Reiss
Center for Family Research
George Washington University Medical Center

The field of quantitative behavioral genetics draws inferences about genetic and environmental influences on behavior using genetically informed designs. Most of these designs employ comparisons between monozygotic (MZ) twins and dizygotic (DZ) twins or, in adoption studies, compare characteristics of birth parents with comparable characteristics of their adopted children. Nowadays, this field is often conceived as a preliminary and indirect peek at the influences of specific genes on behavior. According to this view, we are now on the threshold of a new era in which advances in molecular genetics will provide a much clearer and more precise view of how specific genes shape our thoughts and actions. The recent preliminary maps of the human genome have heightened interest in this prospect. The simple optimism inherent in these hopes obscures a very different role for quantitative genetics. In fact, these familiar tools now promise developments that are more realistic and closer at hand, serving to unravel the relationship between family dynamics and child development. First, they can help us properly weigh the role of children themselves in evoking and influencing the dynamics of their own families. Second, these tools can help clarify reciprocal child and parent influences as they unfold across development. Third, they can help delineate those aspects of families that make them more or less vulnerable to these influences. These new uses of familiar tools may lead us to surprising places. They may improve understanding of the interplay between genetic and social influences in development and provide an even fuller understanding of how genetic influences are expressed in thought and behavior. I will review some of the logic of quantitative behavioral genetics and illustrate its relevance for understanding child effects and reciprocal responses from families.

CHILD EFFECTS AND THE LOGIC OF
QUANTITATIVE BEHAVIORAL GENETICS:
PROSPECTS AND PROBLEMS

The value of quantitative behavioral genetics in delineating child effects depends on the validity of inferences drawn from genetically informed studies. Of central importance, as in most fields in developmental psychology, are the assumptions on which these inferences are drawn. There are two major approaches to research design and each is built around certain assumptions.

The first is the twin-sibling method. The simplest designs use a sample of monozygotic (MZ) and dizygotic (DZ) twins. MZ twins are genetically identical. DZ twins share, on average, 50% of the genes that make us different. If a trait is highly heritable, then MZ twins should be more similar to each other than are DZ twins. Recently, our group has developed this design further by adding ordinary siblings (FS) and full siblings in stepfamilies where both siblings are the biological offspring of the mother (FSS). We also included half siblings in stepfamilies (HSS), both children are mother's, but only one child is the stepfather's. HS share 25% of individual difference genes. We also included genetically unrelated or "blended" siblings (BS), where both the mother and father bring a child from a former marriage. In this design, a heritable trait should show within-pair correlations that approximate this pattern: MZ > DZ = FS = FSS > HS > BS. We have referred to this as a "genetic cascade."

These comparisons across sibling types have been used to draw inferences about environmental influences as well. If the correlations in all six groups are relatively high and show little genetic cascade, we can conclude that environmental factors common to siblings are most important in the trait under investigation. These factors might include shared experiences in the family, such as parental psychopathology, or shared experiences of important extra-family environments, such as the neighborhood. Surprisingly, most studies have shown relatively small influences for shared environment. If the between-sibling correlations are relatively low, also without much genetic cascade, we conclude that experiences unique for each sibling are most important for the traits under study. These might include differential parenting, serious physical illness in one sibling, or the powerful role of a teacher or friend of one sibling. Measurement error can also produce low correlations and must be distinguished from nonshared environment.

The fundamental assumption behind comparisons such as these is that no spurious circumstance, other than variations in genetic similarity, would account for the genetic cascade. This supposition is called the equal environments assumption. In the case of our expanded design, we assume equal correlations across all six groups of all non-genetic influences on the trait under study. At first glance, this seems untenable. For example, in a devastating critique of the twin method over 40 years ago, the family therapist Don Jackson (Jackson, 1960) argued that parents were much more likely to treat MZ twins more similarly, to dress them alike for example, than they were to treat DZ twins. However, data has shown that this form of similar treatment has little effect on any interesting aspects of child development (Lochlin & Nichols, 1976). Moreover, differences in similarity between MZ and DZ twins remain in subsamples of twins whose zygosity has been misdiagnosed (Scarr & Carter-Saltzman, 1979) and in twins reared apart (Pedersen et al., 1991).

Does the equal environments assumption hold for the stepfamily addition to the twin method? For example, full siblings in stepfamilies live together for the entire duration of the younger sibling's life. They live together in a pre-divorce household, again with their mother when she is living without a husband and once more in the stepfamily when she remarries. However, blended siblings may live together for only brief periods (in our study we required a minimum of five years). Further, isn't it possible that mothers in stepfamilies will treat full siblings, both of whom are her biological offspring, more similarly than in blended siblings where they are not? We have shown for a broad range of measures that neither of these factors influence within-pair similarities in stepsiblings (Reiss, Neiderhiser, Hetherington, & Plomin, 2000). Although all these findings support the validity of the equal environments assumption, both for the standard twin method and for our extension of it, there is still good reason to question it, as we will show in the next section.

The other major design in this area is the adoption study. The most common is the retrospective design. Here, children who were adopted soon after birth are assessed in adolescence or adulthood, as are their adoptive parents. Data on their biological parents are usually obtained from public or hospital records. In many cases, these studies attempt to reconstruct the adopted child's family environment by retrospective accounts of both the child and the adoptive parents. Genetic influences are assumed if there is a substantial correlation between characteristics of the biological parents and those of the children they placed in adoptive care. The second approach to design is the prospective adoption study. There is only one example of this kind of adoption study (Plomin, DeFries, & Fulker, 1988). Here, adopted offspring (AO) and their adoptive parents (AP) are enrolled in a longitudinal study soon after the adoption is accomplished and the biological parents are assessed directly. In this design, a control group of biological parents (BP) rear their own children (BO). If a trait were strongly heritable, we would expect that parent-child correlations should be much greater for BP-BO than AP-AO.

One weakness of the adoption design is the difficulty in ascertaining whether we are measuring in children, particularly younger ones, a trait that is comparable to that in the adult. For example, what characteristics of a three-year-old might be correlated with unipolar depression in a biological or an adoptive mother? Further, even if we are reasonably certain we are measuring comparable traits, let us say verbal intelligence in a 6-year-old child and a parent, there is no assurance

that the same genetic factors influence both 6-year-old and adult behavior. Indeed, the influences of genetic factors on the same trait can switch on and off in a
matter of months in young children (Plomin et al., 1994a) and in as little as three
years in adolescents (Reiss et al., 2000). These weaknesses can be offset by the
use of siblings in the adoption design. Adoptive parents often adopt another child
or have one of their own. In either case, the adopted child and its sibling are
genetically unrelated, much like blended siblings. Typically, siblings in families
where biological parents raise their own children are full siblings sharing approximately 50% of their individual difference genes. From a genetic point of view, the
contrast between siblings in families where biological parents rear siblings and
adoptive parents rear siblings is identical to FS and BS in stepfamilies. Further,
the equal environments assumption must hold for genetic inferences to be drawn
from contrasts between within-pair correlations.

Genetic inferences in adoption studies are based on two assumptions. The
first is that adoption agencies or biological parents have not purposefully selected
adoptive parents that are similar in personality, cognitive ability, and psychopathology to biological parents. This assumption is known as selective placement.
The second assumption is that the personality or psychopathology of the biological mother does not exert intrauterine effects on the child. The most conspicuous
examples are impulsive or anxious women who may abuse alcohol or other substances injurious to the fetus. Both assumptions are best investigated in the prospective adoption design. In the only study of this kind ever conducted, selective
placement and intrauterine factors—as measured in the study—were trivial (Plomin,
Devries, & Fulker, 1988). However, adoptions have become more open and biological parents play a greater role in selecting adoptive families. This may lead
not only to selective placement but, even more challenging to the logic of the
design, to biological parents participating in the rearing of their own children.
Further, we have new information on intrauterine factors that influence physical
and psychological development of the child. These include maternal smoking
(Griesler, Kandel, & Davies, 1998; Weissman, Warner, Wickramaratne, & Kandel,
1999) and severe maternal stress (Glover, 1997; Niederhofer & Reiter, 2000)

THE ROLE OF HERITABLE CHARACTERISTICS OF CHILDREN IN EVOKING FAMILY PROCESS

Almost all twin and adoption studies have focused on weighting genetic and environmental influences on a broad range of human behavior, including temperament, personality, cognitive abilities, and psychopathology. In the early 1980s,
David Rowe was the first to explore the use of these methods for studying the
family environment of children (Rowe, 1981, 1983). He asked children about
their family environment; for some measures, particularly those related to

perceived parental acceptance, he found that MZ twins were more similar than DZ twins. He did not find these differences for adolescents' reports of parental control. After these early reports, a number of investigators, comparing MZ twins and DZ twins on measures of the family environment, reported similar findings. For example, using a twins-reared-apart design, Plomin and colleagues reported MZ twins to be more similar in their reports on the family environments they remembered from childhood (Plomin, McClearn, Pedersen, Nesselroade, & Bergeman, 1988), particularly for measures of warmth and conflict but not control. This finding was replicated in another twin-reared-apart study (Bouchard & McGue, 1990). All these studies used the twins' own perceptions of their family environment. Findings suggested heritable factors in children might evoke or influence their family environment, at least as they perceive it. They were the first clues of a genetically-based child effect.

However, personality and psychopathology—characteristics for which genetic influences are well established—might color these perceptions. In studying the effects of heritable characteristics of children on family dynamics, we need more direct evidence of their impact. Thus, it is important that these earlier findings have been replicated by other methods. For example, Goodman and Stevenson (1991) used data from extensive interviews of parents concerning their parenting. A novel feature of this study was that the parents did not recognize the zygosity of many of the MZ twins. Likewise, Braungart and colleagues found greater similarity between biological than adopted siblings in the HOME measure which uses data obtained by trained observers (Braungart, Plomin, Fulker, & DeFries, 1992). Dunn and her colleagues used a similar comparison of siblings from the same study (Dunn & Plomin, 1986; Dunn, Plomin, & Daniels, 1986; Dunn, Plomin, & Nettles, 1985). They used coded videotapes to study mother-child relationships in 3-year-old siblings studied at different points in time but at the same age. Biologically related siblings were more similar to each other than adoptive siblings on videocoded measures of affection and control. This comparison held in follow-up studies when the younger siblings were 4 and the older ones were 7 (Rende, Slomkowski, Stocker, Fulker, & Plomin, 1992b).

Our team at George Washington University, in collaboration with Robert Plomin when he was at Penn State and Mavis Hetherington at the University of Virginia, conducted the most comprehensive investigation of this kind. We studied adolescent twins and siblings at the mean age of 13 and then again at 16 using the full spectrum of sibling similarity, as described above, from MZ to BS. Further, we used child and parent reports of parent-child relationships as well as highly reliable coding of videotaped records of parent child interaction in their own homes. We used similar measurement techniques to assess sibling relationships. The findings replicated and extended the results that had been obtained in the previous two decades.

First, we found that comparisons across our six sibling groups suggested moderate to substantial genetic influences on almost all dimensions of parent–child relationships, particularly for mothers' and fathers' warmth and support and for their conflict and negativity. Figure 1.1 illustrates the genetic cascade for a measure of mother's negativity that combines her report, the child's report, and the coded videotaped record of their interaction. We also found small to moderate genetic influences on parental monitoring of their children and their attempts and success in controlling their misbehavior. Similar to several previous studies (Daniels & Plomin, 1985; Rende, Slomkowski, Stocker, Fulker, et al., 1992a), we also found small genetic influences on sibling relationships. That is, heritable factors in each sibling played a small role in evoking both warmth and negativity from the other sibling. Of particular interest was our analysis of disagreements and conflict between mother and father about each of the siblings. Because this marital conflict is specific for each child, it is possible to compare the marital conflict occasioned by each sibling and correlate these across our six sibling types. We found evidence for moderate genetic influence here as well, suggesting those heritable features of children influence the marital conflict of their parents.

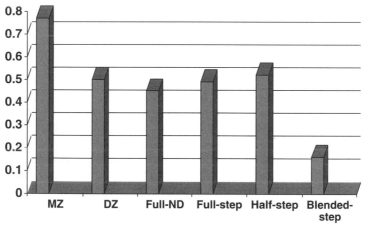

FIG. 1.1. Mother's negativity toward child: Within sibship correlations across sibling types. Numbers on vertical axis are intraclass correlations within sibships.

These findings raise both methodological and theoretical questions. On methods, we may ask whether contrasts among the sibling types we have just summarized suggest that the equal environment assumption has regularly been violated after all. In a recent review, Rutter takes this position (Rutter, Pickles, Murray, & Eaves, 2001). If MZ twins are treated more similarly than DZ twins, is that not reason to be suspicious, once again, that the twin method overestimates genetic influences in general and, in particular, on the family environment? However, this is unlikely to be the case. Violations of the equal environment assumption, when this assumption is precisely defined, refer to inequality of treatment across groups of twins or of siblings only if this inequality *originates* in the non-genetic environment. It expressly does not refer to inequalities across groups that are evoked by the heritable characteristics of the twins or siblings. As we understand more about the reciprocal influences of child and environment, this distinction must be increasingly stringent. Thus, it is important that the genetic influences on family dynamics we have reviewed have been found in twins reared apart and in twins whose zygosity was misdiagnosed. Further initial attempts to determine whether similarities in parental treatments reflect children's initiatives or their own have favored the former (Lytton, 1977; O'Connor, Hetherington, Reiss, & Plomin, 1995).

From a theoretical perspective, these data do argue that heritable features of children influence the principal subsystems of the family: parent-child, sibling, and marital. However, we may ask whether expensive and comprehensive genetic designs are necessary to illustrate child effects of this kind. Isn't this a rather simple update of the analyses carried out by R. Q. Bell over a quarter of a century ago (Bell, 1968)? Most researchers would conclude that if the story stopped here it would hardly be worth the telling. Rather, the fact of the pervasive influence of heritable characteristics of children on their families is a tool for a refreshed and more penetrating investigation of some of the central questions of child development and of family dynamics.

Two lines of investigation have opened. First, these pervasive influences of genetic factors on family systems have proved to be a new tool for understanding the relationship among family systems themselves. For example, in our adolescent twin and sibling study, we explored the well-known relationship between three family subsystems: mother-child relationships, father-child relationships, and sibling relationships. Since heritable factors in the child are associated with all three, it is plausible that these factors could account for any of the observed associations. For example, a child with genetically influenced irritability might evoke negative reactions from each parent and from a sibling. This common influence of a heritable characteristic could account for observed associations across the three subsystems. In fact, the results are just the opposite. Using multivariate techniques we will describe below, we found that genetic factors common to three subsystems accounted for very little of their association. Indeed, environment common to both siblings, the shared environment, account for the preponderance of the associations suggesting social dynamics, not genetics, accounts for the coordination of subsystems within the family. In this instance, a genetically informed design underscores the importance of familywide influences on the coordination of its subsystems. The adolescents' genes play no role in this process.

More pertinent to the topic covered in this volume, however, are the implications of these genetic influences for the development of the children. In contrast *to observed associations among family systems* we have just summarized, when we examine *the observed association between family systems and adolescent development* a very different picture merges. Here genetic factors play a central and perplexing role, one that others and we are still trying to unravel.

FAMILY SYSTEMS AND PSYCHOLOGICAL DEVELOPMENT: THE ROLE OF GENETICALLY INFLUENCED CHILD EFFECTS

All of the results from genetic studies we have summarized so far rely on what is now called "univariate" analyses. We have asked a simple question: is there an association between an individual's genotype and their reported and observed behaviors? The behaviors we have summarized are relationship behaviors—those of the child and those of others in the family who respond to the child. More recently, a number of workers have elaborated multivariate, quantitative behavioral genetic techniques. These are most relevant when we are interested in the association of two or more variables when each of the variables shows genetic influence. Multivariate analyses can estimate, first, whether the same genetic factors influence both variables. Second, it can estimate the percentage of the covariance between the two that is accounted for by common genetic influences. For example, in our data we found that antisocial behavior and negativity between mother and child show heritabilities of over 50%. We also found, as have many other investigators, that the observed association between the two was high, in our case .59. Are the genetic influences on each variable the same and, if so, how much of this association might be accounted for by these common influences?

Our estimates rest on cross-correlations. For each sibling type, for example, we correlate the mother's negativity towards one sibling with the antisocial behavior measured in the other sibling as shown in Figure 1.2. If genetic factors account for the association between the two, then we would

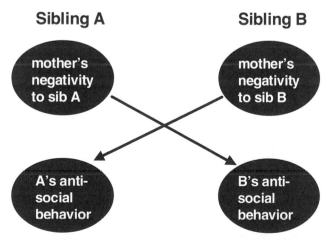

FIG. 1.2.   Illustration of cross-sibling correlations for detecting overlap of genetic influences.

expect very high cross-sibling, cross-variable correlations for MZ twins and almost no correlation for blended siblings. In fact, this is precisely what we found. The cross-correlations, relating maternal negativity towards one sibling with antisocial behavior in the other, for MZ twins were .62 and BS were .06. DZ was .27, FS was .29, FSS was .25, and HS was .27. Figure 1.3 shows these results graphically.

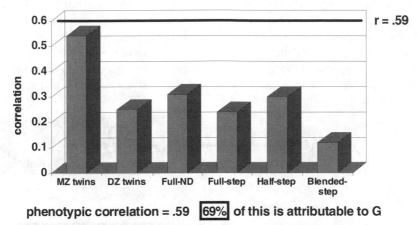

phenotypic correlation = .59 $\boxed{69\%}$ of this is attributable to G

FIG. 1.3. Overlapping genetic influences on mother's negativity and adolescent antisocial behavior: comparing cross sibling correlations across groups.

Only this last was "out of order," but the overall cascade+ suggests genetic factors played a central role in the association. Indeed, we estimated that 71% of the association was attributable to common genetic influences. In our study of adolescent twins and siblings, this finding was quite typical. It held for many associations for a range of dimensions for mother-child and father-child relationships, including their negativity, warmth and support, and monitoring and control of their children. It also held for the relationships between parental conflict about the child and several measures of child adjustment. It held as well for a range of measures of adjustment in our adolescents, including depressive symptoms, social responsibility, and self-worth. In effect, many associations that had previously been attributed to psychological or social mechanisms must now be regarded as, in some way, implicating genetics. The genetic factors influencing the measure of social relationships and the genetic factors influencing the measure of adjustment were highly correlated, a circumstance known as *gene • environment (G • E) correlation.* Other investigators are now searching for links of this kind involving parenting and the behavior of young children (Deater-Deckard, 2000), measures of variation in adolescent-family and adolescent-school "connectedness", on the one hand, with depressive symptoms, on the other (Jacobson & Rowe, 1999) and among socioeconomic status, stress, and social support, on the one hand, and physical health, on the other, in adults (Lichtenstein, Harris,

Pedersen, & McClearn, 1993; Lichtenstein & Pedersen, 1995). Important G • E correlations were found in all these studies but varied depending on gender and the sources of data about the social relationships.

What could account for these astonishing results? There are three possible explanations. First, in the case of parent or sibling relationships the same genetic factors could account for both parenting and adjustment because parents and their biological offspring share 50% of their individual difference genes and siblings share, on average, 50%. Thus, genetic factors that lead to antisocial behavior in children may lead, when these children become parents, to irritable and hostile relationships with *their* children. This is known as *passive G • E correlation* and is illustrated in Figure 1.4. Second, genetic factors may influence major domains of child adjustment such as antisocial behavior, depressive symptoms, self-esteem, and social responsibility.

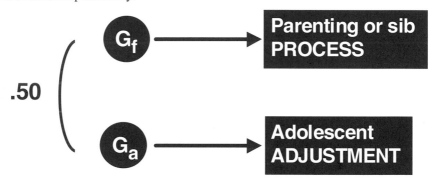

FIG. 1.4.   Passive gene-environment correlation.

These child problems might then, secondarily, disrupt parenting and sibling relationships. We have called this the *child effects evocative model.* Lastly, genetic factors might influence the child's temperament, perceptual styles, and social skills. These heritable features may elicit parental and sibling responses that in turn amplify the child's traits into distinctive features of adjustment. For example, genetic factors influence irritability and distress to limitations in infants and toddlers. (Goldsmith, Lemery, Buss, & Campos, 1999). These same features, according to the work of van den Boom, also elicit withdrawal and nonresponsiveness from parents (van den Boom & Hoeksma, 1994). Those parental responses may amplify the child's adjustment process. The role of parental responses to infant irritability is suggested by the positive results of improving their sensitivity to children's communicative signals (van den Boom, 1994, 1995). We term this the *parent effect evocative model.* A sequence of this kind is illustrated in Figure 1.5 for mother's negativity and child antisocial behavior. Can such a sequence be confirmed using genetically informative designs? At least five separate steps are necessary for verification.

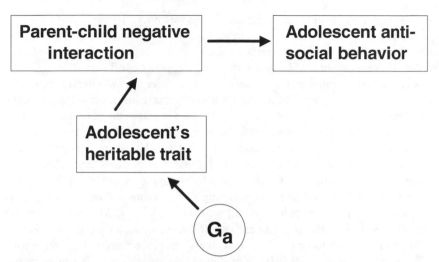

FIG. 1.5.   The parent effects evocative model.

First, there must be evidence of G • E correlation. As indicated, the evidence is strong in our data and initial reports from other investigators note the same phenomena. There may be effects of age, gender, and observer that are not yet understood.

Second, it is important to verify that the genetic effects in question are evocative rather than passive. Twin designs cannot make this distinction clearly, when the social relationships under study are between genetically related members of the same family. Adoption studies are crucial here and it is relevant that two preliminary reports from adoption studies confirm the importance of evocative effects. For example, in a study of adolescents, Ge and his colleagues compared adopted offspring of biological parents with substance/abuse antisocial disorders and those who did not. Adoptive parental responses to the child were associated with the presence or absence of psychopathology in the biological parent and this effect was mediated by hostile and antisocial behavior in the adopted offspring (Ge et al., 1996). A similar finding was recently reported for younger children (O'Connor, Deater-Deckard, Fulker, Rutter, & Plomin, 1998). Both studies also reported associations of parenting factors with child adjustment that were independent of genetic factors.

A third step in pursuing this idea is a variant of a problem that faces all developmental researchers. The parent effects evocative model posits that several developmental events occur in sequence. First comes the genetic influence on a child's behavior that is important to a parent. This is followed by a parental response that, in a third step, amplifies the child's heritable characteristics. Longitudinal studies are an important approach in verifying an hypothesized sequence of this kind and it is no different when one of the steps is a genetic influence. However, longitudinal studies are useful only during periods when we know all the relevant variables are undergoing substantial change. In adolescence, for example, there is ample evidence that both child characteristics and parental responses show a good deal of variation across time. Can we say the same for genetic influence?

This question emphasizes the distinction between an individual's genotype that is fixed at conception and the expression of genetic influences that can occur at any point across development. It is widely known that many heritable diseases, such as Alzheimer's, are not expressed until adult life even though the search for their early antecedents are continuing and important. The same is true of genetic influences on psychological adjustment of children and adolescents. Indeed, we can use the same multivariate techniques for studying emerging genetic influences as those described above for relating two or more variables. These techniques use within-sibling pair, cross-time correlations. For example, we correlate antisocial behavior in sibling 1 in earlier adolescence with antisocial behavior in sibling 2 in later adolescence. This analysis is most informative if genetic influences are strong at both times. If we see the genetic cascade, across sibling types, comparing cross-sibling/cross-time correlations across our six sibling groups we can infer that the genetic factors that influence antisocial behavior in early adolescence are the same as those that influence this same behavior in later adolescence. If there is little or no genetic cascade, we can conclude that the genetic influences that operate in early adolescence are different than those that operate three years later. In other words, the genetic influences in later adolescence are new. Evidence of this kind provides a good estimate of whether we are studying individuals during a time of genetic change, a good period for exploring the parent-effects hypothesis, or a period of genetic quiescence where a test of the hypothesis will be fruitless.

Our data suggest that adolescence is, indeed, a time of genetic change. For example, for adolescent social behavior we found that heritability at earlier adolescence was 67%. Thirty-six percent of these genetic influences operate in early adolescence but are no longer operative three years later. The heritability of antisocial behavior at time 2 does not change—it is 68%. However, new genetic influences operate. Indeed, of the total genetic factors influencing antisocial behavior in later adolescence, 38% were not influential three years before. A more dramatic finding was obtained for sociability. Here about half the genetic influences operating in earlier adolescence were not operating three years later. Further, half the genetic influences operating later were not operating three years before. Similar changes in genetic influence on the same behavior has been found during the toddler period (Plomin et al., 1994a). Initial reports suggest that the age periods from 4 to 10 may show less change in genetic expression (van den Oord & Rowe, 1997). The same stability is true for cognitive and personality measurers across broad spans of adult life (Pedersen & Reynolds, 1998; Plomin, Pedersen, Lichtenstein, & McClearn, 1994b; Viken, Rose, Kaprio, & Koskenvuo, 1994).

The fourth step is to use longitudinal data to determine causal ordering according to the parent effects hypothesis. Does genetic influence on family relationships occur before genetic influence on adjustment? In the case of antisocial behavior, mother-child negativity is positively associated with antisocial behavior and her warmth and support is negatively associated with it. Do the genetic influences on these aspects of the mother-child relationships precede the genetic influences on antisocial behavior? Such a sequence would support but not prove the model in Figure 2. Jenae Neiderhiser has devised the genetic equivalent of a cross-lagged model to answer questions such as these (Neiderhiser, Reiss, Hetherington, & Plomin, 1999). She found that genetic influences on positive relationships for mothers, fathers, and siblings precede genetic influences on antisocial behavior. In only one instance did genetic influences on a negative attribute of relationship precede genetic influence on antisocial behavior—father's negativity. Indeed, a substantial portion of genetic variation in antisocial behavior in later adolescence is associated with a *lack of endearing, heritable qualities* in the child rather with the *presence of objectionable heritable qualities*. This crucial social information might be of considerable benefit in the search for specific genetic polymorphisms that influence antisocial behavior in adolescence.

A fifth step helps make the parent effects model more plausible. The hypothesis proposed that family relationships might mediate the influence of genetic factors on a range of child, adolescent, and adult adjustments. In other words, family process is posited to be a critical component of the mechanisms of the expression of genetic influence on behavior. They may be the last essential step in a long chain of events that begins with the transcription of genetic information from DNA to RNA. RNA is an effective mediator of DNA because all the genetic information inherent in the four-base code of DNA is retained in the coding of RNA. How much genetic information is it possible for family relationships to encode? We know that children differ on a broad array of dimensions of adjustment. Quantitative genetic analyses, and molecular analyses, suggest that a number of different genes may be involved. It seems likely that there is some specificity of association between particular genes or sets of genes and specific types of child and adolescent behaviors. If family relationships serve to mediate the expression of genetic influences on the ontogeny of these distinct genetically influenced behaviors, then it too must show the capacity to "encode" genetic influences. That is, genetic influences acting on one family subsystem or on one quality of family subsystem should be distinct from those acting on another. There should be specificity of genetic influences on family relationships if family relationships serve a central function of mediating these influences on adjustment.

The bivariate methods summarized above for detecting specific genetic influence on distinct measures of adjustment and distinct genetic influences in earlier and later adolescence are applicable here. To perform this analysis we first correlated the entire mother, father, sibling, and marital measures—12 in all, with each other. Of these correlations, 34 equaled or exceeded .20. Of these 34, 30 of them showed a preponderance of distinct genetic influences. That is, the genetic influence on one measure in the pair of relationship variables was, for the most part, distinct from the genetic influence on the other. For example, the warmth and positivity that fathers showed their adolescent children was correlated with the same variable in mothers (r = .42). Further, the genetic influences on mothers and on fathers' warmth were substantial (35% and 31%, respectively). However, there was *no* correlation between these two sets of genetic influences. This suggests that the heritable characteristics in children that elicit maternal warmth are entirely different from the characteristics that elicit paternal warmth.

To cite another striking example, marital conflict about the child and father's negativity towards the child were highly correlated, replicating many previous studies that did not use a genetically informed design. Moreover, the genetic influences on each are substantial. However, there was relatively little correlation between these genetic influences. We also found that the monitoring and control variables, measured across time, showed little common genetic influence between earlier and later influence. Thus, three dimensions of family relationships appear to encode a great deal of genetic "information": the nature of the subsystem (marital, parental, or sibling), the quality of the relationships (negativity, warmth and support, monitoring and control) or the time in development (earlier versus later adolescence). In sum, these first analyses suggest that the family, considered as a whole, is both discriminating and sensitive to distinction and variation among heritable features in their children. On these grounds, it appears well suited to accomplish the final process of transducing genetic influence into variations in adjustment.

The evidence we have just reviewed makes the parent-effects evocative model plausible. More data are needed, however. First, no one has yet shown that family relationships evoked by heritable characteristics of children do, in fact, influence subsequent change in an important index of adjustment. Neiderhiser's data suggest this. However, twin data cannot distinguish evocative from passive G • E correlation. Thus, her data need to be supplemented by those obtained from a longitudinal adoption study where we can determine the temporal sequence of heritable characteristics in the child, evoked responses in adoptive parents, and subsequent change in child adjustment. Second, no one has shown that by altering parental response to heritable characteristics in their children, adverse genetic influences on behavior can be aborted and positive influences can be enhanced. The work of van den Boom suggests that interventions can effectively be made to alter parents' responses to children with difficult temperaments. Further, these interventions encourage development that is more favorable. However, van den Boom's work cannot delineate the role of genetic influences in this process. As we will show, the design of a suitable, longitudinal adoption study, and an informative preventive, intervention study go hand in hand.

FAMILY FACTORS THAT MODERATE GENETICALLY INFLUENCED CHILD EFFECTS

The idea that genetic influence on a range of behaviors is mediated, in specific ways, by family process is a hopeful one. It is another blow to the notion of genetic determinism because it suggests that genetic influences may be as malleable as other risk factors that are now common targets for efforts at preventive intervention. Preventive interventions that focus on the responses of parents and others to heritable features of the child might reduce adverse genetic influence on development and enhance positive influences.

Is there evidence that some characteristics of the family might influence their response to heritable characteristics of their children and thereby alter the expression of genetic influences? The impact of environmental circumstances on gene expression is termed *gene x environment (G x E) interaction*. Adoption studies are the most powerful designs to detect these effects. In nonadoptive families, as we have noted, there is a substantial correlation between the offspring's genotype and the rearing environment. Some of this may be due to passive G • E correlation. In adoption studies where there is no selective placement, children at genetic risk are equally likely to be reared in favorable and unfavorable adoptive family environments. This distribution enhances the likelihood of detecting interaction between family factors and genetic influences. Some have argued that the range of environments in adopted families is restricted and hence environmental effects, or their interaction with genetic influences is impaired (Stoolmiller, 1999). However, such criticism overlooks the elimination of passive G • E correlation in adoption studies. Variation in adoptive families is "pure environment." Moreover, many studies show that adoptive families are well distributed along several measures of parental and marital functioning (e.g., the work of Cadoret, cited below).

Evidence for G x E interaction, particularly where the E is a characteristic of the family, does not address the parent-effects evocative model directly. Data of this kind simply say that attributes of the family affect gene expression. This makes the hypothesis more plausible but more specific data, as we note below, are required. Most evidence of G x E interaction comes from retrospective adoption studies. As noted, these are conducted when the adopted offspring are in adolescence or adulthood. Characteristics of their biological parents are usually ascertained through public or medical records and characteristics of the adoptive family during the offspring's earlier childhood must also be reconstructed. Within these limits, adoption studies have yielded very interesting data. Of particular interest are *cross-fostering studies* in which offspring of affected biological parents and those who are not affected are each equally distributed to favorable and unfavorable adoptive family environments. Are heritable disorders more likely to occur when the rearing environment is unfavorable?

Most work in this area has concentrated on alcoholism and antisocial behavior, in large part because these attributes in biological parents can be readily obtained from public or clinical records. A series of studies has shown that alcoholism, other substance abuse disorders and antisocial behavior are of low frequency in the adopted offspring if the biological parent does not have these disorders but are much more frequent if they do, *particularly when the child is reared in an unfavorable environment* (Cadoret, Troughton, Bagford, & Woodworth, 1990; Cadoret, Yates, Troughton, Woodworth, et al., 1995; Cloninger & Gottesman, 1987; Cloninger, Sigvardsson, Bohman, & von Knorring, 1982). These studies attempted to circumvent the limits of retrospective assessment of the rearing environment by using measures of events that could be documented or easily recollected. Cloninger used social class of the adoptive family in early childhood and the number of postnatal placements of the adopted child, before final adoption, as a retrospective proxy for environmental effects and family stress. The number of temporary placements could, of course, reflect features of the child—perhaps heritable ones. This is a confounding circumstance that cannot be addressed in retrospective studies. Cadoret used major impairment in adoptive parent mental health, severe marital difficulties or divorce, and severe legal difficulties of adoptive parents. None of these are immune to child effects either. In Cadoret's studies, the adopted child and adoptive parents were directly assessed. In other cross-fostering studies similar G x E interactions were observed for depression for women but not for men (Cadoret, Winokur, Langbehn, & Troughton, 1996). Tienari and his colleagues have conducted a cross-fostering study of offspring of women hospitalized for schizophrenia in Finland (Tienari et al., 1994). In this study, the hospital diagnosis of the mothers was confirmed by research interviews of the mothers. Moreover, the overall adoptive family, as a system, was evaluated using a number of well-conceptualized and developed measures. Again, G x E interaction was demonstrated. To date, most of the offspring with schizophrenia have a genetic risk and experience an adverse adoptive family environment. Schizophrenia is rare or absent when at-risk children are raised in favorable adoptive families.

These data suggest that favorable family environments may suppress, in part or entirely, adverse genetic influence on the development of psychopathology. However, these data have three limitations. First, as noted, biological risk was, for most cross-fostering studies, ascertained indirectly through public or medical records. Second, the adoptive family environment was assessed retrospectively and, in most cases, after psychological dysfunction or overt disorder appeared in the adopted offspring. Early phases of the disorder may have disrupted family function rather than the reverse. Family reassembly experiments attest to the power of children with behavior problems to disrupt normal family process. For brief periods, in these studies, children with behavior problems interact with parents of normal children who are strangers to children with problems. The parental behavior in this situation quickly deteriorates in comparison to parents of children with conduct problems who are temporarily matched with normal children (e.g., Anderson, Lytton, & Romney, 1986). Third, the G x E interactions were obtained in studies where the extremes of genetic influences were being compared (e.g., the biological mothers had schizophrenia or they had never had a psychiatric hospitalization or they had antisocial behavior/substance abuse vs. no evidence of disorder). As in any interaction, using extreme values can enhance the interaction and, in this instance, overestimate the role of the environment. Indeed, in two adoption studies using unselected biological parents, interactions were very difficult to detect (Bergeman & Plomin, 1988; Bergeman, Plomin, McClearn, Pedersen, & Friber, 1988). Fourth, most studies that do show G x E interaction have used crude indices of family functioning (e.g., psychiatric disorders in the adoptive parents). These provide few clues as to exact mechanisms by which positive adoptive rearing environments may suppress adverse genetic influences. In particular, it is not clear that they reflect family factors that influence parental response to children.

Recently, three lines of investigation have begun to address these difficulties. First, retrospective adoption studies have begun to address more detailed hypotheses about mechanisms. For example, Riggins-Casper and her colleagues have obtained retrospective ratings of adolescent aggressive behavior and adoptive parents' harsh discipline (Riggins-Casper et al., in press). Criminal, antisocial behavior and/or substance abuse of the biological parents for these adopted offspring indexed genetic risk. Consistent with other findings on G • E correlation, harsh discipline of the adoptive parents towards the adopted child was most frequent when the adopted offspring were at high risk genetically. However, this increase in harsh discipline occurred only when the adoptive parents reported a psychiatric disorder, serious marital problems, or legal difficulties. The greater detail of this retrospective adoption study does suggest that the same family factors—parental psychopathology, parental legal difficulties, and marital difficulties—that influence gene expression in antisocial behavior also moderate parental response to adverse and genetically influenced child behavior. Indeed, the two mechanisms may be closely linked. Positive family environments may counter the expression of adverse genetic influences *because* they reduce harsh responses of parents to difficult children. There is no direct evidence relevant to this hypothesis.

In a second line of study, cross-fostering studies in primates have yielded findings that support the findings of retrospective adoption studies. For example, Suomi and his colleagues compared the development of rhesus monkeys with and without the short form of the serotonin transporter gene. Peer-reared monkeys with this particular polymorphism develop severe aggressive behavior, whereas mother-reared monkeys do not (Suomi, 2000). Suomi's group has begun to map out the metabolic and neurobiological pathways linking rearing conditions to gene expression (Bennett et al., 1998).

Finally, with colleagues in a six-university consortium, I have begun to explore the feasibility of a prospective adoption design. As noted, this design can directly test the parent-effects evocative model. To do so, it must use unselected biological parents and follow offspring through the age of risk for the disorders of interest. Biological parents and adoptive parents should be followed for the same period of time, beginning in the first few months of life. It must also assess intrauterine exposure of the fetus to both severe maternal stresses as well as substances that cross the placenta and may influence later development. A critical question is whether increasing openness in adoptions invalidates the design. The results of a pilot study involving biological and adoptive parents of 100 adopted offspring were very promising. They showed that it is feasible to directly assess biological parents and to estimate intrauterine exposure to substances of abuse as well as severe maternal stress. Further, longitudinal assessment of offspring and their adoptive parents is quite feasible. Of great importance, variation in openness appears to have no effect on the validity of the design. In fact, even in open adoptions, biological parents have little or no contact with their children. Contact with adoptive parents seems to have little systematic effect on the adoptive parents' conception of both parents or of their child.

Thus, the prospect is good of carrying forward a major, prospective adoption study of child effects on family dynamics and the role of these child effects in the expression of genetic influence. The adoption design can also delineate reciprocal child and parent effects that are independent of genetic influence. A study of this kind can make two major contributions to our understanding of genetically influenced child effects. First, we can observe—in detail—their effects on family dynamics and the subsequent reciprocal influences of those family dynamics on the adopted child's development. Also, in this context we can assess—in detail—family factors that moderate the response of the family to these genetically influenced child effects.

More important, we can conduct prevention trials within the context of a genetically informed adoption study. This allows a critical test of the central role of genetically influenced child effects on gene expression. A naturalistic, prospective adoption study will help us identify with precision the parental responses elicited by children with differing genetic risks. Following van den Boom, we should be able to adapt existing parent-child intervention methods to reduce maladaptive parental responses to specific, heritable, and adverse behavior in children. In the control group, in the study we are imagining, we should still observe substantial correlations between biological parent psychopathology and evolving problem behavior in children. In the experimental group, not only will the mean level of problem behavior be reduced but, more critically, its correlation with biological parent psychopathology should be eliminated. In effect, the intervention should produce improved adjustment *and* reduced heritability.

These approaches to intervention are ready now, years before we will have neurobiological tools to alter gene expression in studies of the prevention of psychopathology and even before we have delineated the specific genes associated with common behavior problems in children. Of course, it would be a delicious irony if family therapy techniques were the first to offset adverse genetic influences on behavior. It would be a fitting tribute to R. Q. Bell and his pioneering efforts to underscore the virtuosity of children in shaping their families.

ACKNOWLEDGMENTS

Research reported in this chapter was done in collaboration with Mavis Hetherington, Robert Plomin, and Jenae Neiderhiser, and was supported by NIMH Grants (MH 443373 and MH 48825) and the W. T. Grant Foundation.

REFERENCES

Anderson, K. E., Lytton, H., & Romney, D. M. (1986). Mothers' interaction with normal and conduct-disordered boys: Who affect whom? *Developmental Psychology, 22,* 604–609.

Bell, R. Q. (1968). A reinterpretation of the direction of effects in studies of socialization. *Psychology. Review, 75,* 81–95.

Bennett, A. J., Lesh, K. P., Heils, A., Long, J., Lorenz, J., Shoaf, S. E., Campoux, M., Suomi, S. J., Linnoila, M., & Higley, J. D. (1998). Serotonin transporter gene variation, strain and early rearing environment affect CSF concentrations in rhesus monkeys. *American Journal of Primatology, 45,* 168–169.

Bergeman, C. S., & Plomin, R. (1988). Genotype environment interaction. In M. H. Bornstein & J. S. Bruner (Eds.), *Interaction in human development* (pp. 157–170). Hillsdale, NJ: Lawrence Erlbaum Associates.

Bergeman, C. S., Plomin, R., McClearn, G. E., Pedersen, N. L., & Friber, L. T. (1988). Genotype-environment interaction in personality development. *Psychology and Aging, 3,* 399–406.

Bouchard, T. J., & McGue, M. (1990). Genetic and rearing environmental influences on adult personality: An analysis of adopted twins reared apart. *Journal of Personality, 58,* 263–292.

Braungart, J. M., Plomin, R., Fulker, D. W., & DeFries, J. C. (1992). Genetic mediation of the home environment during infancy: A sibling adoption analysis of the HOME. *Developmental Psychology, 28,* 1048–1055.

Cadoret, R. J., Troughton, E., Bagford, J., & Woodworth, G. (1990). Genetic and environmental factors in adoptee antisocial personality. *European Archives of Psychiatry & Neurological Sciences, 239*, 231–240.

Cadoret, R. J., Winokur, G., Langbehn, D., & Troughton, E. (1996). Depression spectrum disease, I: The role of gene-environment interaction. *American Journal of Psychiatry, 153*, 892–899.

Cadoret, R. J., Yates, W. R., Troughton, E., Woodworth, G., et al. (1995). Genetic-environmental interaction in the genesis of aggressivity and conduct disorders. *Archives of General Psychiatry, 52*, 916–924.

Cloninger, C. R., & Gottesman, I. I. (1987). Genetic and environmental factors in antisocial behavior disorders. In S. Mednick, T. Moffitt, & S. Stack (Eds.), *The causes of crime* (pp. 92–109). New York: Cambridge University Press.

Cloninger, C. R., Sigvardsson, S., Bohman, M., & von Knorring, A.-L. (1982). Predisposition to petty criminality in Swedish adoptees: II. Cross-fostering analysis of gene-environment interaction. *Archives of General Psychiatry, 39*, 1242–1247.

Daniels, D., & Plomin, R. (1985). Differential experiences of siblings in the same family. *Developmental Psychology, 21*, 747–760.

Deater-Deckard, K. (2000). Parenting and child behavioral adjustment in early childhood: A quantitative genetic approach to studying family processes. *Child Development, 71*, 468–484.

Dunn, J., & Plomin, R. (1986). Determinants of maternal behaviour towards 3-year-old siblings. *British Journal of Developmental Psychology, 4*, 127–137.

Dunn, J., Plomin, R., & Daniels, D. (1986). Consistency and change in mothers' behavior towards young siblings. *Child Development, 57*, 348–356.

Dunn, J. F., Plomin, R., & Nettles, M. (1985). Consistency of mothers' behavior towards infant siblings. *Developmental Psychology, 21*, 1188–1195.

Ge, X., Conger, R. D., Cadoret, R. J., Neiderhiser, J. M., Yates, W., Troughton, E., & Stewart, M. A. (1996). The developmental interface between nature and nurture: A mutual influence model of child antisocial behavior and parent behaviors. *Developmental Psychology, 32*, 574–589.

Glover, V. (1997). Maternal stress or anxiety in pregnancy and emotional development of the child. *British Journal of Psychiatry, 171*, 105–106.

Goldsmith, H. H., Lemery, K. S., Buss, K. A., & Campos, J. J. (1999). Genetic analyses of focal aspects of infant temperament. *Developmental Psychology, 35*, 972–985.

Goodman, R., & Stevenson, J. (1991). Parental criticism and warmth towards unrecognized monozygotic twins. *Behavior and Brain Sciences, 14*, 394–395.

Griesler, P. C., Kandel, D. B., & Davies, M. (1998). Maternal smoking in pregnancy, child behavior problems, and adolescent smoking. *Journal of Research on Adolescence, 8*, 159–185.

Jackson, D. (1960). A critique of the literature on the genetics of schizophrenia. In D. Jackson (Ed.), *The etiology of schizophrenia* (pp. 37–90). New York: Basic Books.

Jacobson, K. C., & Rowe, D. C. (1999). Genetic and environmental influences on the relationships between family connectedness, school connectedness, and adolescent depressed mood: Sex differences. *Developmental Psychology, 35*, 926–939.

Lichtenstein, P., Harris, J. R., Pedersen, N. L., & McClearn, G. E. (1993). Socioeconomic status and physical health, how are they related? An empirical study based on twins reared apart and twins reared together. *Social Science & Medicine, 36*, 441–450.

Lichtenstein, P., & Pedersen, N. L. (1995). Social relationships, stressful life events, and self-reported physical health: Genetic and environmental influences. *Psychology & Health, 10*, 295–319.

Loehlin, J. C., & Nichols, R. C. (1976). *Heredity, Environment and Personality.* Austin, TX: University of Texas Press.

Lytton, H. (1977). Do parents create or respond to differences in twins? *Developmental Psychology, 13*, 456–459.

Neiderhiser, J. M., Reiss, D., Hetherington, E. M., & Plomin, R. (1999). Relationships between parenting and adolescent adjustment over time: Genetic and environmental contributions. *Developmental Psychology, 35*, 680–692.

Niederhofer, H., & Reiter, A. (2000). Maternal stress during pregnancy, its objectivation by ultrasound observation of fetal intrauterine movements and child's temperament at 6 months and 6 years of age: A pilot study. *Psychological Reports, 86*, 526–528.

O'Connor, T. G., Deater-Deckard, K., Fulker, D., Rutter, M., & Plomin, R. (1998). Genotype-environment correlations in late childhood and early adolescence: Antisocial behavioral problems and coercive parenting. *Developmental Psychology, 34*, 970–981.

O'Connor, T. G., Hetherington, E. M., Reiss, D., & Plomin, R. (1995). A twin-sibling study of observed parent-adolescent interactions. *Child Development, 66*, 812–829.

Pedersen, N. L., McClearn, G. E., Plomin, R., Nesselroade, J. R., Berg, S., & DeFaire, U. (1991). The Swedish Adoption Twin Study of Aging: An update. *Acta Geneticae Medicae et Gemellologiae: Twin research, 40*, 7–20.

Pedersen, N. L., & Reynolds, C. A. (1998). Stability and change in adult personality: Genetic and environmental components. *European Journal of Personality, 12*, 365–386.

Plomin, R., DeFries, J. C., & Fulker, D. W. (1988). *Nature and nurture during infancy and early childhood.* Cambridge, England: Cambridge University Press.

Plomin, R., Emde, R. N., Braungart, J. M., Campos, J., Corley, R., Fulker, D. W., Kagan, J., Reznick, J. S., Robinson, J., Zahn-Waxler, C., & DeFries, J. C. (1994a). Genetic change and continuity from fourteen to twenty months: The MacArthur Longitudinal Twin Study. *Child Development, 64*, 1354–1376.

Plomin, R., McClearn, G. E., Pedersen, N. L., Nesselroade, J. R., & Bergeman, C. S. (1988). Genetic influence on childhood family envirnment perceived retrospectively from the last half of the life span. *Developmental psychology, 24*, 738–745.

Plomin, R., Pedersen, N. L., Lichtenstein, P., & McClearn, G. E. (1994b). Variability and stability in cognitive abilities are largely genetic later in life. *Behavior Genetics, 24*, 207–215.

Reiss, D., Neiderhiser, J., Hetherington, E. M., & Plomin, R. (2000). *The relationship code: deciphering genetic and social patterns in adolescent development.* Cambridge, MA: Harvard University Press.

Rende, R. D., Slomkowski, C. L., Stocker, C., Fulker, D. W., et al. (1992a). Genetic and environmental influences on maternal and sibling interaction in middle childhood: A sibling adoption study. *Developmental Psychology, 28*, 484–490.

Rende, R. D., Slomkowski, C. L., Stocker, C., Fulker, D. W., & Plomin, R. (1992b). Genetic and environmental influences on maternal and sibling interaction in middle childhood: A sibling adoption study. *Developmental Psychology, 28*, 484–490.

Riggins-Casper, K., Cadoret, R. J., Knutson, J. F., & Langbehn, D. Biology-environment interaction and evocative biology-environment correlation: Contributions of harsh discipline and parental psychopathology to problem adolescent behaviors (submitted).

Rowe, D. C. (1981). Environmental and genetic influences on dimensions of perceived parenting: A twin study. *Developmental Psychology, 17*, 203–208.

Rowe, D. C. (1983). Biometrical genetic models of self-reported delinquent behavior: Twin study. *Behavioral Genetics, 13*, 473–489.

Rutter, M., Pickles, A., Murray, R., & Eaves, L. (2001). Testing hypotheses on specific environmental causal effects on behavior. *Psychological Bulletin, 127*, 291-324.

Scarr, S., & Carter-Saltzman, L. (1979). Twin method: Defense of a critical assumption. *Behavioral Genetics, 9*, 527–542.

Stoolmiller, M. (1999). Implications of the restricted range of family environments for estimates of heritability and nonshared environment in behavior-genetic adoption studies. *Psychological Bulletin, 125*, 392–409.

Suomi, S. J. (2000). A biobehavioral perspective on developmental psychopathology: Excessive aggression and serotonergic dysfunction in monkeys. In A. J. Sameroff, M. Lewis, & S. M. Miller (Eds.), *Handbook of developmental psychopathology* (pp. 237–256). New York: Kluwer Academic/Plenum.

Tienari, P., Wynne, L. C., Moring, J., Lahti, I., Maarala, M., Sorri, A., Wahlberg, K. E., Saarento, O., Seitamaa, M., Kaleva, M., & Laksy, K. (1994). The Finnish Adoption Family Study of Schizophrenia: Implications for family research. *British Journal of Psychiatry, 164,* 20–26.

van den Boom, D. C. (1994). The influence of temperament and mothering on attachment and exploration: An experimental manipulation of sensitive responsiveness among lower-class mothers with irritable infants. *Child Development, 65,* 1457–1477.

van den Boom, D. C. (1995). Do first-year intervention effects endure? Follow-up during toddlerhood of a sample of Dutch irritable infants. *Child Development, 66,* 1798–1816.

van den Boom, D. C., & Hoeksma, J. B. (1994). The effect of infant irritability on mother-infant interaction: A growth curve analysis. *Developmental Psychology, 30,* 581–590.

van den Oord, E. J. C. G., & Rowe, D. C. (1997). Continuity and change in children's social maladjustment: A developmental behavior genetic study. *Developmental Psychology, 33,* 319–332.

Viken, R. J., Rose, R. J., Kaprio, J., & Koskenvuo, M. (1994). A developmental genetic analysis of adult personality: Extraversion and neuroticism from 18 to 59 years of age. *Journal of Personality & Social Psychology, 66,* 722–730.

Weissman, M. M., Warner, V., Wickramaratne, P. J., & Kandel, D. B. (1999). Maternal smoking during pregnancy and psychopathology in offspring followed to adulthood. *Journal of the American Academy of Child & Adolescent Psychiatry, 38,* 892–899.

2

On the Meaning of Models: A Signal Amidst the Noise

Kathleen McCartney
Harvard University

O chestnut tree, great-rooted blossomer,
Are you the leaf, the blossom or the bole?
O body swayed to music, O brightening glance,
How can we know the dancer from the dance?
— "Among School Children" by W. B. Yates

Two questions have guided most of developmental psychology: What is the typical course of development? And what are the causes of individual differences in development? The first question is the easier of the two to address, because it merely requires description. Using careful, sometimes painstaking, observational methods, researchers have identified milestones across a wide range of behaviors. Importantly, there is agreement about stages, phases, and sequences of development. By most standards, developmentalists have made good progress in describing normative development.

In contrast, progress in explaining individual differences has been more limited, because explanation is more difficult than description. Causes imply mechanisms, and only two possible mechanisms can explain individual differences in behavior: genes and environments. As Turkheimer (2000) noted, social scientists have faced two formidable problems in the quest to model the effects of genes and environments. The first is that randomized trials, the gold standard for evaluating causality, are not possible for work on individual differences in humans. The second is that the list of possible sources of influence on any psychological trait is great, potentially too great for statistical modeling. Consider the complexity of the task at hand.

POSSIBLE SOURCES OF INFLUENCE

Heritability

Conception results in a genetic heritage that reflects characteristics of the mother and father. Despite recent advances in mapping the human genome, we are not yet able to assess a child's genotype. Even if we could, as Plomin (1986) pointed out, most, if not all, psychological traits are no doubt influenced by multiple genes (polygeny), and most genes are likely to have an impact on different behaviors (pleiotropy). Complicating matters further, the effect of genes may change over time.

Toward a Taxonomy of the Environment

There is no accepted theory of the environment that unites the field. That notwithstanding, existing theories include hypothetical constructs that cannot be measured, for example, reinforcement histories and social ecologies. Sensibly, developmentalists have reduced their focus to hypothesized constructs that can be measured, and, not surprisingly, have focused on the environment provided by parents to children (see Parke & Buriel, 1998). Some researchers have operated within a social address approach to assess parent effects by measuring distal variables. The list of distal variables that have been studied is quite long. Some pertain to individual differences in the parents themselves—for example, age, gender, ethnicity, sexual orientation, mental health, intelligence, and dimensions of personality. Others refer to the context in which parents raise their children—for example, family constellation variables, such as group size, birth order, gender, and spacing; or family structure variables, such as single-parent status, divorce status, and number of adults living with the child; or family income dynamics. Distal models are merely indicators of the processes through which parents influence their children. Researchers also have modeled proximal variables via constructs such as parental discipline style, instruction, responsivity, sensitivity, management of children's time, monitoring of children's lives, storytelling, and rituals, to name but a few.

In time, developmentalists came to realize that children influence their parents, beginning with the pioneering work of Bell (1968). Soon, it was clear that the results of early socialization research had been "overstated" (Collins, Maccoby, Steinberg, Hetherington, & Bornstein, 2000). Sameroff's (1983) work on transaction and developmental systems followed. The child develops in multiple settings and multiple systems, a situation Sameroff described as "daunting" with respect to its complexity. To the list of family variables came constructs such as martial climate, coercive relationships, and family myths. Moreover, developmentalists began to consider non-familial influences as important contributors to experience. To Sameroff's daunting world, Plomin and Daniels (1987) voiced a potential "gloomy prospect" that the salient environment might be unsystematic.

GENOTYPE-ENVIRONMENT INTERPLAY

Plomin, DeFries, and Loehlin's (1977) classic *Psychological Bulletin* paper on genotype-environment correlation and interaction added another layer. These terms are familiar enough to social scientists now, but were not then. Although developmentalists had always talked about "interactionism," the term seemed to connote little more than the notion that there was some kind of interplay at work— interplay that could not be operationalized. Plomin and his colleagues defined their terms. Genotype-environment correlation refers to any process through which "genotypes are selectively exposed to different environments" while genotype- environment interaction refers to any process through which "individuals of dif- ferent genotypes may respond differently to environments" (p. 309). The heuristic value of this paper for developmental science has been great. It left developmentalists wondering how to interpret constructs such as socialization and heritability.

Socialization research was criticized as uninterpretable, because of the con- founding effects of heredity (Scarr & McCartney, 1983). Conservatively, developmentalists have known this for twenty-five years. Yet, researchers con- tinue to make fundamental attribution errors by attributing associations between environmental inputs and child outcomes to the effects of experience per se. This is actually a more general problem in psychology, as noted by Harré (2000, as quoted in Proctor and Capaldi (2001, p. 760), who puzzled over the fact that "Conceptual muddles long exposed to view are evident in almost every issue of standard psychology journals."

The implications of the paper by Plomin, DeFries, and Loehlin (1977) were problematic for behavior genetics estimates of heritability as well, because of the confounding effect of socialization. At that time, behavior genetics models were additive. Variation in a trait was assumed to be the sum of heredity, environment, and error; in other words, the influence of genotype-environment interaction and correlation was assumed to be negligible. To the extent that environmental influ- ences were correlated or interacted with genetic influences, then additive models would yield inflated estimates of heritability and deflated estimates of the envi- ronment, especially the shared environment. Recent claims that parents have little influence on their children (Harris, 1995; Rowe, 1994) were derived from synthe- ses of univariate genetic analyses that no doubt underestimated the effect of the shared environment.

So as not to create a "straw man," it is important to acknowledge that from the beginning of the nature-nurture debate there were those who wondered whether it made sense to partition the variance between heredity and environment. Collins et al. (2000) began their paper on the case for nature and nurture with Gesell and Thompson's (1934) great quote that the two can be separated "only in analytic thinking." More recently, Gottlieb, Wahlstein, and Lickliter (1998) argued that the question of whether nature or nurture is more important is "nonsensical."

LIMITATIONS OF METHODS

Developmentalists knew that there must be genotype-environment interplay before Plomin, DeFries, and Loehlin's paper (1977), just as they knew about child
effects before Bell's book (1968). Unfortunately, this knowledge could not be
translated to method because *theory and conceptualization in developmental science far exceed method.* I do not mean to imply that the glass is half empty or
worse. Instead, my thesis is that while behavior genetics and socialization methods are each useful, neither of them enables developmentalists to move beyond
description to explanation. The reason for this is that researchers lack the tools to
model complexity well.

We are limited by our methods, each and every one of which is additive,
unidirectional, static, and/or simplistic. As such, our models are not only reduc-
tionistic, but also based on assumptions that finally cannot be true. Behavior genetics studies can only provide evidence "suggestive of genetic effects of behavior" (Gottlieb, Wahlsten, & Lickliter, 1998, p. 251), just as socialization studies
can only provide evidence suggestive of environmental effects; however, statements beyond this (for example, statements about the percent of variance in a trait
that is accounted for by a given mechanism) cannot be justified logically. This
argument can be extended to the study of child effects. Studies that demonstrate
child effects essentially demonstrate that the child is not passive. There is no means,
at least not yet, to assign meaningful weights to child effects, because models do
not reflect the recursive nature of parent-child interaction. Consider the state of
the art with respect to method.

Genetic Studies of Family Process

Behavior genetics studies rely on sibling and adoption data, each with its own set
of methodological problems as outlined by Reiss (this volume). Reiss and his
colleagues have extended the sibling method in innovative ways. For example,
Reiss's research group has advanced the twin method by including a range of
sibling types as comparisons. Within-pair correlations should be greatest for
monozygotic twins, followed by dizygotic twins and ordinary siblings, followed
by half siblings, followed by unrelated or blended siblings. Reiss describes this
pattern as a genetic cascade. Yet, as he also explains to the reader, a spurious
circumstance, the equal environments assumption, calls into question any conclusion that variations in genetic similarity alone account for any identified genetic
cascade. In other words, an environmental cascade might confound any genetic
cascade. The same problem arises when assessing within-sibling pair, cross-time
correlations.

Adoption studies are more powerful than twin studies for assessing genetic
and environmental influences on development, because they offer a quasi-experi-

mental approach in which associations between adopted parents and children reflect pure environmental effects, unaffected by gene-environment correlation or interaction. The primary concern about adoption studies, however, is selective placement, which would result in covariation between heredity, as provided by biological parents, and environment, as provided by the selected adopted parents. There may be good reason to be concerned about selective placement, especially in light of Stoolmiller's (1999) concerns about range restriction in the environments provided by adopted families. Consider, however, that adoptive siblings in the Colorado Adoption Study (Plomin & DeFries, 1985) became less similar over time; selective placement would seem to predict greater similarity between adoptive siblings over time. Replication and extension of this kind of study, along the lines proposed by Reiss, are badly needed.

Newer behavior genetics models include direct assessments of the environment as components. Reiss and his colleagues (Pike, McGuire, Hetherington, Reiss, & Plomin, 1996) have been at the forefront of developing bivariate statistical models that include direct assessments of the environment so that genotype-environment correlation and interaction can be estimated. Studies using these bivariate models suggest that the shared environment and genotype-environment components account for substantial variance in children's outcomes. In fact, Deater-Deckard (2000) argued that externalizing behavior reflects mostly genotype-environment correlation variance rather than heritability variance per se. Bivariate models hold great promise because they offer the best of both the behavior genetics and socialization worlds.

Parenting

In addition to the augmented behavior genetics design, Collins et al. (2000) outlined three contemporary research approaches to the study of parenting. First, they discuss the value of studying how children with different predispositions, for example children with different temperaments, respond to different kinds of parenting. It is easy to imagine how strategies like this could be used to study child effects as well. This method offers a mechanism to study genotype-environment interplay to the extent that true predispositions can be assessed. Second, they suggest experimental parenting intervention studies to assess change in both parents' and untreated children's behaviors. Experimental strategies are powerful, especially with longitudinal follow-up. Building on social ecology theory, Collins et al. advocate a third strategy, which involves examining how parenting effects vary by ecological niches, such as neighborhoods. This is perhaps the weakest strategy offered, because neighborhood selection could have genetic confounds. In general, Turkheimer (2000) argued that these methods are not as precise as behavior genetics methods, because they do not offer a means to assess differences in experience across individuals, whereas the twin method offers a means to assess differences in genetic background across individuals.

Moving Outside the Family

Some developmentalists have moved outside the family to other important contexts of development. Consider child care, an applied problem, because data from child-care studies can inform social policies for children and families. Child care is a potential context to assess early experience in development without genotype-environment confounds. In fairness, genotype-environment confounds would be absent only if children were randomly assigned to varying child-care programs, and this is not likely to ever be the case. No truly experimental study of child care has ever been conducted for ethical as well as practical reasons, although there have been several quasi-experimental studies in which some children were randomly assigned to high-quality programs, while other children, participating in a variety of programs, served as the comparison group (e.g., Ramey, Ramey, Lanzi, & Cotton, 2002). These kinds of child-care studies function as interventions in that they tell us whether early experience outside the home matters for children's development. For the most part, children's predispositions are ignored, although researchers occasionally model temperament by child-care interactions. It would be fair to ask child-care researchers, where is the interplay?

Researchers have attempted to control for family selection effects into child-care experience. Sometimes, they have used family correlates of a child-care parameter like quality, which results in a highly conservative test (McCartney, 1984). Sometimes researchers select a set of control variables based on their conceptual relation to predictors and outcomes in the models (Peisner-Feinberg & Burchinal, 1997). And sometimes researchers use several sets of covariates so as to model the influence of more and less conservative models (NICHD Early Child Care Research Network, 2002). There is no consensus among child-care researchers about how to control for selection. There is not even agreement about whether the models are too liberal or too conservative.

Molecular Genetics

Plomin and Rutter (1998) outlined a program of research for developmentalists interested in modeling genotype-environment interplay. Associations between genes and behaviors are beginning to be identified, the best example of which is the association between the 7-repeat alleles for DRD4 and novelty seeking. According to Plomin and Rutter, developmentalists could use this kind of information to ask whether children who are at genetic risk are more sensitive to environmental risks (genotype-environment interaction) and whether children who are at genetic risk are more likely to seek out environmental risks (genotype-environment correlation). We should be concerned about the fact that genetic effects are dynamic, polygenous, pleiotropic, and probabilistic; nevertheless, molecular genetics offers a potentially powerful tool for developmentalists.

STATISTICAL INNOVATIONS

As Turkheimer (2000) reminded us, "the disconnect between the analysis of variance and the analysis of causes" is "the bedrock methodological problem of contemporary social science" (p. 162), both with respect to behavior genetics and
socialization research. Two statistical innovations offer new techniques to model
individual differences, but neither can move the research enterprise to the level of
explanation, as statisticians have recognized.

Longitudinal Methods

As Gottlieb et al. (1998) noted, "to understand the origin of any phenotype, it is
necessary to study its development in the individual" (p. 234). Ironically, most of
developmental psychology is not particularly developmental. The reason for this
seemingly sad state of affairs is that we have lacked the statistical tools to model
development. Our standard tools, difference or change scores as well as residualized
change scores, were criticized for their poor validity. It was not until the 1980s
that methodologists developed individual growth models that enabled researchers
to study change well (see Willett & Singer, manuscript in preparation).

Modeling change requires two levels of analysis. The first is to model within-
individual change, that is, the shape of each person's individual growth trajectory;
the second is to model inter-individual differences in change, that is, whether predictors can account for different patterns of within-individual change. Changes in
an outcome variable can then be regressed on changes in a predictor. As in static
models, however, it is important to control for possible motivations, conditions,
and events that might be operating as third variables, causing changes in outcomes and predictors. Longitudinal models resolve some issues, such as the sepa-
ration of observed status from measurement error, but they cannot really help with
causal arguments.

Time Series

Time series data consist of observations obtained at equally spaced time intervals,
where the time intervals could be seconds, minutes, hours, days, or even years.
Time series techniques can be used when there are at least fifty observations; with
fewer observations, panel analysis or repeated measures analysis of variance is
more appropriate. Consider a face-to-face social interaction study in which a behavior of a parent and child was coded every 15 seconds. The first step would be
to determine whether there were non-random patterns in the data. Typically, there
are meaningful trends, cycles, or some other kind of serial dependence in social
interaction data. The next step would be to determine whether there is a relationship between a pair of time series. For parent and child data, one merely treats the

two time series as two variables and then computes a correlation between the two. If, however, one predicts a child effect, then the parent's response to the child should occur after a brief time lag. To model this, one examines time-lagged dependence. For example, the parent's behavior at time t could be correlated with the child's behavior at some previous time, say t-1 or t-2. However, a common environmental event could lead to a spurious correlation between two time series. Removal of patterns within each time series might deal with some potential sources of spuriousness, but probably cannot get rid of all of them. For this reason, Warner (1998) argued that time series cannot be used to make causal arguments. Instead, she suggested that researchers be content with a modest goal, namely, "a relatively simple, clear, and reasonably complete description of interrelated patterns in the pair of time series" (p. 123).

FINAL THOUGHTS

Claims about the direction of an effect and the size of an effect must be approached cautiously. A significant association probably tells us little more than there might be something there, a kind of signal amidst the noise. Gottlieb and his colleagues made a compelling case that "the probable nature of epigenetic development is rooted in the reciprocal coactions that take place in complex systems" (Gottlieb et al., 1998, p. 262). The result of this, they argue, is bidirectionality and indeterminacy. This was Yates's point, too, when he queried, "*How can we know the dancer from the dance?*" For this reason, we may need to be content with *description* of genetic, environmental, and gene-environment interplay as our goal—at least for now. Effect sizes will be useful to those who wish to relate findings across studies to characteristics of samples and to measures; however, they cannot tell us anything about the importance of mechanisms yet.

I do not intend my words to lead to a kind of nihilism about the value of our field. Specifically, I am not advocating abandoning logical positivism for postmodern musings or for an interpretive psychology. With respect to applied issues, it is reasonable to draw conclusions from developmental science that inform programs and practices for children, despite the fact that the established knowledge base is limited. Because policies will be made for children, with or without our input, there is no other ethical course of action. We can and should go beyond our data as long as we do not make unwarranted assertions that misrepresent the knowledge base (Shonkoff, 2000). With respect to theoretical issues, it is reasonable to continue to use our methods, imperfect as they are, and to search for replications as well as failed replications across designs, as long as an evaluation of method is a critical part of our discussions. Proctor and Capaldi (2001) suggested that naturalism, a new movement in philosophy of science, may help guide us. In this view, methodological statements are evaluated "on the same basis as all other empirical statements" (p. 771). Existing dialectics across research traditions should point the way towards needed evaluations of method.

ACKNOWLEDGMENTS

I gratefully acknowledge Kristen Bub, Eric Dearing, Kirby Deater-Deckard, and William Hagen for their comments on an earlier draft of this manuscript. Their constructive criticisms and direction to relevant literatures helped me to sharpen my thinking.

REFERENCES

Bell, R. Q. (1968). A reinterpretation of the direction of effects in studies of socialization. *Psychological Review, 75*, 81–95.

Collins, W. A., Maccoby, E. E., Steinberg, L., Hetherington, E. M., & Bornstein, M. H. (2000). Contemporary research on parenting. *American Psychologist, 55*, 218–232.

Deater-Deckard, K. (2000). Parenting and child behavioral adjustment in early childhood: A quantitative genetic approach to studying family processes. *Child Development, 71*, 468–484.

Gesell, A., & Thompson, H. (1934). *Infant behavior: Its genesis and growth*. New York: McGraw-Hill.

Gottlieb, G., Wahlsten, D., & Lickliter, R. (1998). The significance of biology for human development: a developmental psychobiological systems view. In R. M. Lerner (Ed.), *Handbook of child psychology, Vol. 1* (pp. 233–274). New York: Wiley.

Harris, J. R. (1995). Where is the child's environment? A group socialization theory of development. *Psychological Review, 102*, 458–489.

McCartney, K. (1984). Effect of quality of day care environment on children's language development. *Developmental Psychology, 20*, 244–260.

NICHD Early Child Care Research Network. (2002). Early child care and children's development prior to school entry: Results from the NICHD Study of Early Child Care. *American Education Research Journal, 39*, 133–164.

Parke, R., & Buriel, R. (1998). Socialization in the family: Ethnic and ecological perspectives. In N. Eisenberg (Ed.), *Handbook of child psychology, Vol. 3* (pp. 463–552). New York: Wiley.

Peisner-Feinberg, E., & Burchinal, M. (1997). Relations between preschool children's child-care experiences and concurrent development: The cost, quality and outcomes study. *Merrill-Palmer Quarterly, 43*, 451–477.

Pike, A., McGuire, S., Hetherington, E. M., Reiss, D., & Plomin, R. (1996). Family environment and adolescent depressive symptoms and antisocial behavior: A multivariate genetic analysis. *Developmental Psychology, 32*, 590–604.

Plomin, R. (1986). *Development, genetics, and psychology*. Hillsdale, NJ: Lawrence Erlbaum Associates.

Plomin, R., & Daniels, D. (1987). Why are children in the same family so different from one another? *Behavioral and Brain Sciences, 10*, 1–60.

Plomin, R., & DeFries, J. C. (1985). *Origins of individual differences in infancy*. New York: Academic Press.

Plomin, R., DeFries, J. C., & Loehlin, C. C. (1977). Genotype-environment interaction and correlation in the analysis of human behavior. *Psychological Bulletin, 84*, 309–322.

Plomin, R., & Rutter, M. (1998). Child development, molecular genetics, and what to do with genes once they are found. *Child Development, 69*, 1223–1242.

Proctor, R. W., & Capaldi, E. J. (2001). Empirical evaluation and justification of methodologies in psychological science. *Psychological Bulletin, 127*, 759–772.

Ramey, C. T., Ramey, S. L., Lanzi, R. G., & Cotton, J. N. (2002). Early educational interventions for high-risk children: How center-based treatment can augment and improve parenting effectiveness. In J. G. Borkowski & S. L. Ramey (Eds.), *Parenting and the child's world: Influences on academic, intellectual, and social-emotional development. Monographs in parenting* (pp. 125–140). Mahwah, NJ: Lawrence Erlbaum Associates.

Rowe, D. (1994). *The limits of family influence: Genes, experience, and behavior*. New York: Guilford Press.

Sameroff, A. J. (1983). Developmental systems: Contexts and evolution. In W. Kessen (Ed.), *Handbook of child psychology, Vol. I* (pp. 237–294). New York: Wiley.

Scarr, S., & McCartney, K. (1983). How people make their own environments: A theory of genotype → environment effects. *Child Development, 54*, 424–435.

Shonkoff, J. (2000). Science, policy, and practice: Three cultures in search of a shared mission. *Child Development, 71*, 181–187.

Stoolmiller, M. (1999). Implications of the restricted range of family environments for estimates of heritability and nonshared environment in behavior-genetic adoption studies. *Psychological Bulletin, 125*, 392–409.

Turkheimer, E. (2000). Three laws of behavior genetics and what they mean. *Current Directions in Psychological Science, 9*, 160–164.

Warner, R. (1998). *Spectral analysis of time-series data*. New York: Guilford.

Willett, J. B., & Singer, J. D. (manuscript in preparation). *Twice is not enough: Analyzing longitudinal data in education, psychology, and the social sciences.*

3

Are We Finally Ready to Move Beyond "Nature vs. Nurture"?

Xiaojia Ge
M. Brent Donnellan
Lawrence Harper
University of California-Davis

If we could ask one of the alumni of our developmental sciences courses to identify a topic that he or she still remembers long after his or her graduation, most likely the topic of the intellectual confrontation between nature and nurture would be recalled. Indeed, this is one of the most fascinating issues in our field, and the battle for supremacy of genes (G) vs. the environment (E) has been long and hard fought. Unfortunately, researchers on either side of the issue have been guided by the assumption that genetic influences on individual characteristics can be isolated from environmental influences and vice versa. This assumption has justified a preoccupation with partitioning of variance into tidy packages labeled as either "genetic" or "environmental" influences. Partisans on either side of the nature/nurture debate often point to these summary statistics as evidence that their preferred "cause" is the primary influence on a given behavior. Hopefully, this will no longer be the view among social scientists once they read this work by David Reiss (this volume). Reiss's recognition of the complex ways in which genetic and environmental influences play out over time should help to end the polarized rhetoric about the rival influence of nature versus nurture and finally move the field forward.

"HOW MUCH?" OR "HOW?": THE LEGACY OF TWIN AND SIBLING DESIGNS

For reasons that are not apparent to us, researchers using twin and sibling designs continue to focus attention on estimating the relative contributions of G and E for the development of the child. This preoccupation occurs despite repeated warnings that the critical question is not "how much," but rather, "how" G and E transact at different times to influence development (Anastasi, 1958; Hoffman, 1991; Wachs, 1983). In these designs, data analyses usually center on comparisons of the correlations between siblings of different degrees of genetic relatedness, typically between monozygotic (MZ) and dizygotic (DZ) twins.

A common result from these twin and sibling comparisons is that sibling similarity decreases as a function of decreasing genetic relatedness, with MZ twins more similar than DZ twins. By partitioning the variance and covariance, researchers derive estimates of the extent to which observed variability in each measure, or the association between various pairs of measures, is due to genetic, shared environmental, or nonshared environmental influences. From these analyses it is often concluded that siblings are alike because they share genes—not because they have been raised in similar ways. To the extent that siblings are different, it is said to be due to their different experiences that are thought to occur mainly outside the family. Despite the contributions such a practice of variance partitioning have made to our awareness of genetic influence on behaviors, these interpretations have little to say about "how" nature and nurture transact to influence a child's phenotype.

GENE-ENVIRONMENT CORRELATION: THE ISSUE OF THE EQUAL ENVIRONMENT ASSUMPTION

Although not elaborated in much detail, Reiss suggests a significant redefinition of what constitutes a violation of equal environment assumption (EEA). He writes:

> Violations of the equal environment assumption, when this assumption is precisely defined, refers to inequality of treatment across groups of twins or of siblings only if this inequality *originates* (emphasis is original) in the nongenetic environment. It expressly does not refer to inequalities across groups that are evoked by the heritable characteristics of the twins and siblings (Reiss, this volume).

The implication of this redefinition is far-reaching: It represents a significant departure from the definition used in "traditional" twin and sibling designs and has important relevance for the study of child effects.

In traditional twin or sibling designs, the EEA simply refers to the assumption that environments are comparable for all sibling pairs. For example, neighborhood contexts are typically thought of as a shared environmental influence. According to the EEA, MZ twins thus should reside in neighborhoods that are no more or less disadvantaged than those for DZ twins. If the EEA is satisfied, then we are in a position to argue that the differential degree of similarity in phenotypic behaviors between MZ and DZ twins is due to genetic influence. However, under the EEA, parents of MZ twins are also expected to treat each of their twins no more similarly than parents of DZ twins treat their twins. This aspect of the EEA may be far less plausible than assumptions about neighborhoods. Importantly, any violation of the EEA reflects a confounding of genetic and environmental influences. If parents raise MZ twins in more similar ways than they raise DZ twins, the G and E influences become confounded: the greater similarity between MZ twins than DZ twins could be attributed either to parents' more equal rearing of MZ twins than DZ twins or to the greater proportion of shared genes in MZ twins than DZ twins. Indeed, in a large-scale twin study conducted in the United States (Carbonneau, Rutter, Silberg, Simonoff, & Eaves, 2000), the variance in parents' differential criticisms toward DZ twins was more than twice the size of the variance in parents' differential criticisms toward MZ twins, suggesting that parents tend to treat DZ twins more differently than MZ twins.

The EEA may not hold in at least two additional situations. First, MZ twin pairs may interact more with one another, have more shared experience together, and generally be closer to each other than DZ twins or biologically unrelated siblings. Thus MZ twins may have more opportunity to shape each other's phenotypic behaviors toward greater similarity (Patterson, Leve, & Stoolmiller, 1997). Indeed, in a reanalysis of the Danish twin study data, Carey (1992) showed that MZ twins imitate each other's antisocial behavior more than do DZ twins. In their analysis of the Finnish twin cohort, Rose and Kaprio (1987) found that the more frequent contact between MZ twins than between DZ twins was associated with different degrees of behavioral similarity between MZ and DZ twins. Similarly, Tambs, Harris, and Magnus (1995), in a Norwegian twin study, reported MZ twins were closer to each other than DZ twins and that closeness was significantly related to higher behavioral similarity in MZ than DZ twins. This inequality applies even more when non-twin siblings, particularly unrelated siblings, are concerned. For example, Hetherington, Henderson, and Reiss (1999) demonstrated that biologically related siblings show both more positivity and negativity in their relationships than do stepsiblings. In addition, age differences between non-twin siblings could very well mean that they interact with each other less often than twins and thus have even fewer opportunities to influence each other towards similarity. Second, biologically unrelated siblings in stepfamilies may have environments that differ more than biologically related siblings (Hetherington, Henderson, & Reiss, 1999). Moreover, if parents are warmer, more nurturant, more supportive, and more involved with their biological children than their stepchildren, as Hetherington, Henderson, and Reiss (1999) demonstrated, it also casts doubt on the applicability of the equal environment assumption.

Perhaps less appreciated by traditional behavior geneticists is the very fact that genetic and environmental measures are correlated in the twin and sibling designs, making the EEA less tenable. It is often noted that environment measures covary with different degrees of genetic relatedness (Rowe, 1981). For example, in the brilliantly designed Nonshared Environment of Adolescent Development project (NEAD; Reiss, Neiderhiser, Hetherington, & Plomin, 2000), gene-environment correlations may mean that the similarity of siblings' environments decreases along with the genetic cascade. If this is the case, as it has been repeatedly reported, then inferences based on traditional quantitative analyses of the sources of phenotypic variation in twin or sibling designs should be taken with great caution. This is because the attribution of the decreasing similarity across the cascade to the decreasing genetic relatedness of siblings hinges upon the equal environment assumption. However, if, for example, MZ twins are more likely to reinforce or imitate each other's behavior than DZ twins, or parents treat MZ twins more similarly than DZ twins, then there is also a cascade of environmental similarity across sibling types. Given this scenario, it would be difficult to definitively attribute any observed differences in sibling similarity to either G or E because there are two parallel cascades of both genetic and environmental similarity.

Reiss's redefinition, if we understand it correctly, and the design he proposes imply that our analyses no longer need to be predicated on the EEA because we are no longer preoccupied with partitioning variance. Rather, the inequality of environments provided by parents or by sibling interaction across sibling types (e.g., MZ twins, DZ twins, full-siblings) provides an opportunity to explore a totally new avenue—an evocative gene-environmental correlation with the following sequence: $G \rightarrow E \rightarrow Phenotype$ or $G \rightarrow$ Phenotype $\rightarrow E$. Because the EEA only become crucial if we try to answer the question of "how much" variance in a behavior is due to G or E, and because the question that interests us now is "how" G and E work together to influence development, the question of whether the inequality of environments across the cascade *originates from*, or is a *response to*, the different degrees of genetic relatedness becomes more relevant than whether the EEA is met or not.

A departure from a focus on the partitioning variance to G or E opens a much greater window of opportunity for understanding how G and E transact to influence human development. As carefully outlined by Reiss (this volume), we can begin to ask whether parents' greater similarity in the treatment of MZ twins as compared to DZ twins or other types of siblings is a response to simple zygosity or to some genetically influenced characteristics of the child. We can address these questions without worrying about violations of the EEA. Assuming that differential treatment was influenced by the child's genotype, we could further inquire about which specific characteristics of the child are so salient to parents (i.e., child effects). Moreover, we could then proceed to ask how these parental responses further shape the child's development over time. These are richer and more fruitful questions to ask about G and E.

GENE X ENVIRONMENT INTERACTION: BEYOND ADDITIVE MODELS

We have been puzzled by the reluctance of traditional behavior genetics to deal with the possibility of $G \times E$ interaction. One possibility is that the existence of this interaction makes quantification of the "degree" of genetic effects difficult

(Plomin, DeFries, & Loehlin, 1977). Because the standard twin and sibling models are additive models, that is, *Phenotype = G + E*, a presence of an interactive term, *Phenotype = G + E + (G x E)*, would mean a violation of the assumption of additivity. For example, if the DZ twin correlation is far smaller, say $\rho_{DZ} = .13$, than that of MZ twins, say $\rho_{MZ} = .65$, then the classic formula for "heritability," 2 $(\rho_{MZ} - \rho_{DZ})$, would result in an inexplicable number that is larger than unity (1.04). Another speculation is more technical: It is much more difficult to parameterize an interaction term in so-called "biometric" twin and sibling models with limited degrees of freedom. Only when the sample size is very large, such as in the Add Health (Rowe, Almeida, & Jacobson, 1999; Rowe, Jacobson, & van den Oord, 1999) or in the FinnTwin16 (Rose, Dick, Viken, & Kaprio, 2001), can one estimate the variability in "genetic" effects across different environmental contexts.

By the term "*G* x *E* interaction," we mean that the relation between genotypes and child phenotypic behaviors varies as a function of environment. Contrary to a more restrictive assumption that *G* has to contribute equally to development at all levels of *E*, *G* x *E* interaction simply means that genetic influences on phenotypic behavior vary at different levels of environment. For example, it is well known that genetically "dull" rats placed in an enriched environment can perform as well as their genetically "bright" counterparts reared in typical laboratory environments. Alternatively, consider two children with an equal genetic propensity for obesity who were raised in very different environments. One would expect the likelihood of developing obesity to be significantly greater for the child raised on a steady diet of fast food in comparison to the child raised on a more healthful diet.

Unlike many other behavior geneticists, Reiss shows a much greater enthusiasm for *G* x *E* interaction. As he remarks, finding *G* x *E* interaction "is another blow to the notion of genetic determinism because it suggests that genetic influences may be as malleable as other risk factors" (p. 17, this volume). Indeed, these types of findings are beginning to accumulate. For example, the studies by Cadoret et al. (1995, 1996) cited in Reiss demonstrated clearly that the genetically at-risk child placed in a highly aversive environment is most likely to develop antisocial and substance use problems.

The term "environment" in *G* x *E* interaction is not limited to parenting or the home environment. Environment can be broadly construed to include an individual's life experiences, schools they attend, peers they are associated with, historical eras in which they lived, and their developmental stage. For instance, in the Add Health data, the measured genetic influences on aggression have been shown to vary significantly across school contexts (Rowe et al., 1999a). In the same data, estimated genetic contributions to variations in verbal IQ vary systematically with parental education levels (Rowe et al., 1999b). In a recent Finnish twin study, measured genetic influences on alcohol use were shown to vary between adolescents residing in rural and urban areas (Rose et al., 2001).

An interesting secular trend in genetic influences was found on educational attainment (Heath et al., 1985) and intelligence (Sundet, Tambs, Magnus, & Berg,

1988), with an increasing genetic contribution in more recent cohorts. Even the very finding that estimated genetic influences change over development, as Reiss reports, can be construed as a form of $G \times E$ interaction. While it is true that genes turn on and off at different times in development, it is equally true that social contexts differ at different ages: For example, behavior that may be tolerable at a younger age may be unacceptable at a later age. Not only can the environment serve as moderator of genetic influences, but genetic factors can also play a significant role in individual differences in susceptibility to environment risks. Many negative life events appear to have no effect on individuals without a genetic propensity for emotional disorders but exert a significant effect among those with a genetic propensity for emotional disorders (Silberg, Rutter, Neale, & Eaves, 2001).

Even genetically influenced environments can moderate the influence of G on phenotypic behavior. It is a dubious notion to argue that once an environmental measure is shown to be associated with G, it somehow becomes automatically disqualified as a potential moderator of genetic influences. For example, using an adoption design, consider a situation in which an adoptive mother's negativity were found to be affected by her adopted son's impulsive behaviors, which were likely genetically influenced. This negative response of the adoptive mother should still be considered to be a moderator of genetic influences on the adopted child's behavior, particularly on his future developmental outcomes.

We can understand the statistical argument for the reduction in power for detecting a significant interaction when the two variables involved in the product term $(G \times E)$ are not perfectly orthogonal. However, we wonder if this technical reason justifies the denial of the existence of $G \times E$ interaction. A likely explanation for the reluctance of behavior genetics to deal with $G \times E$ interaction may be that a genetically influenced environmental measure is no longer thought of as a "pure" measure of the environment that could be cleanly separated from G. However, this concern may only be a vestige from the focus on the partitioning of variance into G or E, an analytical focus that is no longer of interest to us. In the evocative parent effect model proposed by Reiss, we would be able to escape from the straitjacket that once forced us to draw a "clean and simple" distinction between G and E, and can begin to address the far more interesting issue of "how" G and E are exquisitely intertwined in affecting development.

A GREAT LEAP FORWARD: PROSPECTIVE ADOPTION DESIGNS

One of Reiss's major accomplishments was to highlight the elegance of the prospective adoption design for studying child effects. This is a welcome contribution to a field that has struggled with the methodological and conceptual issues surrounding the investigation of child effects for well over 30 years (e.g., Anderson, Lytton, & Romney, 1986; Bell, 1981a, 1981b; Bell & Chapman, 1986; Bell

& Harper, 1977; Brunk & Henggeler, 1984; Grusec & Kuczynski, 1980; Keller, 1981; Keller & Bell, 1979; Lytton, 1990; Yarrow & Waxler, 1971). Before emphasizing the strengths of the prospective adoption design, it is useful to consider previous research strategies for investigating child effects in order to engender a greater appreciation for Reiss's suggestion.

Much of the first work inspired by Bell's (1968) seminal analysis was designed to empirically demonstrate the existence of child effects by using cross-sectional experimental designs. One common strategy, known as the functional pairs approach (Keller, 1981), involved the experimental manipulation of the behavior of child-actors and the subsequent examination of its impact on adult participants (e.g., Brunk & Henggeler, 1984; Keller & Bell, 1979). For example, Brunk and Henggeler (1984) found that adult participants used lower-limit control strategies with child actors who demonstrated anxious-withdrawn behavior and upper-limit control strategies with child actors who demonstrated aggressive non-compliance in a semi-structured play setting.

A major assumption of this approach was that the interaction of these functional pairs was a workable approximation of the parent-child interaction process. However, Halverson and Waldrop (1970) pointed out that, in a laboratory context, parents are likely to treat their own children differently (the "ownness" problem). Indeed, they showed that mothers treated their own children more negatively and less positively than they treated other children. Anderson, Lytton, and Romney (1989) addressed some of these issues by combining mother-child observation with the functional-pairs approach in a study of the role of conduct disorder (CD) on adult-child interactions. Mothers were paired with their own sons (half of whom had a CD diagnosis) for one observation and paired with the sons of other women for two other observations (one with a CD diagnosis and one without a CD diagnosis). Anderson, Lytton, and Romney (1989) found that boys with CD elicited more negative responses than boys without CD from all mothers in the study. However, mothers exhibited more coercive behaviors in response to the behavior of their own sons with CD than to the behavior of other boys with CD. Thus, "ownness" did have an impact on adult-child interactions.

Collectively, these experimental investigations were useful in demonstrating that children influence the behavior of adults. Several issues remained unaddressed by this literature, however. First, it is unclear if experimental settings approximate the "real" and complex interactions between parents and children over time. The Hetherington, Henderson, and Reiss (1999) study also found the impact of "ownness" but in a different direction. Second, cross-sectional experiments do not provide much insight on how child effects operate over time and how child effects impact behavior in the long term (Rutter et al., 1997). Thus, experimental studies provide no clues to the significance of child effects for the development of *future* outcomes of interest (e.g., achievement, competency, delinquency). Finally, and most relevant to the topic at hand, these designs were not helpful in understanding the transactions between G and E influences involved in child effects.

In addition to experimental designs, another strategy for investigating child effects has been to examine the impact of temperament (or some other "congenital" child characteristic) on subsequent parent-child interactions in longitudinal data sets. For example, Buss (1981) correlated activity level measurements taken during the preschool years with parent-child interactions at age 5. He found that highly active preschoolers were more likely to be involved with power struggles and have difficult relationships with their parents. However, because these designs are often not genetically informed, they provide little insight into how G and E factors work together in development. Moreover, these designs are unable to distinguish between passive and evocative G - E correlations when looking at parent-child interactions.

Prospective adoption designs such as the one proposed by Reiss may be the best method yet devised for studying child effects for several reasons. First, this design is more ecologically valid than experimental designs and therefore conclusions drawn from the results should be more generalizable. Second, adoption studies with a long-term focus have the potential to inform the field about the developmental significance of child effects, which was not addressed in the Ge et al. (1996) study. When participants are followed from birth onward it may be possible to trace the development of child effects from their earliest roots to their long-term consequences.

Third, prospective adoption studies are genetically informed. Data from these designs will provide us with a more nuanced view of nature, nurture, and family dynamics. For example, adoption studies provide an opportunity to clearly identify evocative gene-environment correlation because there should be no systematic, passive gene-environment correlations. We finally have a method for investigating the processes whereby genetically influenced characteristics of the child evoke certain parental responses that, in turn, influence the child's phenotype. Moreover, as Reiss proposes, with prospective adoption designs, we have the ability to distinguish between parent-effect evocative models and child-effect evocative models. We can start to tease apart and understand the characteristics of parents that elicit developmentally significant responses in their children from the characteristics of children that elicit developmentally significant responses in their parents.

Finally, prospective adoption studies provide an avenue to explore G x E interaction. With prospective adoption designs, we may understand how children with genetic predispositions for psychopathology are placed at greater or lesser risk for the development of these problems by their family environments. These are undoubtedly complex questions but the answers will provide us with much more effective strategies for prevention and intervention efforts. These questions need to be addressed if we are ever to understand the "how" question of nature and nurture.

The prospective adoption design holds the promise to bring about a truly exciting era in the study of behavioral development and for the ultimate understanding of the "how" question of nature and nurture. Almost 50 years after it was posed by Anastasi (1958), an answer to the question of "how" may be within our grasp.

CONCLUSION

Individual differences are influenced by the coaction of genetic factors and environmental circumstances throughout development. This is a simple statement that reflects the complex reality of human development. Whether our characteristic differences are mainly a product of nature or nurture is no longer a question of much interest. How we develop is, after all, as much *natural* as it is *nurtured*. The context in which genes are expressed is as much biological as environmental. The boundaries between genes and environment—between nature and nurture—are much fuzzier than we often realize and than traditional models presumed. Only after we acknowledge this proposition and discard outdated assumptions about the separability of nature and nurture, can we begin to address the much more exciting and intriguing question of how nature and nurture transact to make us who we are.

ACKNOWLEDGMENTS

Writing of this manuscript was supported partially by the California Agriculture Experiment Station (CA-D*-HCD-6092-H) and a Faculty Research Grant by the Academic Senate of the University of California, Davis. The authors would like to thank Dannelle Larsen-Rife, Claire Vallotton, and Vivian Wong for their participation in a discussion group on "Child Effects on Parents."

REFERENCES

Anastasi, A. (1958). Heredity, environment, and the question "how?" *Psychological Review, 65,* 197–208.

Anderson, K. E., Lytton, H., & Romney, D. M. (1986). Mothers' interaction with normal and conduct-disordered boys: Who affect whom? *Developmental Psychology, 22,* 604–609.

Bell, R. Q. (1968). A reinterpretation of the direction of effects in studies of socialization. *Psychological Review, 75,* 81–95.

Bell, R. Q. (1981a). Symposium on parent, child, and reciprocal influences: New experimental approaches. *Journal of Abnormal Child Psychology, 9,* 299–301.

Bell, R. Q. (1981b). Four new research approaches to socialization: An evaluation of their advantages and disadvantages. *Journal of Abnormal Child Psychology, 9,* 341–345.

Bell, R. Q., & Chapman, M. (1986). Child effects using experimental or brief longitudinal approaches to socialization. *Developmental Psychology, 22,* 595–603.

Bell, R. Q., & Harper, L. V. (1977). *Child effects on adults.* Hillsdale, NJ: Lawrence Erlbaum Associates.

Brunk, M. A., & Henggeler, S. W. (1984). Child influences on adult controls: An experimental investigation. *Developmental Psychology, 20,* 1074–1081.

Buss, D. M. (1981). Predicting parent-child interactions from children's activity level. *Developmental Psychology, 17,* 59–65.

Cadoret, R. J., Winokur, G., Langbehn, D., & Troughton, E., Yates, W., & Stewart, M. (1996). Depression spectrum disease, I: The role of gene-environment interaction. *American Journal of Psychiatry, 153,* 892–899.

Cadoret, R. J., Yates, W. R., Troughton, E., Woodworth, G., & Stewart, M. A. (1995). Genetic-environmental interaction in the genesis of aggressivity and conduct disorders. *Archives of General Psychiatry, 52,* 916–924.

Carbornneau, R., Rutter, M., Silberg, J. L., Simonoff, E., & Eaves, L. J. (2000). *Assessment of genetic and environmental influences on differential ratings of within family experiences and relationships in twins.* Manuscript submitted for publication.

Carey, G. (1992). Twin imitation for antisocial behavior: Implications for genetic and family environment research. *Journal of Abnormal Psychology, 101,* 18–25.

Ge, X., Conger, R. D., Cadoret, R. J., Neiderhiser, J. M., Yates, W., Troughton, E., & Stewart, M. A. (1996). The developmental interface between nature and nurture: A mutual influence model of child antisocial behavior and parent behaviors. *Developmental Psychology, 32,* 574–589.

Grusec, J. E., & Kuczynski, L. (1980). Direction of effect in socialization: A comparison of the parent's versus the child's behavior as determinants of disciplinary techniques. *Developmental Psychology, 16,* 1–9.

Halverson, C. F., & Waldrop, M. F. (1970). Maternal behavior toward own and other preschool children: The problem of "ownness." *Child Development, 41,* 839–845.

Heath, A. C., Berg, K., Eaves, L. J., Solaas, M. H., Corey, L. A., Sundet, J., Magnus, P., & Nance, W. E. (1985). Educational policy and the heritability of educational attainment. *Nature, 314,* 734–736.

Hetherington, E. M., Henderson, S., & Reiss, D. (1999). Adolescent siblings in stepfamilies: Family functioning and adolescent adjustment. *Monographs of the Society for Research in Child Development, 64* (Serial No. 259).

Hoffman, L. W. (1991). The influence of the family environment on personality: Accounting for sibling differences. *Psychological Bulletin, 110,* 187–203.

Keller, B. B. (1981). The study of reciprocal influences through experimental modification of social interaction between functional adult-child pairs. *Journal of Abnormal Child Psychology, 9,* 311–319.

Keller, B. B., & Bell, R. Q. (1979). Child effects on adult's method of eliciting altruistic behavior. *Child Development, 50,* 1004–1009.

Lytton, H. (1990). Child and parent effects in boys' conduct disorder: A reinterpretation. *Developmental Psychology, 26,* 683–697.

Patterson, G. R., Leve, L., & Stoolmiller, M. (1997). *A critique of some well-known method problems in additive twin models: An alternative developmental model.* (Unpublished manuscript). Eugene, OR: Oregon Social Learning Center.

Plomin, R., DeFries, J. C., & Loehlin, J. C. (1977). Genotype-environment interaction and correlation in the analysis of human behavior. *Psychological Bulletin, 84,* 309–322.

Reiss, D., Neiderhiser, J., Hetherington, E. M., & Plomin, R. (2000). *The relationship code: Deciphering genetic and social patterns in adolescent development.* Cambridge, MA: Harvard University Press.

Rose, R. J., Dick, D. M., Viken, R. J., & Kaprio, J. (2001). Gene-environment interaction in patterns of adolescent drinking: Regional residency moderates longitudinal influences on alcohol use. *Alcoholism: Clinical and Experimental Research, 25,* 637–643.

Rose, R. J., & Kaprio, J. (1987). Shared experience and similarity of personality: Positive data from Finnish and American twins. *Behavioral and Brain Sciences, 10,* 35–36.

Rowe, D. C. (1981). Environmental and genetic influences on dimensions of perceived parenting: A twin study. *Developmental Psychology, 17,* 203–208.

Rowe, D. C., Almeida, D. M., & Jacobson, K. C. (1999a). School context and genetic influences on aggression in adolescence. *Psychological Science, 10,* 277–280.

Rowe, D. C., Jacobson, K. C., & van den Oord, C. G. (1999b). Genetic and environmental influences on vocabulary IQ: Parental education level as moderator. *Child Development, 70,* 1151–1162.

Rutter, M., Dunn, J., Plomin, R. Simonoff, E., Pickles, A., Maughan, B., Ormal, J., Meyer, J., & Eaves, L. (1997). Integrating nature and nurture: Implications of person-environment correlations and interactions for development psychopathology. *Development and Psychopathology, 9,* 335–364.

Silberg, J., Rutter, M., Neale, M., & Eaves, L. (2001). Genetic moderation of environmental risk for depression and anxiety in adolescent girls. *British Journal of Psychiatry, 179*, 116–121.

Sundet, J. M., Tambs, K., Magnus, P., & Berg, K. (1988). On the question of secular trends in the heritability of intelligence test scores: A study of Norwegian twins. *Intelligence, 12*, 47–59.

Tambs, K., Harris, J. R., & Magnus, P. (1995). Sex-specific causal factors and effects of common environment for symptoms of anxiety and depression in twins. *Behavior Genetics, 25*, 33–44.

Wachs, T. D. (1983). The use and abuse of environment in behavior-genetic research. *Child Development, 54*, 396–407.

Yarrow, M. R., & Waxler, C. Z. (1971). Child effects on adult behavior. *Developmental Psychology, 5*, 300–311.

4
How to Spin Straw Into Gold

J. Richard Udry

Carolina Population Center at the University of North Carolina-Chapel Hill

Most social science theories assume parent-to-child effects as the basic causal sequence because they do not believe that children have inherent attributes. If children do not have inherent attributes, then there is no starting point in the child. It is tabula rasa all over again.

If you believe that individuals differ from one another from birth because of inherent attributes, then no assumption of parent-to-child as the starting point makes any sense. Longitudinal designs will not solve the problem. Nor will starting your investigations at younger and younger ages.

I have two daughters. While they grew up with the same parents in similar shared environments (as laymen think of this), I was from the beginning struck with how different the two children were in their responses to the same situations. This was in the 1960s before I believed in genes. One smiled at strangers, the other frowned at strangers. When I talked to other parents, they had the same observations about their own children. One was a fussy and cranky baby, the other was a placid baby. Then research with parents and their parenting strategies began to show that parents were sensitive to the differences in children's responses and developed different strategies with each child. Parents generally recognize the uniqueness of each child, and encourage the development of their strengths, unless their strengths are unpleasant or antisocial.

Most behavior genetic (BG) studies have shown relatively small or nonexistent influences for shared environment. Now in BG talk, any experience that makes siblings more alike is by definition a shared environment.

Since similar family experience is what most social scientists mean by shared environment, I thought that we should conclude that children react *differently* to similar family experience. We would not reasonably conclude that children are not *affected* by similar family experience. If the difference in their response is a function of their degree of biological relatedness, this variance is called genetic. If the difference in their response is *not* a function of their biological relatedness, it will show up in BG analysis as *nonshared variance*, even though the events associated with it are within-family events.

But now listen to how Reiss et al. (2000), in their recent co-authored book, *The Relationship Code*, summarize the findings of his adolescent genetic panel study:

Thirteen years after beginning this unusual venture, we have concluded that the household family is not an important source of non-shared environment for adolescence (p. xii).

This doesn't mean that adolescent behaviors are not explained by nonshared variance from *somewhere*. Adolescent behaviors have plenty of nonshared variance. Later, Reiss et al. say, "Non-shared factors are the most important source of environmental influence on most domains of adolescent adjustment" (p. 421). They just don't originate in the household family experience of the adolescent. Where do they originate? Reiss and his colleagues don't know:

Further, our preliminary assessments of other social worlds of the adolescent have provided few, if any, clues as to what the main sources might be (p. xii).

This is a bitter pill to swallow at the conclusion of a study, the most important purpose of which was to explicate the sources of nonshared variance, especially those originating in the family household. Fortunately, they learned an enormous amount about other aspects of adolescence on the way to this conclusion.

So now where do we go with nonshared variance—residual unexplained variance? For adolescents it isn't related to family relationships, peer group quality, or stressful life events, among other things, according to Reiss and his colleagues. Maybe it is just where we were afraid it would be before this all started. As they say in *The Relationship Code* (p. 422):

The non-shared environment might simply turn out to be the residue of random but influential events that pile up in the course of most people's lives. Although this explanation "fits" all our findings on the non-shared environment, it is highly unsatisfactory. It is the precise equivalent of the statement, "We don't know what the non-shared environment is, and have no good ideas about it."

If so, this is good to know. But it cannot contribute any more deeply to our understanding because there is nowhere to go from there. Or is there? What about gene-environment interactions? Gene-environment interactions are illustrated by Reiss (this volume). We particularly note his examples from adoption studies. Here, children with a genetic risk of schizophrenia from a biological parent are most likely to develop schizophrenia when placed in an adverse adoptive family environment, and unlikely to develop schizophrenia when placed in a favorable family environment, in spite of their genetic risk. In a decomposition of variance in BG, such gene-environment interactions are lumped into nonshared environment.

Reiss says such interactions are hard to find in sibling designs, and usually show up only in adoption designs. But Rowe, Jacobson, and van den Oord (1999) show gene-environment interactions in Add Health, using a twin design. Here, verbal IQ was shown to be mostly genetic among children of more educated parents, and hardly genetic at all among children of less educated parents. Dunne et al. (1997) used the Australian national twin sample to show that age at first sex was highly genetic among twins who came of age after the sexual revolution when youth were more free to express their natural inclinations, and hardly at all genetic among twins who came of age in an earlier period of greater social restrictions on opportunities and attitudes toward sex. And Carver and Udry (1997) used the Add Health BG sample to show that religiosity was more highly genetic among adolescents living under permissive parental supervision than among those living under more restrictive parental controls. All of these examples of gene-environment interactions come from straightforward sibling designs of population samples. This should lead us to be optimistic that gene-environment interactions are about us awaiting discovery by those who have good theoretically driven hypotheses. These discoveries depend on data sets with measures of the right contexts of behavior. As Bo Cleveland says, it looks like in the short run BG has more to gain from sociologists than from microbiologists.

Reiss tells us that behavior genetics has been thought of in this heyday of molecular genetics as a preliminary "peek at the genes." Some people have thought that molecular genetics would replace BG, and at best BG could be thought of as a way of deciding what relationships are probably genetic and are therefore worth the effort to locate the molecules that control the genetics. Nothing could be further from the facts. Many of the issues raised by Reiss can never be approached as easily through molecular routes. I would be interested in seeing an explication of how BG and molecular genetics can be partners in science, playing different but complementary roles.

Recently, I was part of a planning group at the National Institutes of Health on how NIH could plan a research agenda on "gene-environment interactions." People were asking, "how do gene-environment interactions manifest themselves at the molecular/biochemical/neurological level?" When you think about gene-environment interactions, especially in humans, you quickly realize the complexity of the problem when you can not produce 50 inbred strains of humans the way you can drosophila. Reiss has only touched on the role of BG designs that can examine many genetic research problems that are beyond the scope of molecular genetics, and are not amenable to experimental research designs in humans for resolving interactions. But I am afraid that NIH will bet its dollars on molecular routes to gene-environment interaction.

Developmental behavior genetics is central to many of the problems we as developmentalists want to look at. Reiss calls our attention to the fact that many genes are expressed during a specific age span. Some of the changes seem to involve genes whose expression begins at a certain age, while in others the expression stops at a certain age. Adolescence seems to be an age at which genetic expressions are changing rapidly. Is this because of biological maturation, as we imagine the case in Alzheimer's as related to old age? My guess is probably not. In adolescence, but particularly just after adolescence, environmental opportunities for adolescents are proliferating. Adolescents are suddenly facing a much greater variety of environments. The actual environmental variation faced by a cohort increases after adolescence. Now one of the rules that non-BG scholars overlook in BG is that the decomposition of variance in BG only holds for the same population in the same environments. As adolescents age, we have a situation in which the population stays the same but the environmental variance increases a lot. Environments become more and more idiosyncratic to individuals.

I see the following four developments in behavior genetic analysis as adolescents move into adulthood.

1. Decline of the influence, if any remains, of shared environments because siblings will not share much environment.

2. Increase in variance explained by genetics because adolescents will select environments that provide opportunities to express their long-time genetic propensities but as adolescents found no opportunities to express.

3. Decrease in explained variance (or what is the same thing, increased nonshared variance) because of the proliferation of environments that are more and more idiosyncratic, each individually explaining less and less, and therefore being harder and harder to identify.

4. Increase in gene-environment interactions as we learn to extract them from the nonshared (unexplained) variance. To do this we need to incorporate measures of the social contexts of adult life which adults must accommodate.

Reiss and his colleagues planned their monumental study on nonshared environments in the late 1980s. In a partly overlapping period, my colleagues and I were planning a study of environmental effects on adolescents. We were worried that we would mis-identify the sources of effects on adolescents if we didn't have a genetically informative sample. We engaged Robert Plomin, who had just finished planning the nonshared environment design, as a consultant. As a consequence of this fortunate move on our part, we were able to incorporate a genetically informative sample into the study that became Add Health. Further, we used the same expanded genetic design as that used by Reiss et al. (including not only twins, but full siblings and half siblings, and unrelated adolescent pairs living in the same household). Because we incorporated this design into a multi-stage school-based survey plan, we were able to have the best of both worlds: a large representative survey sample, and a representative expanded genetic sample of the same population of adolescents. Add Health is now collecting its fourth round of data on this sample. Thank you, David Reiss, for having developed your design for us to incorporate.

Reiss and his colleagues came up with many surprises. While their goal of explicating the meaning of nonshared environment effects on adolescents produced results that were frustrating to them and to us, their study provides a foundation for answering questions about the effects of children on families. The usual social science design provides no grasp of genetic effects.

Add Health has hundreds of researchers using its data, and only a handful using the genetic sample for analysis. It is a great source of frustration to me that Add Health data users never make comparisons of results from behavior-genetic analysis with those not using it. I am sure that one reason for this absence is that most researchers do not know how to do the simplest genetic analysis.

I myself am not a behavior geneticist, but I recently had Bo Cleveland, a student of David Rowe, working with me as a post-doctoral fellow. Another analyst, Kim Chantala, and I had been working on a measure of sex typicality (masculinity-femininity) that we could construct for all Add Health respondents using questions answered differently by males and females. We constructed a measure I call PrBoy (probability of being a boy). Values for boys run from .01 to .99, and values for girls run from .01 to .99 using the same scale. We then used the genetically informative sample from Add Health to compute the heritability of PrBoy. For girls, the heritability was about .38, while for boys it was about .25 (Cleveland, Udry, & Chantala, 2001). Interestingly, for both boys and girls, shared environment as a contributor to sex-typical behavior was *zero*. Now I need a theory that explains why sex typicality is more heritable for girls than for boys.

In another recent study, this time using biological measures that have their effects through prenatal uterine environments, I showed that prenatal maternal hormones have effects on adult female offspring's sex-typical behavior. These effects would presumably show up in a twin study as "shared environment." But those prenatal hormone effects actually interact with the offsprings' own adult hormones to produce their effects (Udry, 2000). Since these adult hormones are hypothetically genetically controlled, we might imagine that we have what in a behavior genetic model would be a gene-environment interaction between adult women's genes and their prenatal "shared environment." So the behavior turns out in the BG study to be genetic, but in an entirely different design turns out to be a gene-environment interaction. Maybe these are two entirely different sources of the genetic effects on sex-typicality.

There are many questions raised in my mind about the evidence Reiss gives us for the effects of genes appearing and disappearing over a period of three years. Now I realize that I don't have the foggiest idea what we mean when we say gene expression turns on or turns off. How can we tell the difference between a gene turning on and off and a gene interacting with an environmental element at one time and not at another? Evidently they may mean the same thing. Reiss says that "The impact of environmental circumstances on gene expression is termed gene x environment interaction" (p. 17, this volume). Let me take as an example one that Reiss provides in his ingenious strategy for combining an intervention with a panel adoption design. Reiss says that "no one has shown that by altering a parental response to heritable characteristics in their children that adverse genetic influences on behavior can be aborted and positive influences can be enhanced" (p. 16). Now suppose we could show that we could do this. Let us say we have observed at time 1 a trait we will call antisocial behavior in some 10-year-old boys, and have determined it to be 60 percent heritable.

Suppose we have determined from other studies that punishment by fathers evoked by this behavior causes increased in antisocial behavior. We divide our group of antisocial boys into two groups and allow some fathers to proceed with punishment, while in another group we teach the father to respond with an alternate response—spending more time with the boy but no punishment. Now at time 2 we test again the heritability of boys' antisocial behavior, and find in the punished group, antisocial behavior is 60% heritable when punished, and 10% heritable when treated with the alternate response. Would we conclude that the gene for antisocial behavior had been turned off by the new environmental treatment? Is that different from concluding that there is a gene-environment interaction between genes for antisocial behavior and the element of the environment we have manipulated? You can see how much I still have to learn.

So my instruction for spinning the straw of nonshared variance into gold is to discover the gene-environment interactions through BG *sibling designs*. I am betting that the current follow-up of Add Health respondents will provide the spinning wheel through which behavior geneticists can do this.

REFERENCES

Carver, K., & Udry, J. R.. (1997). *The biosocial transmission of religious attitudes*. Presented at the annual meeting of the American Sociological Association, Toronto, Canada.

Cleveland, H. H., Udry, J. R., & Chantala, K. (2001). Environmental and genetic influences on sex-typed behaviors and attitudes of male and female adolescents. *Personality and Social Psychology Bulletin, 27*, 1587–1598.

Dunne, M. P., Martin, N. G., Statham, D. J., Slutske, W. S., Dinwiddie, S. H., Bucholz, K. K., Madden, P. A., & Heath, A. C. (1997). Genetic and environmental contributions to variance in age at first sexual intercourse. *Psychological Science, 8*, 211–216.

Reiss, D., Neiderhiser, J. M., Hetherington, E. M., & Plomin, R. (2000). *The relationship code: Deciphering genetic and social influences on adolescent development*. Cambridge, MA: Harvard University Press.

Rowe, D. C., Jacobson, K. C., & van den Oord, E. J. C. G. (1999). Genetic and environmental influences on vocabulary IQ: Parental education level as moderator. *Child Development, 70*, 1151–1162.

Udry, J. R. (2000). Biological limits of gender construction. *American Sociological Review, 65*, 443–457.

II

What Role Does Infant and Early Childhood Temperament Play in the Development of Relationship With Parents?

5

Infant Negative Emotionality, Caregiving, and Family Relationships

Susan Crockenberg
Esther Leerkes
University of Vermont

Thirty-five years ago, when researchers investigated parents' influence on children's development, recognition that children affect their caregivers constituted a significant shift in paradigm (Bell, 1968; Thomas, Chess, Birch, Hertzig, & Korn, 1963). In the wake of that shift, developmental psychologists began to investigate the nature and pervasiveness of these child effects (Bell & Harper, 1977).

For a number of reasons having to do with both the field and the culture, researchers focused disproportionately on how infant temperament, and more specifically infant "difficulty," affected *maternal* caregiving behavior. The thesis that such an effect was likely to be negative was widely held. Excessive infant crying, the keystone of the difficulty construct, was thought to be aversive to caregivers both because the sound itself was irritating and because crying required a response that interfered with managing other (family) responsibilities and getting enough sleep. As a consequence, mothers of infants with a temperamental predisposition to cry often and intensely were expected to develop negative feelings about their babies and over time to respond less quickly and less appropriately to their cries.

For nearly 20 years, empirical findings accumulated, and like much developmental research, results were mixed (Crockenberg, 1986). In some studies, the expected negative association between infant irritability and maternal sensitivity was confirmed. However, in almost equal numbers, the opposite association was apparent; mothers engaged more sensitively with highly irritable than with less irritable infants. These differences were linked with sample characteristics. When mothers of irritable infants were at risk for less optimal parenting by virtue of their own personalities or their social contexts, they were *less* positive, sensitive, or responsive toward their infants. In the absence of any obvious risk characteristics, mothers of irritable infants were *more* positive, sensitive, and responsive toward their infants. Based on this analysis, Crockenberg (1986) proposed that infant temperament effects on caregiving are conditional on other aspects of the family context. It followed that to assess the effect of infant irritability on maternal behavior, researchers had to test interactive effects.

In the 15 years since that review, few researchers have taken that advice. In studies of infant temperament effects on caregiving, researchers continue to test and report main effects, with only a few exceptions (Calkins, Gill, Dedmon, &

Johnson, under review; Clark, Hyde, Essex, & Klein, 1997; Crockenberg & Leerkes, under review; Leerkes & Crockenberg, in press), which we consider in detail below. Despite this design limitation, research on "temperamental effects" has evolved in a number of potentially productive directions. We provide a brief tour of the burgeoning research on infant temperament in family context, beginning with the post-1986 studies linking infant negative emotionality with maternal well-being and maternal behavior. We review evidence of a moderating effect of parental behavior on infant negative emotionality through emotion regulation and consider the few studies linking infant negative emotionality with paternal behavior and with the marital and co-parental relationships. Then we identify directions for future research on infant temperament in the family context.

NEGATIVE EMOTIONALITY AS A TEMPERAMENTAL CHARACTERISTIC

As a temperamental characteristic, negative emotionality refers to individual differences in the experience and expression of negative emotions, including both reactive and regulatory components (Rothbart & Bates, 1998). Typically, in infancy negative reactivity is measured as some combination of the frequency and intensity of vocal, facial, motor, and physiological indices of distress, whereas regulation is operationalized in terms of the timing and/or degree of reductions in the same measures (Goldsmith & Rothbart, 1996; Kagan, Reznick, & Gibbons, 1989; Rothbart, 1981). In addition, for at least the last 20 years (Rothbart & Derryberry, 1981), researchers have acknowledged two types of negative emotionality associated with different types of eliciting stimuli: distress to novelty (i.e., fear) and distress to limitations (i.e., frustration). Although the import of this distinction for the question at hand is uncertain, support for its neurological underpinnings has grown quickly in the last 15 years.

There is evidence that fear and anger/frustration are associated differentially with the right and left frontal lobes of the cerebral cortex, respectively (see Dawson, 1994, for a review), and that the intensity of both reactions relates to activation of both frontal lobes. Although some researchers have interpreted these data as consistent with a genetic basis of temperament, Dawson and her colleagues report data indicating that the infant's parenting environment plays a part in shaping patterns of frontal activation asymmetries (Dawson, Grofer Klinger, Panagiotides, Hill, & Spieker, 1992).

Both interpretations may be correct. According to LeDoux (1987, 1993), emotions are distributed throughout reciprocally acting subcortical and cortical regions. Thus, general arousal is controlled by the ascending influence of subcortical structures on the cortex, preparing the infant to interpret and respond to external stimuli. It follows that individual differences in generalized activation are present very early in infancy because they do not involve the later-developing frontal cortex, and therefore may be influenced little by the postnatal caregiving environment. Other subcortical limbic regions (e.g., the amygdala) appear to be specialized for the rapid appraisal of events related to biological survival and are linked with innate action tendencies toward approach and withdrawal. Even decorticate animals engage in approach-withdrawal responses including rage, escape, attack, fear, and exploration. Thus, individual differences in the tendency to engage in approach or withdrawal likely exist before postnatal experience has had the opportunity to influence them.

How then might infants' post-birth experiences influence their temperamental characteristics associated with negative emotion? Dawson's (1994) thesis, drawing on LeDoux (1987), is that more complex discrimination and interpretation of emotional stimuli require the neocortex. The frontal region in particular specializes in functions necessary for the regulation of emotion, and these abilities are thought to be strongly influenced by experience.

It is noteworthy in this context that the results of behavioral genetic research carried out with infants are consistent with the view that measures of infant negative emotionality and behavioral inhibition represent both genetic and environmental influences. Typically, the heritability of these characteristics ranges from .30–.50, depending on both the measures of temperament used and size and characteristics of the sample, indicating that as much or more of the variation is a function of infants' pre and postnatal experience (see Goldsmith, Buss, & Lemery, 1996; Goldsmith, Lemery, Buss, & Campos, 1999 for reviews).

This discussion of the physiological basis of temperamental differences may seem an unnecessary digression from the question of how infant temperament impacts the family. I assure you that it is relevant. If emotion regulation is influenced by learning and if the developing frontal cortex is implicated in this process, by the second half of the first year of life even physiological assessments of infant temperament, not to mention maternal reports, likely reflect the interplay of genetic and environmental factors. As a consequence, investigating the impact of infant temperament on caregivers, and on the family generally, will be challenging indeed. Certainly, attempts to operationalize reactive components of negative emotionality without at the same time considering regulating components will confound the search for causal mechanisms to the extent that family characteristics thought to influence emotion regulation are the same characteristics thought to be affected by infant negative emotionality. Thus, in this review we highlight studies in which researchers reduce the impact of experience on infant negative emotionality by controlling pre-existing characteristics of caregivers thought to influence infant emotion regulation through their association with caregiver behavior.

INFANT NEGATIVE EMOTIONALITY AND MATERNAL EMOTIONAL WELL-BEING

Investigations of the effect of infant negative emotionality on maternal confidence, self-efficacy, and depression tell a reasonably consistent story. With only minor exceptions or qualifications, mothers of fussier, less soothable infants report significantly less confidence, lower efficacy, and more stress and depressive symptoms than mothers of less fussy, more soothable infants. This association is apparent as a main effect (Cutrona & Troutman, 1986; Hubert, 1989; Murray, Stanley, Hooper, & King, 1996; Papousek & von Hofacker, 1998; Teti & Gelfand, 1991; van Egeren & Lower, 2001; Ventura & Stevenson, 1986; Wilkie & Ames, 1986) and in interaction with other variables (Crockenberg & Leerkes, under review; Leerkes & Crockenberg, in press; Martin, Clements, Crnic, Pollack, & Boreck, 2001).

In most of the above studies, pre-birth characteristics of mothers that may have confounded the results (e.g., prenatal depression or low self-esteem) were *not* controlled, leaving open the possibility that mothers influenced infant temperamental characteristics, rather than the reverse. Notably, however, in the studies in which these variables were covaried, associations between infant temperament and mothers' well-being remained significant, even in low-risk samples, as main (Murray et al., 1996) or interactive effects. In Leerkes and Crockenberg (in press), high infant distress to novelty in conjunction with low soothability was associated with low maternal self-efficacy at 5 months postpartum, controlling for prenatal maternal self-esteem, which also predicted maternal self-efficacy. In Crockenberg and Leerkes (under review), infant distress to novelty interacted with mothers' childhood acceptance by parents to predict maternal postpartum depressive symptoms. Mothers of easily distressed infants whose own parents were rejecting reported more depression postpartum than mothers of comparable infants with accepting parents, controlling for prenatal depressive symptoms, marital aggression, and self-esteem (see Figure 5.1). In Martin et al. (2001), with infant and maternal variables covaried, infant negative affect predicted maternal stress only when mothers' negative emotion was high.

In a high-risk sample, we might expect to find main effects, rather than interactions, because protective factors are less prevalent. To illustrate, in Papousek and von Hofacker's (1998) research, mothers of infants who were persistent criers scored lower on feelings of self-efficacy, and higher on depression, anxiety, and anger than control mothers, but higher also on adverse childhood memories and marital distress. In such a sample, it would be difficult to find a subgroup of mothers with high-crying infants and supportive relationships with either parents or partners, and probably impossible to test moderating effects. Nevertheless, the so-called main effect of infant irritability on maternal well-being in this study is more accurately viewed as an untested cumulative effect of multiple risk factors, rather than a simple main effect.

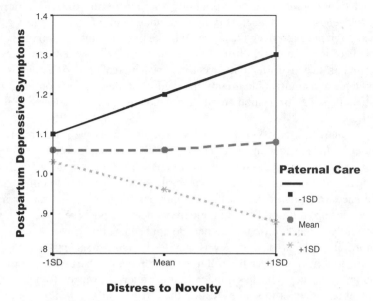

FIG. 5.1.   Interactive effect of infant distress to novelty and remembered paternal care/acceptance on maternal postpartum depressive symptoms.

NEGATIVE EMOTIONALITY AND MATERNAL SENSITIVITY

For the most part, patterns of association between negative emotionality and maternal sensitivity obtained in the last 15 years parallel earlier ones (Crockenberg, 1986).

High-risk Samples

Under conditions of high risk, mothers of infants high in negative emotionality behave differently and less optimally than mothers of infants low in negative emotionality (Papousek & von Hofacker, 1998; Susman-Stillman, Kalkose, Egeland, & Waldman, 1996; van den Boom & Hoeksma, 1994). But it appears that they may be insensitive in different ways, depending on the nature of the risk.

van den Boom and Hoeksma (1994) alerted us to the possibility that some "high risk" mothers (i.e., those whose risk was defined by low socioeconomic status) may behave insensitively when their infants are quiet and alert, rather than when they are fussing and crying. They reported differences in the behavior of mothers of infants identified as extremely irritable or not at all irritable during the neonatal period, using a standardized assessment of the speed, frequency, and intensity of infant negative arousal. Infant and maternal behavior was observed from 1 to 6 months of age. Surprisingly, there were no differences in mothers' responsiveness to fussing and crying as a function of infant irritability at any observation point. Moreover, the decrease in the initially higher level of soothing by mothers of irritable infants from 1 and 6 months corresponded with decreases in their infants' negative affectivity over the same period of time. At 6 months, mothers of irritable and nonirritable infants engaged in similar rates of soothing, suggesting that the behavior of mothers of the irritable infants was normative in this respect.

In contrast, mothers of the highly irritable infants were noninvolved more frequently and engaged in less effective stimulation (i.e., less contact, fewer positive vocalizations and expressions of affect) when their infants were in positive affective states than mothers of less irritable infants. As shown in Figure 5.2, this difference was apparent across the 6-month period, despite the fact that infants in the two groups did not differ in their frequencies of positive affect at 6 months. Apparently, some "high-risk" mothers do not become less responsive over time to their irritable infants' distress as was previously assumed, at least when the infants become less irritable over time. Rather, they remain less responsive to their infants' *positive* cues. This has implications for intervention and for the assessment of maternal behavior in studies testing the effect of infant negative emotionality on maternal sensitivity. If differences in maternal sensitivity associated with infant irritability are apparent primarily in response to positive cues, using mothers' reactions to infant *distress* as an index of sensitivity reduces the likelihood of finding an effect. However, other risk factors may be associated with insensitivity to infant distress.

Responsiveness to positive signals

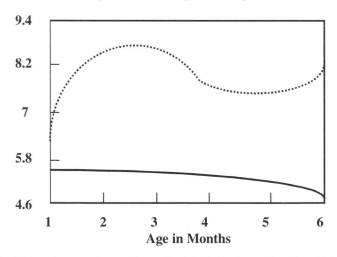

FIG. 5.2. Maternal responsiveness to positive infant signals as a function of infant irritability. – represents irritable infants, ▪ ▪ represents non-irritable infants.

We speculate that there are two types of risk, with different implications for maternal behavior. In the first type, risk occurs because competing demands associated with the family context interfere with mothers' engagement with their infants when they are *not* distressed. This pattern would occur when mothers have been highly attentive when their babies were distressed and use the time when the babies are calm to take care of other responsibilities. Risk of this type might be apparent in low-income samples in which mothers are responsible for tasks that more affluent mothers hire others to perform, when cultural values (e.g., regarding household cleanliness) require behaviors that interfere with attention to the infant, or when other family members compete with the infant for attention.

In the second type, risk occurs when mothers' characteristics increase the likelihood that they will experience negative emotion when their infants cry frequently and intensely, and therefore respond slowly or inappropriately (i.e., insensitively) when their infants are distressed. Risk of this type would occur when mothers are predisposed to depression or anger by virtue of their childhood-based working models of attachment or current life circumstances (e.g., a dysfunctional partner relationship). These distinctions have implications for intervention and for research investigating the effect of infant negative emotionality on families (see below).

Low-risk Families

Above, we document the empirical support for one side of the hypothesized interaction: that under conditions of high risk, a negative association exists between infant irritability and maternal sensitivity. Support for the other half of the interaction is mixed. In the absence of risk, infant negative emotionality as a main effect is either positively associated with (Washington, Minde, & Goldberg, 1986), unrelated to (Calkins et al., under review; Crockenberg & Leerkes, under review; Hann, 1989; Leerkes & Crockenberg, in press), or negatively associated with maternal sensitivity (Clark et al., 1997; Mangelsdorf, Gunnar, Kestenbaum, Lang, & Andreas, 1990; Seifer et al., 1996; Spangler, 1990) as a main effect.

Possibly the failure to control pre-existing maternal characteristics in some studies, as we propose above, or differences in the way infant negative emotionality or maternal sensitivity were measured explain the discrepant findings. We might argue also that the preponderance of evidence supports a negative association because typically we would not consider the absence of association as compelling evidence in support of a hypothesis, and this pattern characterizes most of the studies congruent with the hypothesis of conditional temperamental effects.

Alternatively, it appears to us that the interactive effects reported by Clarke et al. (1997), Leerkes and Crockenberg (in press), and Calkins et al. (under review) explain both the lack of association and the negative association between infant negative reactivity and maternal sensitivity under conditions of low risk and lend credibility to the hypothesis. In Leerkes and Crockenberg, there was no main effect of infant distress to limits or novelty on maternal sensitivity, before or after controlling for prenatal maternal characteristics and partner support. However, consistent with the hypothesized interactive effect, high *distress to limits* in conjunction with maternal self-efficacy predicted less sensitive maternal behavior. In Calkins et al. (under review), high infant *distress to limits* was associated with less sensitive maternal behavior *only* when mothers reported high stress associated with their infants' characteristics.

The results of Clark et al. (1997) are particularly compelling because they demonstrate dramatically how interactions can fully explain an apparent main effect. As shown in Figure 5.3, mothers with shorter maternal leaves (i.e., returned to work by 6 weeks postpartum) and infants high in *distress to limits* engaged in less positive affective involvement and were less sensitive and responsive than mothers with equally distressed infants, but longer maternal leaves. Consistent with the thesis that infant negative emotionality temperament adversely affects maternal behavior under conditions of high risk, only when mothers take short maternal leaves is infant negative emotionality associated negatively with maternal sensitivity. This could be useful information for mothers with easily distressed infants who have control over the length of their leaves, and for establishing social policies that allow flexibility in parental leave when infants have special needs. Unfortunately, lack of control for prebirth characteristics of mothers that might influence both the decision to return to work quickly and ratings of their infants' distress undermines our ability to interpret the interactive effect.

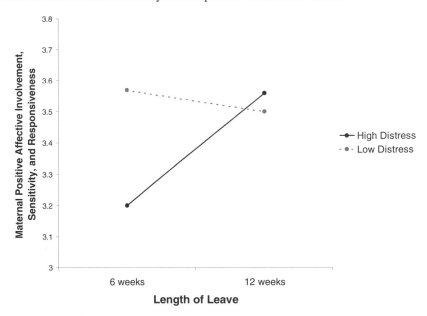

FIG. 5.3. Interactive effect of distress to novelty and length of maternal leave on maternal responsiveness.

Nevertheless, the question of whether infant negative emotionality adversely impacts maternal sensitivity only when risk is high remains unanswered in 2001. This is largely because so few researchers have controlled for pre-existing characteristics of mothers and tested interactive effects, although issues related to the context in which infant negative emotionality and maternal sensitivity are assessed may also play a role. In the studies reviewed above, it is distress to limits that interacts with risk to predict maternal sensitivity. Whether distress to novelty is similarly moderated remains to be determined, although Crockenberg and Leerkes (under review) who tested the interactive effects of that dimension of infant reactivity found no significant results. However, in the studies reviewed below, it is distress to novelty that is moderated by caregiver behavior, suggesting that interactive effects may be apparent for both dimensions of reactivity, possibly with different risk factors relevant for different dimensions of negative emotionality. We consider some reasons for these differences below in our discussion of temperament by gender interactions.

As we suggested earlier, the impact of infant negative emotionality on maternal behavior may vary as a function of the type of risk involved. If risk is the result of competing responsibilities and lack of assistance, mothers may be less engaged when their infants are positive or neutral and appear not to need them. If risk is a function of depression, lack of empathy, or childhood rejection, we would expect infant irritability to be negatively associated with maternal sensitivity to crying. Global measures of maternal sensitivity could obscure these distinctions and make it more difficult to find associations between infant temperament and maternal behavior when they exist. Thus, in research of this kind, it is essential to match operational measures of maternal behavior with the type of risk involved. On the other hand, it may be difficult to accurately test the moderating impact of risk on the link between infant temperament and maternal behavior if there are multiple risk factors (maternal depression, poor self-esteem, childhood rejection or abuse), only one of which is identified in the interaction. Creating a composite of risk factors *expected to have the same negative impact on maternal behavior* when they occur in conjunction with high negative emotionality would allow researchers to test interactive effects more effectively in such samples.

Finally, there is the challenge of obtaining accurate measures of maternal sensitivity from observations of mothers and infants in constrained circumstances. Mothers strive to be good mothers, *especially* when they are being observed. The briefer the observation and the fewer the distractions (i.e., telephone, television, other children), the more responsive we would expect them to be. Moreover, the absence of distractions should have a disproportionately greater impact on mothers who are more distracted by them when they are present (i.e., the less sensitive mothers), making them appear more sensitively attuned than they are typically. It behooves us, therefore, to consider carefully the conditions in which we assess maternal behavior if we are to adequately test the hypothesis of conditional temperamental effects.

INFANT NEGATIVE EMOTIONALITY, PARENTAL BEHAVIOR, AND EMOTION REGULATION

Despite the enormous number of articles on emotion regulation in the last decade, investigations of the moderating effect of parental behavior on infant negative emotionality as a temperamental characteristic are limited. Often researchers test and report associations between different parental behaviors and infant emotion regulation, rather than the differential effects of those behaviors on infants who differ in negative emotionality. Nevertheless, some provide useful direction for researchers interested in the differential effects of caregiver behavior on infants who differ in negative emotionality. For example, Stifter and Grant (1993) reported that 10-month-old infants who expressed frequent anger when a toy was removed and also when the toy was returned (i.e., infants who regulated anger less well) had fathers who displayed *low* levels of negative affect. The researchers speculated that fathers who expressed negative affect frequently inhibited the expression of negative emotion in their infants, citing Termine and Izard's (1988) finding, that mothers' expression of negative affect inhibited play and increased gaze aversion, in support of this interpretation. We could speculate further that the infants who regulated anger poorly in Stifter and Grant's study were temperamentally reactive infants whose less expressive fathers withdrew from their negative reactivity, depriving them of the assistance they needed to regulate negative emotion.

Other data demonstrate reduced behavioral inhibition over the course of infancy for highly reactive infants with less accommodating parents. In Arcus (2001), infants identified as highly reactive at 4 months were observed with their mothers from 5 to 13 months. Differences in behavioral inhibition at 14 months varied as a joint function of maternal selective attentiveness to infant distress and limit setting during the intervening months. For first-born children, reactive infants whose mothers were highly attentive to infant crying, but less responsive when their infants were positive or neutral, and low in limit-setting later in the first year were more inhibited at 14 months. Highly reactive infants whose mothers did not attend differentially to fussing and crying early in the first year of life and who were firm and direct in their discipline later on were less inhibited at 14 months. Park, Belsky, Putnam, and Crnic (1997) reported similarly that 3-year-old boys identified as highly reactive in infancy were less inhibited when their mothers were more intrusive and their fathers less sensitive, with fathers' behavior somewhat more predictive than mothers'.

Arcus (2001) theorized that firm, consistent parental behavior provides infants with opportunities to develop strategies for coping with minor stresses in the security of the home. Presumably, they use these strategies when they are exposed to unfamiliar stimuli in the laboratory and demonstrate less behavioral inhibition as a result of their enhanced emotion regulation. Certainly, we would not expect this pattern of adaptation if the parent's behavior was frightening; and Arcus pointed out that in her study negative control was comprised primarily of directives, which some investigators code as control, rather than negative control (Crockenberg & Litman, 1990). Nor is it responsiveness to crying per se that is associated with greater behavioral inhibition at 14 months among highly reactive infants, but a mother's responsiveness to crying *at the expense of responsiveness during quiet, alert periods*. Such a mother may overlook opportunities to encourage her infant to approach unfamiliar situations when she is available to serve as a secure base and the infant is in an optimal state for learning. Additionally, her inconsistent responsiveness may undermine the development of a secure infant-mother attachment, which Nachmias, Gunnar, Mangelsdorf, Parritz and Buss (1996) found to moderate the association between behavioral inhibition and stress reactivity during the toddler period.

Based on this research, there is reason to think that experiences orchestrated by caregivers alter patterns of extreme infant reactivity during infancy, probably by fostering the development of effective emotion regulation. Moreover, it appears that different parental responses may be needed during different phases of infancy and perhaps also in relation to different types of negative reactivity. Early on, sensitive responsiveness to the infant's negative *and positive* cues likely reduces the amount and degree of negative affect experienced by infants who tend to react strongly and negatively to novelty. In doing so, it counteracts their tendency to withdraw from novelty and simultaneously fosters secure attachment relationships. As infants become mobile later in the first year of life and increasingly autonomous in the second year, they come in contact with more novel events and more barriers to achieving their goals, conditions that elicit strong negative reactions from infants so disposed. During this period of development, parents who support, but do not force, their infant's exposure to novelty and who limit their infant's pursuit of dangerous, age-inappropriate, or socially disruptive goals firmly, but not harshly, foster the development of adaptive emotion regulation.

As Eleanor Maccoby points out (this volume), it may be necessary also to consider temperament and gender simultaneously in tracing transactive infant-family effects in the second year of life. In a 1984 study, Maccoby, Snow, and Jacklin observed mothers and infants at 12 and again at 18 months, in a series of teaching tasks. Both temperament and gender influenced the across-time correlations. Mothers of 12-month-old boys who expressed more negative affect reduced their teaching effort subsequently, and the infant sons of mothers who exerted greater teaching effort at 12 months became less difficult during the subsequent 6 months. No comparable effects were observed for girls, suggesting that parents respond differentially to negative emotionality in male and female infants by the second year of life. Certainly, to the extent that families embrace the cultural stereotypes regarding the gendered expression of negative emotion (e.g., that anger is tolerated less in girls than boys, whereas fear is tolerated less in boys than girls), we would anticipate different reactions to children high in distress to limits and novelty as a function of gender (Crockenberg & Langrock, 2001). Evidence that negatively reactive, inhibited male infants were more likely than similar female infants to become less inhibited over the course of development (Arcus, 2001) is consistent with such a gendered pattern of socialization.

Ultimately, we need to know the conditions under which extreme negative reactivity is moderated over the course of infancy and the immediate and long-term impact of those changes on the infant, other family members, and the family system as a whole. van den Boom's (1994) experimental intervention tests these questions for infants. Fifty mothers of irritable neonates were taught to identify infant cues, interpret them accurately, and implement an appropriate response, behaviors indicative of maternal sensitivity. At 9 months, experimental mothers were significantly more responsive, stimulating, attentive, and appropriately controlling than control mothers, and their infants were more self-soothing and cried less than infants of control mothers. Positive intervention effects were still apparent at 3 ½ years (van den Boom, 1995).

By demonstrating that caregivers vary in their responses to highly reactive infants, both naturally and through intervention, the reviewed data lends additional credibility to the hypothesis of conditional, (i.e., risk-linked) temperament effects on caregivers. It suggests further that differences in the way parents respond to their temperamentally irritable infants are important precursors of healthy development and psychopathology.

INFANT NEGATIVE EMOTIONALITY AND THE FAMILY SYSTEM

In the past 15 years, we have witnessed a broadening of views on the effect of easily distressed infants on families. Whereas in earlier studies researchers focused exclusively on the infant-mother dyad, more recently they have begun to consider how negatively reactive infants affect their fathers and also the parents' marital relationship. We review that undeniably scant research below.

Infant Temperament and Fathers

In their 1986 study, Wilkie and Ames found that a high amount of mother-reported infant crying correlated positively with fathers' depression, anxiety, and concern about the changes in their lives. Ventura and Stevenson (1986) reported similarly that infants' optimal temperaments were negatively associated with fathers' depressive symptom. Sirignano and Lachman (1985) found negative changes in self-reported personality among parents who perceived their infants as having less positive temperaments, an effect that was greater for fathers than for mothers.

But the pattern is not uniform. In a recent study, Van Egeren and Lower (2001) found that mothers' ratings of fussiness were *positively* associated with fathers' self-efficacy, which may reflect the increased sense of competence some fathers experience when they are more involved in the care of their infants. Moreover, as we discuss in greater detail below, fathers' greater involvement with their negatively reactive infants may serve as a buffer against the potentially negative impact of the infants' temperament on mothers' caregiving.

In contrast, in the only investigation of the effect of infant negative emotionality on father's behavior early in the second year of life, Woodworth, Belsky, and Crnic (1996) reported that observed negative or positive infant emotionality at 12 to 13 months was not associated with fathers' positive or negative engagement, or with their child management behavior. Although the limited amount of data on fathers precludes generalizations, the findings for these low-risk fathers are similar to those for low-risk mothers and consistent with the hypothesis that high infant irritability impacts parents adversely only when it occurs with other risk factors.

Infant Temperament and the Marital Relationship

Wilkie and Ames (1986) reported that infant crying correlated negatively with fathers' views of themselves as husbands and their wives as wives and mothers, and positively with greater concern about the changes in their lives since their babies' births. Using more traditional measures of infant temperament, Belsky and Rovine (1990) found similarly that infant unpredictability and unadaptability[1] were associated with decreases in love and increases in conflict in marital relationships, as reported by mothers. Hakulinen, Laippala, and Paunonen (1998) reported links between infant negative mood and family dynamics in a Finnish sample. When infants had low thresholds for reactivity, mothers reported less role reciprocity with fathers. (As 98% of fathers reported high role reciprocity, it is not surprising that no comparable effects were obtained when they were the reporters.) Whether this reflects lower father participation in infant care and family maintenance when infants are reactive, or the mother's perception that he is participating less than needed under the circumstances, is uncertain because the researchers did not document the amount of time fathers spent doing these tasks. However, the finding is consistent with the results of two other studies. Jones and Heerman (1992) reported that fathers participated later in the provision of care when their infants had negative than when they had positive temperaments. Leerkes and Crockenberg (in press) reported similarly that mothers reported lower satisfaction with partner support when they rated their infants as high in distress to novelty and greater satisfaction when they rated them as highly soothable. We

---

[1] Although infant negative mood was not similarly predictive, entering the four temperament constructs simultaneously might have obscured such an effect.

speculate in that article that fathers are likely no better prepared than mothers to respond effectively to their negatively reactive infants, and further that professional intervention may be necessary when the needs of the infant differ substantially from the norm.

In sum, there is evidence that negatively reactive infants adversely affect fathers, as well as mothers, in ways that could undermine the marital relationship during the transition to parenthood. If fathers' views of themselves and their wives as marital partners are diminished by having a negatively reactive baby, the scene is set for increased marital conflict around these issues and for lower marital satisfaction as a result of both the perceptions and the conflict. Whether in fact it does so is less certain. Only Belsky and Rovine (1990) report data on change in the marital relationship as a function of infant temperament, and only from the mother's perspective. Nor is it clear whether such an effect endures as infants become less negatively reactive or parents work through the issues raised by their infants' special needs. Herein lies the crux of the issue. Everything else we know suggests that the effects of infant negative reactivity on the family vary as a function of other characteristics of family members and family contexts. It follows that we should anticipate interactive effects of infant negative reactivity in relation to the marital and co-parental relationships as well.

Infant Temperament and the Co-parental Relationship

Preliminary data from Berkman, Alberts, Carleton, and McHale (2001) are consistent with such a prediction, although they do not test the interaction directly. In their study of 40 low-risk families, babies who were rated as more negative and inhibited on an observational assessment of infant temperament had more cooperative interactions with their parents during triadic play at 3-months postpartum. These same families displayed more warmth during triadic play, between parents as well as from parent to child, suggesting that when they have the resources, parents pull together around a child who appears to need them to do so. Their efforts may be reflected in the infants' ability to maintain a more positive affective state during play than would have been expected on the basis of temperament alone.

In contrast, unpublished longitudinal data from Carmola Hauf, Leerkes, and Crockenberg (n.d.), based on 41 low-risk families with 2 ½-year-olds, indicate the opposite effect. Mothers of infants high in *distress to novelty* at 5 months postpartum rated the parenting alliance, a questionnaire-based measure of the co-parental relationship, more negatively when the infants were 2 ½ years of age. This association was independent of the other significant predictors of the parenting alliance, a prenatal measure of fathers' engaged coping and a 6-month measure of fathers' marital aggression. Additionally, infant distress to novelty interacts with fathers' disengaged coping and distress to limits interacts with fathers' engaged coping to predict parenting alliance. It is intriguing that distress to novelty is negatively associated with the parental alliance when fathers report low disengaged coping, whereas distress to limits is negatively associated with the parental alliance when fathers report low engaged coping. Taken together, these findings suggest a mismatch between the father's preferred coping style and the infant's approach-withdrawl-linked emotions is detrimental to the parenting alliance during the infant's third year of life.

As we have argued above, the discrepancy in the results of these two studies may reflect differences in the analyses employed, as only the latter controlled for confounding variables and tested interactive effects. It could also reflect the age of the infants at the time the co-parental relationship was assessed (3 months versus 2 ½ years) or the different measures of the co-parental relationship. Possibly the ability to maintain a positive co-parental relationship around a child who is highly distressed by novelty becomes more challenging over the course of infancy as opportunities for exposure to novelty increase and as parents adapt to the birth of a second child. It is these transactive infant-family effects throughout infancy (Sameroff, 1975) that we consider below.

DIRECTIONS FOR FUTURE RESEARCH

A number of methodologies may be used to investigate the interplay of infant temperament and family functioning, but knowing how to proceed presupposes a conceptualization of the process to guide decision-making. We present such a model in Figure 5.4. In the model, pathways diverge and destinations differ depending on the characteristics of both parents individually, their relationship, and the way both they and their infant change over the course of early development.

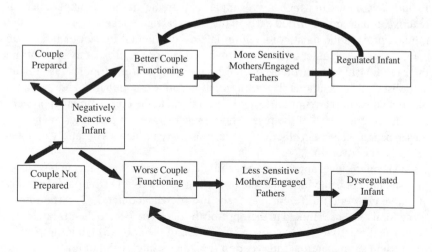

FIG. 5.4.   A transactive model of infant negative emotionality and family relationships.

Specifically, negatively reactive infants enter families that differ in their suitability for supporting their infants' healthy development. When parents are psychologically prepared for having a baby, the infant's temperament may draw them together as a couple and as parents, supporting maternal sensitivity and paternal engagement, and facilitating adaptive emotion regulation thereby. Presumably their success in this significant family task feeds back positively to their sense of themselves as partners and parents, and in doing so maintains the infant's positive developmental trajectory.

In contrast, when parents are psychologically unprepared for the challenges of having a new baby, individually or as a couple, we expect the infant's negative reactivity to contribute to decreases in marital and co-parental functioning, less sensitive maternal behavior and less engaged fathers, and dysfunctional patterns of emotion regulation. Whether this negative trajectory endures depends in turn on other factors, including the infant's exposure to alternate caregivers, developmental changes in the infant that alter or compensate for their negative emotionality, and parents' ability and opportunity to learn different ways of interacting. For example, intervention-related changes in mothers' and fathers' ability to facilitate adaptive emotion regulation could reduce their infants' negative affect and simultaneously alter their perceptions of each other as partners and parents. Together, these changes may improve parents' abilities to respond appropriately and consistently to their infants during the challenging second year of life.

METHODOLOGIES FOR STUDYING TRANSACTIVE PROCESSES

In our view, studies in which large samples of extreme groups of temperamentally reactive infants are identified early in the first year and tracked over the course of infancy provide the most compelling data on the mutual impact of infants and caregivers on each other over time. Obtaining data on the prospective parents and their relationship pre-birth and including them as control variables ensures that any observed associations (between infant negative emotionality and the family outcome measure) are not artifactual. In addition to the correlational approaches that characterize most of the research reviewed above, several other methodologies appear promising in elucidating the transactive influences of family members on each other over time.

One micro-level approach we use involves second-by-second analyses of infant and mother behavior to test the following questions. (1) Do infants' negative affective cues elicit different responses in different mothers? (2) Are mothers' behavioral responses linked to their pre-birth characteristics, to their infants' temperamental reactivity, or to some combination of the two? (3) Do infants' affective responses to maternal intervention (i e , increasing, maintaining, or decreasing in negativity) differ as a function of the sensitivity of the mothers' responses? 4) Do negatively reactive infants respond disproportionately more negatively (i.e., increase or fail to decrease their negative affect) in response to less sensitive maternal interventions? This allows us to identify how infants and mothers influence each other during a single observation and to understand how characteristics of each contribute to the process. By repeating these analyses at different times during infancy, we may track changes in the dyad as a function of their earlier dyadic interaction using growth curve data.

Halvorsen and Deal (2001) used growth curve data successfully with older children to track individual changes in both temperament and the family context over the course of development. We refer you to those researchers for a detailed presentation of latent growth curve modeling. Suffice it to say that this approach yields information on the slope of the temperament scores that describe increasing (positive slope) or decreasing (negative slope) scores for individuals, as well as the magnitude of the change (as larger slopes indicate more change in a specific direction). By including measures of the family context (at one time point) and changes in other temperament characteristics in regression analyses, they were able to predict within-child differences in temperament across four years. With this approach, it would be possible to track changes in family context in the same way, using both initial negative reactivity and changes over time in reactivity to predict changes in family context. And, by replacing infant temperament scores with dyadic measures, we could track the dyadic process longitudinally. Keep in mind, however, that this is a labor-intensive endeavor as a minimum of four observations are recommended to obtain reliable assessments of change.

Another potentially profitable approach involves the collection and analysis of qualitative data. Because qualitative methods are diverse, it is challenging to define them in a way that is clear and at the same time accurately represents all that go by that name. Nevertheless, Hayes' (1997, p. 4) statement that "qualitative methodology has tended to be associated with a concern on the part of the researcher with meanings, context, and a holistic approach to the material," does as good a job as any of identifying the set of criteria that fits this methodology. As a psychologist educated under the arc of the logical positivists, I (speaking as the senior author) viewed qualitative data suspiciously. I have changed my mind as I have grown to appreciate the way we make sense of and give meaning to our experiences and how that meaning influences behavior (Crockenberg & Langrock, 2001). This being the case, we believe that information about the way others make meaning in their lives by interpreting experience is essential to understanding stability and change in their behavior over time (i.e., development).

We propose a theory-driven qualitative approach that may be useful in elucidating the complex ways infant negative emotionality affects *and is affected by* mothers and fathers and their relationships over time. Like the quantitative methods described above, this approach is time-consuming and labor-intensive, but no more so, we believe, than is necessary to obtain valid data on children and families. Unlike other qualitative approaches, it can be applied to a large sample of people with the possibility that patterns may be sufficiently consistent to allow a claim of generalizability (Stratton, 1997). Used in conjunction with quantitative data, as Phil and Carolyn Cowan have done so brilliantly in their 1992 book about their "Becoming Partners" project, qualitative data can be used to "provide a moving picture of how change in any one family domain affects all the individuals and relationships in the family" (p. 5).

To illustrate: we might want to explain an interaction between infant age and negative reactivity on mothers' responsiveness (i.e., decreases in mothers' responsiveness to their negatively reactive infants over the first year) and its prediction of infants' subsequent noncompliance to fathers. From the qualitative data we could ascertain reasons for the change in maternal behavior by identifying common themes in parents' narratives about their reactions to their infants. We might discover that partners' pressure on mothers to be more attentive to them was mentioned consistently by families in which noncompliance occurred, but infrequently by families in which mothers were equally unresponsive to their negatively reactive infants, but children were compliant with fathers. In the latter group, we might find that mothers' burn-out, associated with the amount of care required by highly reactive infants, was reported consistently in the narratives and that fathers spent more time caring for their babies. In this way, qualitative analyses increase knowledge by moving the analysis to another level of explanation and by providing information on process-level questions that otherwise would not be addressed.

In closing, we wish to acknowledge the possibility of investigating transactive infant-parent and parent-infant effects on a variety of individual and family outcomes using the elaborated behavioral genetic approach proposed by David Reiss (this volume). Not surprisingly in view of our thesis about the primacy of interactive infant-mother effects, we are intrigued by the potential of a cross-fostering design, in which the negative emotionality of infants of *parents* high in negative emotionality, placed in more and less favorable adoptive family environments, is assessed over the course of development to study temperament by environment (G x E) interactions.

ACKNOWLEDGMENTS

We wish to thank Amy Carmola Hauf and Tabitha Holmes, Psychology Department graduate students at the University of Vermont, for their assistance in developing our ideas about qualitative analyses, and Shamila Lekka, a member of our research team, for her help in locating references.

REFERENCES

Arcus, D. (2001). Inhibited and uninhibited children: Biology in the social context. In T. D. Wachs & G. A. Kohnstamm (Eds.), *Temperament in context* (pp. 43–60). Hillsdale, NJ: Lawrence Erlbaum Associates.

Bell, R. Q. (1968). A reinterpretation of the direction of effects in studies of socialization. *Psychological Review, 75,* 81–95.

Bell, R. Q., & Harper, L. V. (1977). *Child effects on adults.* Hillsdale, NJ: Lawrence Erlbaum Associates.

Belsky, J., & Rovine, M. (1990). Patterns of marital change across the transition to parenthood: Pregnancy to three years postpartum. *Journal of Marriage and the Family, 52,* 5–19.

Berkman, J., Alberts, A., Carleton, M., & McHale, J. (2001). *Are there links between infant temperament and coparenting processes at 3 months postpartum?* Poster submitted to the World Association for Infant Mental Health Meetings, 2002.

Calkins, S. D., Gill, K. L., Dedmon, S. E., & Johnson, L. M. (under review). *Mothers' interactions with temperamentally frustrated infants.*

Carmola Hauf, A., Leerkes, E. & Crockenberg, S. (n.d.) Infant temperament, parental characteristics and the parenting alliance. (Unpublished raw data)

Clark, R., Hyde, J. S., Essex, M. J., & Klein, M. H. (1997). Length of maternity leave and quality of mother-infant interactions. *Child Development, 68,* 364–383.

Cowan, C. P., & Cowan, P. A. (1992). *When partners become parents: The big life change for couples.* New York: Basic Books.

Crockenberg, S. (1986). Are temperamental differences in babies associated with predictable differences in caregiving? In J. V. Lerner & R. M. Lerner (Eds.), *New directions for child_development: No. 31. Temperament and social interaction in infants and children_*(pp. 53–73). San Francisco, CA: Jossey-Bass.

Crockenberg, S. C., & Langrock, A. (2001). The role of specific emotions in children's responses to interparental conflict: A test of the model. *Journal of Family Psychology, 15,* 163–182.

Crockenberg, S. C., & Leerkes, E. M. (under review). Parental acceptance, postpartum depression, and maternal sensitivity: Mediating and moderating processes. *Journal of Family Psychology.*

Crockenberg, S. C., & Litman, C. (1990). Autonomy as competence in two-year-olds: Maternal correlates of child compliance, defiance, and self-assertion. *Developmental Psychology, 26,* 961–971.

Cutrona, C. E., & Troutman, B. R. (1986). Social support, infant temperament, and parenting self-efficacy: A mediational model of postpartum depression. *Child Development, 57,* 1507–1518.

Dawson, G. (1994). Development of emotional expression and emotion regulation in infancy: Contributions of the frontal lobe. In G. Dawson & K.W. Fischer (Eds.), *Human behavior and the developing brain* (pp. 346–379). New York: Guilford.

Dawson, G., Grofer Klinger, L., Panagiotides, H., Hill, D., & Spieker, S. (1992). Frontal lobe activity and affective behavior of infants of mothers with depressive symptoms. *Child Development, 63*, 725–737.

Goldsmith, H. H., Buss, K. A., & Lemery, K. S. (1997). Toddler and childhood temperament: Expanded content, stronger genetic evidence, new evidence for the importance of environment. *Developmental Psychology, 33*, 891–905.

Goldsmith, H. H., Lemery, K. S., Buss, K. A., & Campos, J. J. (1999). Genetic analyses of focal aspects of infant temperament. *Developmental Psychology, 35*, 972–985.

Goldsmith, H. H., & Rothbart, M. K. (1996). *Laboratory temperament assessment battery: Prelocomotor version 3.0.* Personality Development Laboratory, University of Wisconsin, Madison.

Hakulinen, T., Laippala, P., & Paunonen, M. (1998). Relationships between infant temperament, demographic variables, and family dynamics of childrearing families. *Journal of Advanced Nursing, 27*, 458–465.

Halverson, C. F., & Deal, J. E. (2001). Temperamental change, parenting, and the family context. In T. D. Wachs & G. A. Kohnstamm (Eds.), *Temperament in context* (pp. 61–79). Mahwah, NJ: Lawrence Erlbaum Associates.

Hann, D. M. (1989). A systems conceptualization of the quality of mother-infant interaction. *Infant Behavior and Development, 12*, 252–263.

Hayes, N. (1997). *Doing qualitative analysis in Psychology.* East Sussex, UK: Psychology Press.

Hubert, N. C. (1989). Parental subjective reactions to perceived temperament behavior in their 6- and 24-month old children. *Infant Behavior and Development, 12*, 185–198.

Jones, L. C., & Heermann, J. A. (1992). Parental division of infant care: Contextual influences and infant characteristics. *Nursing Research, 41*, 228–234.

Kagan, J., Reznick, J. S., & Gibbons, J. (1989). Inhibited and uninhibited types of children. *Child Development, 60*, 838–845.

LeDoux, J. E. (1987). Emotion. In F. Plum & V. Mountcastle (Eds.), *Handbook of physiology: Section I. The nervous system. Vol. 5. Higher functions of the brain* (pp. 419–460). Bethesda, MD: American Physiological Society.

LeDoux, J. E. (1993). Emotional networks in the brain. In M. Lewis & J. M. Haviland (Eds.), *Handbook of emotions* (pp. 109–118). New York: Guilford.

Leerkes, E. M., & Crockenberg, S. C. (in press). The development of maternal self-efficacy and its influence on maternal behavior. *Infancy.*

Maccoby, E., Snow, M., & Jacklin, C. (1984). Children's dispositions and mother-child interaction at 12 and 18 months: A short-term longitudinal study. *Developmental Psychology, 20*, 459–472.

Mangelsdorf, S., Gunnar, M., Kestenbaum, R., Lang, S., & Andreas, D. (1990). Infant proneness-to-distress temperament, maternal personality, and mother-infant attachment: Associations and goodness of fit. *Child Development, 61,* 820–831.

Martin, S. E., Clements, M. L., Crnic, K. A., Pollack, K., & Borek, A. (April, 2001). *The emotional experience of parenting: Links to parent-child interaction, parenting stress, and maternal depressive symptoms.* Poster presented at the Biennial Meeting of the Society for Research in Child Development, Minneapolis, MN.

Murray, L., Stanley, C., Hooper, R., & King, F. (1996). The role of infant factors in postnatal depression and mother-infant interactions. *Developmental Medicine & Child Neurology, 38,* 109–119.

Nachmias, M., Gunnar, M., Mangelsdorf, S., Parritz, R. H., & Buss, K. (1996). Behavioral inhibition and stress reactivity: The moderating role of attachment security. *Child Development, 67,* 508–522.

Papousek, M., & von Hofacker, N. (1998). Persistent crying in early infancy: A non-trivial condition of risk for the developing mother-infant relationship. *Child Care, Health, and Development, 24,* 395–424.

Park, S., Belsky, J., Putnam, S., & Crnic, K. (1997). Infant emotionality, parenting, and 3-year inhibition: Exploring stability and lawful discontinuity in a male sample. *Developmental Psychology, 33,* 218–227.

Rothbart, M. K. (1981). Measurement of temperament in infancy. *Child Development, 52,* 569–578.

Rothbart, M. K., & Bates, J. E. (1998). Temperament. In W. Damon (Series Ed.) & N. Eisenberg (Vol. Ed.), *Handbook of child psychology: Vol. 3. Social, emotional, and personality development* (pp. 105–176). New York, NY: Wiley.

Rothbart, M. K., & Derryberry, D. (1981). Development of individual differences in temperament. In M. Lamb (Ed.), *Advances in developmental psychology* (Vol. 1, pp. 37–86). Hillsdale, NJ: Lawrence Erlbaum Associates.

Sameroff, A. (1975). Transactional models in early social relations. *Human Development, 18,* 65–79.

Seifer, R., Schiller, M., Sameroff, A. J., Resnick, S., & Riordan, K. (1996). Attachment, maternal sensitivity, and infant temperament during the first year of life. *Developmental Psychology, 32,* 12–25.

Sirignano, S. W., & Lachman, M. E. (1985). Personality change during the transition to parenthood: The role of perceived infant temperament. *Developmental Psychology, 21,* 558–567.

Spangler, G. (1990). Mother, child and situational correlates of toddlers' social competence. *Infant Behavior and Development, 13,* 405–419.

Stifter, C. A., & Grant, W. (1993). Infant responses to frustration: Individual differences in the expression of negative affect. *Journal of Nonverbal Behavior, 17,* 187–204.

Stratton, P. (1997). Attributional coding of interview data: Meeting the needs of long haul passengers. In N. Hayes (Ed.), *Doing qualitative analysis in psychology* (pp. 115–142). East Sussex, UK: Psychology Press.

Susman-Stillman, A., Kalkoske, M., Egeland, B., & Walman, I. (1996). Infant temperament and maternal sensitivity as predictors of attachment security. *Infant Behavior and Development, 19*, 33–47.

Teti, D. M., & Gelfand, D. M. (1991). Behavioral competence among mothers and infants in the first year: The mediational role of maternal self-efficacy. *Child Development, 62*, 918–929.

Termine, N. T., & Izard, C. E. (1988). Infants' responses to their mothers' expressions of joy and sadness. *Developmental Psychology, 24*, 223–229.

Thomas, A., Chess, S., Birch, H. G., Hertzig, M. E., & Korn, S. (1963). *Behavioral individuality in early childhood*. New York, NY: New York University Press.

van den Boom, D. C. (1994). The influence of temperament and mothering on attachment and exploration: An experimental intervention of sensitive responsiveness among lower-class mothers with irritable infants. *Child Development, 65*, 1457–1477.

van den Boom, D. C. (1995). Do first-year intervention effects endure? Follow-up during toddlerhood of a sample of Dutch irritable infants. *Child Development, 66*, 1798–1816.

van den Boom, D. C., & Hoeksma, J. B. (1994). The effect of infant irritability on mother-infant interaction: A growth curve analysis. *Developmental Psychology, 30*, 581–590.

van Egeren, L. A., & Lower, R. J. (April, 2001). *Predictors of parental efficacy over the transition to parenthood*. Poster presented at the Biennial Meeting of the Society for Research in Child Development, Minneapolis, MN.

Ventura, J. N., & Stevenson, M. B. (1986). Relations of mothers' and fathers' reports of infant temperament, parents' psychological functioning, and family characteristics. *Merrill-Palmer Quarterly, 32*, 275–289.

Washington, J., Minde, K., & Goldberg, S. (1986). Temperament in preterm infants: Style and stability. *Journal of the American Academy of Child Psychiatry, 25*, 493–502.

Wilkie, C. F., & Ames, E. W. (1986). The relationship of infant crying to the transition to parenthood. *Journal of Marriage and the Family, 48*, 545–550.

Woodworth, S., Belsky, J., & Crnic, K. (1996). The determinants of fathering during the child's second and third years of life: A developmental analysis. *Journal of Marriage and the Family, 58*, 679–692.

6

Child Effects on the Family: An Example of the Extreme Case and a Question of Methodology

Cynthia A. Stifter
The Pennsylvania State University

In 1987, several temperament researchers came together to discuss and come to some agreement about the concept of temperament (Goldsmith, Buss, Plomin et al., 1987). They converged on several points, including two principles: that temperament represents individual differences, and is constitutionally based. Whereas it was agreed that temperament is modifiable, each theorist believed temperament to be a personological rather than relational construct. Such a view likely influenced researchers to investigate how children's temperament directly affected parenting behaviors. Operating on the assumption that parents react differentially to their children's predispositions to react emotionally, for example, temperament researchers have examined how extremes in temperament such as infant "difficultness" impact parenting ability. In both of her reviews, Crockenberg (1986; Crockenberg & Leerkes, this volume) has made excellent points about the effects of temperament on the family, specifically parental behavior and perceptions, pointing out that these effects are largely conditional. In other words, infant temperament's affect on the environment is likely moderated by other aspects of the environment. Crockenberg and Leerkes concluded that there is still more thinking and research to be accomplished, particularly around the conceptualization and measurement of "difficult" temperament and parental sensitivity, and made some important suggestions for getting this task underway. In this response to their review, data from two studies conducted in my laboratory will be presented to further illustrate the points raised. In addition, comments about the methods used when investigating child effects on the family, specifically how maternal sensitivity was measured, will be offered.

THE EXTREME CASE: INFANT COLIC

As Crockenberg and Leerkes point out, the majority of studies done on the effects of infant temperament on the family have focused on infant difficultness, a temperament category characterized by excessive negativity or crying. Another behavioral type defined by bouts of excessive crying is infant colic. Infant colic has been defined in numerous ways but the most widely used definition is the one provided by Wessel and his colleagues (Wessel et al., 1954) who described colic as "paroxysms of fussing or crying lasting for a total of more than three hours a day and occurring on more than three days in any one week" (p. 426), giving us what is popularly called the "Rule of 3's." Another "3" that characterizes infant colic is that it generally is resolved by three months of age. Finally, a more recent addition to the definition of colic agreed upon by many researchers is that of inconsolability (Stifter & Braungart, 1992). The extreme nature of the colic infant's crying is best illustrated by the data we collected from parental diaries. Parents recorded the state of their infant (sleeping, feeding, crying, fussing, awake/content) every 5 minutes when infants were approximately 6 weeks of age. When compared to infants without colic, infants with colic cried and fussed significantly longer and more frequently. As can be seen in Figure 6.1, these infants fussed and cried a total of 247 minutes, well over the 3-hour/day cut-off. In addition, these bouts were frequent and occurred during all periods of the day.

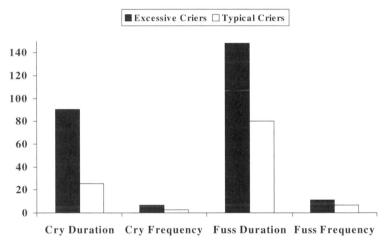

FIG. 6.1. Frequency and duration of fussing and crying for excessive (colic) and typical criers.

The current consensus is that colic is less likely due to an organic condition than to temporary regulatory difficulties (Barr, St. James Roberts, & Keefe, 2001). Indeed, only 5% of colic cases are believed to be attributable to organic causes. The time-limited nature of infant colic also suggests that colic is not a manifestation of an extreme temperamental trait. Whereas a difficult child is often described as highly negative and hard to soothe, their crying is less intense and can eventually be calmed. Moreover, it is expected that their difficult disposition will be stable across development, although perhaps manifested in different ways. Even though the evidence suggests that colic is not a temperamental trait, the intense quality and inconsolability of the colicky infants' crying makes it an important developmental condition with which to test the effect of infant characteristics on the family. Because colic begins and ends within the first 3 months of life, a longitudinal study of infant colic could be construed as a natural experiment and as such provides an excellent opportunity to investigate whether intense, negative states of the infant stress parent-infant interactions and subsequently affect short- and long-term family outcomes.

Effects on Maternal Behavior and the Attachment Relationship

Two prospective longitudinal studies on infants with colic which recruited families into the study before colic emerged and followed them into their first year of life, have been conducted in my laboratory (Stifter, 2001; Stifter & Bono, 1998; Stifter & Braungart, 1992; Stifter & Spinrad, in press). In following infants and their families after their colic had resolved we were able to examine how infant colic affects parenting. For example, the impact of having an excessive crier on maternal sensitivity and later attachment was investigated. Based partially on the literature reviewed by Crockenberg and Leerkes, it was hypothesized that the dynamic between a new mother and her inconsolable infant would have a long-lasting effect on maternal behavior and that this effect would, in turn, impact the developing relationship (attachment) between the mother and child. A child's attachment is considered secure if there is a history of successful, meaningful mother-infant interactions that include sensitive, appropriate and timely responses to infant crying. Thus, we expected that infants with colic would be at risk for insecure attachment. Surprisingly, our hypotheses were not confirmed. Rather, in both studies we found no difference in maternal sensitivity between mothers of infants with and without colic (Stifter & Braungart, 1992; Stifter & Spinrad, in press). And, contrary to expectation, no differences in attachment classification emerged. Indeed, only 20% of the colic infants were found to have insecure attachments, while 27% of the noncolic infants were insecurely attached to their mothers (Stifter & Bono, 1998).

Although no differences in observed parenting behavior were found, we did find colic to affect how the mother perceived herself as a parent. Using a parent self-efficacy questionnaire (Fish, Stifter & Belsky, 1991) when infants were 5 months of age, mothers of previously colicky infants rated themselves as lower on parenting self-efficacy than mothers whose infants did not have colic (see left-hand-side of Figure 2). In light of the intensity of crying and that self-efficacy was measured close to when colic ended, this finding was not surprising. The ability to console or soothe one's infant is the cornerstone of parenting self-efficacy, so that if a child was not able to be soothed a parent might easily attribute this to her inability to parent (Stifter & Bono, 1998). However, it was expected that once a mother had experience with successfully soothing her child her self-efficacy would return to normal levels. This was not the case, as demonstrated in our findings from a second longitudinal study in which parenting self-efficacy was measured at 5 months and again at 10 months (see right-hand side of Figure 6.2). While the

5-month findings replicated the results from our previous study, mothers of colic infants continued to rate themselves as less efficacious at 10 months, suggesting that the effect of excessive crying in a young infant has a long-term effect on perceptions of parenting (Stifter, 2001). It is important to note that the colic infants themselves were not more negative than the noncolic infants at 5 and 10 months of age, nor were they rated by their parents as more negative (Stifter & Braungart, 1992). Thus, mother's feelings about her ability to parent appear be unrelated to the child's current level of negative reactivity.

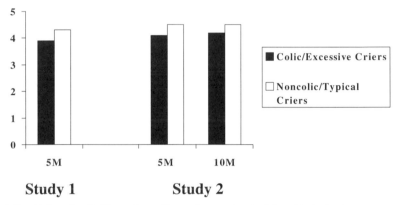

FIG. 6.2. Maternal self-efficacy for mothers of excessive (colic) and typical criers.

Taken together, the data suggest that mothers may be able to separate their feelings from their behavior when interacting with their infants. Importantly, maternal self-efficacy and maternal behavior were not related in our study confirming this conclusion. This finding is consistent with Leerkes and Crockenberg (in press), who found no relation between maternal self-efficacy and sensitivity. However, Teti and Gelfand (1991) did show a strong positive relation between ratings of parenting self-efficacy and maternal behavior, even after controlling for other factors. Teti and Gelfand's sample, however, included a subsample of clinically depressed mothers and although depression was controlled for in the analyses, the significance of the relation was diminished.

The relationship between infant negative reactivity and maternal behavior, therefore, may not be as direct as previously assumed, even in the extreme case. Rather, as indicated by Crockenberg and Leerkes, the effects of infant behavior on parents may be moderated or mediated by other factors. That is, infant difficultness may only impact mothers under certain circumstances such as stress, depression, or low self-efficacy. As reported above, when attempting to examine the direct effect of infant colic on attachment no such relation was revealed. However, when we considered the condition of self-efficacy a significant interaction effect was found. Although drawn from a very small sample, infants with colic whose mothers rated themselves as lowest in self-efficacy were found to be at greatest risk for insecure attachment. Interestingly, these same mothers also displayed the lowest sensitivity scores. It may be that having a colicky infant does not put the mother-infant relationship at risk unless the mother has significantly lowered self-efficacy. The question still remains, does this lowered self-efficacy reflect mothers' interactions with an inconsolable child, or low self-esteem or neuroticism—personality characteristics related to self-efficacy (Jain, Stifter, & Fish, unpublished manuscript).

Effects on the Marital Relationship

Caring for an inconsolable child not only has the potential to affect the infant-parent relationship, it may also affect other relationships within the family. It is well documented in the transition to parenthood literature that the birth of a child into a family has an impact on the marriage (Belsky & Kelly, 1994). To explore the impact of having an infant with colic on the marital relationship, mothers and fathers of both colic and noncolic infants completed a marital satisfaction questionnaire when their infants were 5 and 10 months of age. Remarkably, infant colic's effect on marriage satisfaction was long term for both parents. Mothers of infants who had colic rated their marriages as less positive and more negative at both 5 and 10 months, while fathers of infants rated their marriages as more negative at both ages (Stifter, 2001). This finding may be attributed to differences in how mothers and fathers perceive their marriages. According to Cowan and Cowan (1988), while mothers and fathers agree about who should care for the crying child (mother), they differ about what determines marital satisfaction, e.g., the degree to which fathers are involved in child care. Mothers reported more marital satisfaction when fathers were involved, whereas fathers' satisfaction with their marriage was due to the division of labor. This may explain why mothers and fathers of previously colic infants reported less satisfaction. To confirm this we went back to the diary data which, in addition to asking parents to keep a record of their infants' states, asked parents to note who was with the infant during each of the states. An examination of this data revealed that even though fathers of colic infants spent significantly greater amounts of time with their crying baby than fathers whose infants were not colicky, the proportion of time compared with mothers was not different. In other words, fathers, regardless of whether their infant was colicky or not, spent 40% of the time mothers spent with their infants when they were crying. The negative feelings expressed by mothers of colic infants about their marriage partner may be due to the fact that fathers did not step up and relieve them when dealing with an inconsolable child. The finding that fathers also felt dissatisfaction may be due to the mothers' dissatisfaction as the two scales were correlated for both groups at both ages (Stifter, 2001).

QUESTIONING METHODOLOGY

The findings of our studies are consistent with those reviewed by Crockenberg and Leerkes and support their conclusion that infant temperament, specifically infant negative reactivity, has little or no effect on maternal sensitivity except under certain circumstances. However, as suggested by Crockenberg and Leerkes, there are several methodological concerns with the measurement of maternal sensitivity that preclude any definitive conclusions from being made. In addition to providing evidence to support and contradict some of their conclusions, I would like to add a few more methodological constraints followed by some suggestions on how researchers might improve their ability to understand the influence of temperament on parenting behavior.

As Crockenberg and Leerkes note, when mothers are asked to interact with their infants they are likely putting forward their best behavior. This is not a difficult task given that the typical observation period used to measure sensitivity is relatively short—around five minutes. Because the observation period is brief, mothers can focus their energies on their infants' cues and respond in a contingent, responsive manner. Little variation in maternal responsiveness, therefore, is likely to be observed. In an attempt to elicit more variability in maternal sensitivity we extended the length of the mother-infant interaction period with the hypothesis that mothers would be more stressed by the longer free-play session and would not be able to "keep up appearances." Rather than the standard 5 minutes, we asked mothers to interact with their 5- and 10-month-olds for 15 minutes. Contrary to our expectation, mothers did not decline in sensitivity over the 15-minute session. Indeed, instead of decreasing, sensitivity significantly increased. It is important to note that our sample was low risk. It may be that high-risk dyads would show a different pattern of sensitivity during these extended interaction periods.

One explanation for the increase in sensitivity across a 15-minute interaction may be the context under which the mother's behavior was observed. As with most of the studies examining the effect of temperament on maternal sensitivity (see Crockenberg & Leerkes, this volume), we used a free-play situation. Free-play sessions are generally conducted in the laboratory or home with a basket of toys and instructions for the mothers to "play as you would normally." Given that infant researchers are very careful to schedule visits around the infant's best time (not hungry, not tired) it can be assumed that the majority of the interactions observed in these studies, even those with irritable infants, were primarily positive interactions that allowed the mother to respond sensitively to her infant's cues. For example, in one of our studies the average infant negative reactivity score during a free-play interaction was .12 using a scale ranging from 0 (no negative reactivity) to 3 (high distress) (Wiggins & Stifter, 2001). The context under which mothers' behavior was observed in previous studies, therefore, may have obscured the effect of infant temperament on maternal sensitivity.

Recently, we examined maternal behavior across the "still face" procedure conducted with 4-month-old infants (Wiggins & Stifter, 2001). In this task, mothers interacted with their infants normally for three minutes, after which they were cued to maintain a neutral face and refrain from further interaction for one minute. After this "still face" interval mothers were then cued to re-engage their infants and soothe them if necessary. The lack of maternal interaction during the "still face" portion generally elicits infant negativity because it violates the infant's expectancy that the mother will interact with them when in the face-to-face configuration. In this study we coded maternal sensitivity during both the free-play portion to be consistent with other studies, and during the re-engagement period which for the majority of mothers consisted of soothing their child who was either mildly agitated or greatly distressed. As you can see in Figure 6.3, as infant negativity increased from the free-play interval to the re-engagement interval, maternal sensitivity decreased. This figure includes the entire sample of infants, 40% of whom did not get upset during the still face procedure.

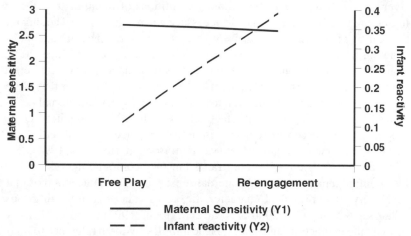

FIG. 6.3.   Change in maternal sensitivity and infant negative reactivity across the still-face procedure.

The same analysis was conducted with only those infants who became distressed to the "still face" and the same significant change was found for both maternal sensitivity and infant reactivity. Thus, even though maternal sensitivity remained high in this low-risk sample (2.5 on a 1-3 point scale), mothers' ability to respond to their children's needs was more taxed when their children were more distressed. If most mothers find it more difficult to interact responsively to a distressed infant, the mother of a temperamentally irritable child may, through a history of stressed interactions, develop a less sensitive style of interaction. In most previous studies, however, this temperamentally influenced interaction style would not be observable since maternal sensitivity was measured during more positive, less stressful conditions. Future research should consider observing mother-infant interaction across several contexts (feeding, free play, distress) and analyzing maternal sensitivity exhibited under each context separately so as to better clarify the relation between infant temperament and maternal behavior (Seifer et al., 1996).

Alternatively, the finding that maternal sensitivity decreases as infant negativity increases may be due to a bias in coding. Maternal sensitivity is often coded using a global coding system that incorporates a list of possible sensitive/insensitive behaviors. Many of the coding systems currently in use follow the 9-point scale of maternal sensitivity introduced by Ainsworth (Ainsworth, Blehar, Waters, & Wall, 1978). Although the parenting behaviors that constitute high sensitivity are well defined and fairly exhaustive, the application of a code for sensitive behavior may be affected by the presence of infant distress. For example, coders may be less likely to ascribe a high degree of sensitivity if the infant is not easily soothed by the mother. Our finding of lowered maternal sensitivity, therefore, may simply be due to the fact that infants were more irritable and not due to any differences in mothers' ability to respond appropriately. Indeed, sensitive responsiveness may look very different under conditions of infant distress than when infants are more positive. It may be necessary when using a global coding method to clearly operationalize sensitivity so that it captures parental adaptations in behavior when interacting with a crying infant (Clausen & Crittenden, 2000). For example, including appropriate attempts to soothe as a criterion for sensitivity would put the emphasis on the parents' attempts and not whether they were successful or not. Finally, coding systems that focus on specific maternal behaviors, as well as the contingency and effectiveness of these behaviors in soothing distress might also be considered in addition to or in place of global coding systems as a way to eliminate coding biases (van dem Boom & Hoeksma, 1994).

Another methodological constraint that may confound the relationship between infant temperament and maternal sensitivity is the conception of maternal sensitivity as a individual characteristic, rather than one reflecting the dyad (Claussen & Crittenden, 2000). As van dem Boom (1997) asserted, "sensitivity is ... about the interaction, and, hence, is meaningless without reference to both partners" (p. 593). Surprisingly, few studies take into account the infants' state during mother-infant interaction; when they do, significant relations between maternal and infant behavior emerge. For example, maternal sensitivity was found to be negatively related to infant negative affect (r's = -.40) measured during a free-play session at 4 months by both Braungart-Rieker, Garwood, Powers, and Wang (2001) and Wiggins and Stifter (2001). These findings confirm that mother's responsiveness is affected contemporaneously by infant distress and suggest that any measure of maternal sensitivity should control for or include a measure of infant state.

CONCLUSION

In this response to Crockenberg and Leerkes' review, data on the effects of excessive crying in early infancy, often referred to as infant colic, on maternal behavior and consequently, on the mother-infant relationship were presented. Our findings are consistent with many of the studies reviewed by Crockenberg and Leerkes, that maternal sensitivity does not appear to be affected by either infant difficult temperament, or excessive crying, a characteristic of difficult temperament. In discussing these findings the methods for observing and coding maternal behavior were questioned and suggestions were made. Although maternal sensitivity has been shown to be a rather robust construct related to the development of attachment (see De Wolff & van Ijzendoorn for a meta-analysis) in order to demonstrate infant temperament's influence on parenting behavior in low-risk samples, if indeed there is one, researchers may need to examine maternal behavior during a more demanding task, i.e., when the child is stressed. Not only would this simulate conditions under which the difficult child is "difficult" but it would also pull for more variability in maternal responsiveness. Likewise, it may be necessary to code more specific maternal behaviors and their effectiveness in reducing infant distress. A more focused observation of maternal behavior would not only contribute to a clearer understanding of infant temperament's impact on parental behavior but would also validate parental perceptions of "difficultness."

REFERENCES

Ainsworth, M., Blehar, M., Waters, E., & Wall, S. (1978). *Patterns of attachment: A psychological study of the strange situation*. Hillsdale: NJ: Lawrence Erlbaum Associates.

Barr, R., St. James Roberts, I., & Keefe, M. (Eds.)(2001). *New evidence on unexplained early infant crying: Its origins, nature and management*. N.P.: Johnson & Johnson Pediatric Institute.

Belsky, J., & Kelly, J. (1994). *Transition to parenthood*. New York: Delacorte Press.

Braungart-Rieker, J., Garwood, M., Powers, B., & Wang, X. (2001). Parental sensitivity, infant affect, and affect regulation: Predictors to later attachment. *Child Development, 72,* 252–270.

Claussen, A., & Crittenden, P. (2000). Maternal sensitivity. In P. Crittenden & A. Claussen (Eds.), *The organization of attachment relationships* (pp. 115–122). New York: Cambridge University Press.

Cowan, C., & Cowan, P. (1988). Who does what when partners become parents: Implications for men, women, and marriage. *Marriage and Family Review, 12,* 105–131.

Crockenberg, S. (1986). Are temperamental differences in babies associated with predictable differences in caregiving? In J. Lerner & R. Lerner (Eds.), *New directions for child development: No. 31. Temperament and social interaction in infants and children* (pp. 53–73). San Francisco, CA: Jossey-Bass.

DeWolff, M., & van Ijzendoorn, M. (1997). Sensitivity and attachment: A meta-analysis on parental antecedents of infant attachment. *Child Development, 68,* 571–591.

Fish, M., Stifter, C., & Belsky, J. (1991). Conditions of continuity and discontinuity in infant negative emotionality: Newborn to five months. *Child Development, 62,* 1525–1537.

Goldsmith, H., Buss, A., Plomin, R., Rothbart, M., Thomas, A., Chess, S., Hinde, R., & McCall, R. (1987). Roundtable: What is temperament: Four approaches. *Child Development, 58,* 505–529.

Jain, A., Stifter, C., & Fish, M. *The Parenting Self-efficacy Scale: A psychometric analysis.* Unpublished manuscript.

Leerkes, E., & Crockenberg, S. (in press). The development of maternal self-efficacy and its impact on maternal behavior. *Infancy.*

Seifer, R., Schiller, M., Sameroff, A., Resnick, S., & Riordan, K. (1996). Attachment, maternal sensitivity, and infant temperament during the first year of life. *Developmental Psychology, 32,* 12–25.

Stifter, C. A. (2001). "Life" after unexplained crying: Child and parent outcomes. In R. Barr, I. St. James Roberts, & M. Keefe (Eds.), *New evidence on unexplained early infant crying: Its origins, nature and management* (pp. 273–288). N.P.: Johnson & Johnson Pediatric Institute.

Stifter, C. A., & Bono, M. (1998). The effect of infant colic on maternal self-perceptions and mother-infant attachment. *Child: Care, Health and Development, 24,* 339–351.

Stifter, C. A., & Braungart, J. (1992). Infant colic: A transient condition with no apparent effects. *Journal of Applied Developmental Psychology, 13,* 447–462.

Stifter, C. A., & Spinrad, T. (in press) The effect of excessive crying on the development of emotion regulation. *Infancy.*

Teti, D., & Gelfand, K. (1991). Behavioral competence among mothers of infants in the first year: The mediational role of maternal self-efficacy. *Child Development, 62,* 918–929.

van dem Boom, D. (1997). Sensitivity and attachment: Next steps for developmentalists. *Child Development, 64,* 592–594.

van dem Boom, D., & Hoeksma, J. (1994). The effect of infant irritability on mother-infant interaction: A growth curve analysis. *Developmental Psychology, 30,* 581–590.

Wessel, M., Cobb, J., Jackson, E., Harris, G., & Detwiler, A. (1954). Paroxysmal fussing in infancy, sometimes called "colic." *Pediatrics, 14*, 421–434.

Wiggins, C., & Stifter, C. A. (2001). *Re-engagement following the still-face: Maternal behavior and the regulation of infant distress.* Poster presented at the biennial meetings of the Society for Research in Child Development, Minneapolis, MN.

7

Sensitivity to Infants' Cues: As Much a Mandate for Researchers as for Parents

James P. McHale
Kathryn C. Kavanaugh
Julia M. Berkman
Clark University

Twenty years ago, Susan Crockenberg (1981) charted new and important territory for researchers studying the interplay of child and family factors in development when she reported that social support was the best predictor of secure infant attachment among the participants in her study—particularly among mothers of irritable babies. Unfortunately, as attested to by Crockenberg and Leerkes (this volume), progress has been quite limited since the time of that 1981 report. Thus, they strive to nudge us forward again, and do a much more thorough job of localizing the effects of infant temperament within the broader system of the family than has been the case in most previous reports. Appropriately perhaps, their review mirrors the state of the field—focusing principally on mothers and infants, but giving some thoughtful attention to father-infant, marital, and coparenting dynamics as well.

Here, we will augment several points made both by Crockenberg and Leerkes, and by other contributors to this volume. As we will argue, striking the right balance between the nomothetic and the idiographic in family research is difficult but important work. When researchers back up far enough, and call upon adjustment markers such as arrest records and psychiatric disturbance (Reiss, this volume), genes turn out to be tremendously important factors. If we zero our lenses in too close, all salient differences among children and their families appear due to the machinations of child-family interactions. We have chosen to run this latter risk in the present chapter, emphasizing both the uniqueness and the goodness of fit of the infants and families we see in our research studies. We emphasize the importance of listening with a better tuned ear to what babies are actually signaling to parents and to researchers, but don't go so far as to suggest that lawfulness in child-family connections cannot be found amidst the very real and important individual differences we underscore. We also share some thoughts about the complexities of studying infants in the context of systems involving multiple caregiving others.

POINT ONE: RESEARCHERS NEED TO PAY
CLOSER ATTENTION TO WHAT IT IS THAT BABIES
ARE SIGNALING

Who is labeled a difficult neonate, difficult 1-month-old, or difficult 2-month-old? Usually, it's a baby who gets distressed easily and often and does not soothe quickly. Crockenberg and Leerkes also draw our attention to an important theoretical distinction between infant signals of fear and of anger. We wish to echo and extend their point that babies cry for all kinds of reasons, and that what they are trying to tell the adults around them is not inconsequential. Indeed, understanding the messages infants are trying to convey to adults is a basic step in charting the infant's impact on the family system.

For decades, psychologists have debated whether the cry sounds of human infants are unique to the eliciting condition—that is, whether there are discernible hunger, pain, startle, or fatigue cries—and if so, whether such cries are perceived uniformly and accurately as such by infants' caregivers (e.g. Gustafson, Wood, & Green, 2000). But asking whether cries signal different states is itself a rather limited question. The bigger issue, at least from the perspective of enduring individual differences, concerns the messages the crier reliably intends to send–trait rather than state communiqués. Beyond transient discomfort signals—which researchers and clinicians alike agree need to be responded to contingently and sensitively—there are also cyclical, fitness-related messages sent out by babies with different constitutional make-ups, in their efforts to help create the particular kinds of environs in which their constitutions will best thrive.

Implicit in research pursuing such topics as the stability of crying, the predictability of distress from neonatal assessments, or the stability of temperamental features, is the notion that such early behaviors or dispositions are prescient, and that they are telling us something about the potential developmental paths down which different children may be heading. Hence, researchers anticipate that early infant propensities for fearfulness, soothability, distress to limitations, activity, and reactivity prime babies to become children who are hypersensitive and fearful; or fearless and active; or stubborn and defiant; or withdrawn, tuned-out escapers into fantasy; or inattentive children with information-processing difficulties (Greenspan, 1992). Of course, what infants are trying to tell their parents and others around them about their internal states frequently does not get encoded by adults in the manner the infants intended. Hence, the basic point is that crying or other signs of distress (typically taken as indices of the integrity of the infant's nervous system; see Lester, 1984) may be tied to later child dispositions largely through their indirect effects on infant-caregiver interaction.

One of the clearest illustrations of the complexities of the infant-caregiving nexus can be found in Belsky and Rovine's (1987) analysis, which sorts through linkages between temperament and attachment. Their synthesis of numerous studies on this topic indicated that infants later classified as A1, A2, B1, or B2 displayed more autonomic stability, alertness, and positive responses as newborns than did infants later classified as B3, B4, C1, or C2, and that these same infants impressed as easier to care for at 3 months. They concluded that infant temperament is formative insofar as it helps shape the manifest *expression* of the infant's eventual attachment security or insecurity, rather than over-determining whether or not the infant comes to develop a secure or insecure attachment per se. Broadening this perspective further, we would echo Crockenberg and Leerkes' observation (this volume) that both direct and indirect effects of infant temperament are further moderated both by sociocultural and contextual factors and by the infant's medical history (Lester, 1984).

Given the myriad factors that need to be taken into account to explain any given infant's travels through time, it is perhaps no wonder that researchers often fall back on such global constructs as "negative reactivity", "irritability", or "difficult infant" to cover the "infant" end of the equation. What we would advocate, however, is a careful reading of any evidence that an infant cries and cries often. Without such an informed understanding, tracking all subsequent sequencing and unfolding of infant-caregiver-context dynamics would seem a fruitless task.

WHAT DOES IT MEAN WHEN OUR EVIDENCE SUGGESTS A DIFFICULT, EXCESSIVELY CRYING BABY?

Clinicians and researchers must consider any number of possibilities when faced with evidence of infant irritability. First, it is incumbent upon professionals to determine whether parents actually have a normally developing (and crying) baby, but are themselves overly attuned to distress signals—if not above clinical thresholds on neuroticism, ego blurring, or AAI insecurity.

Alternatively, parents may have a hypersensitive or tactilely defensive infant who responds strongly to external stimuli and becomes exhausted from taking in and processing these stimuli (DeGangi, Porges, Sickel, & Greenspan, 1993; Greenspan & Weider, 1993). Highly sensitive babies are thought to see, hear, smell, or feel more than others and their cries are intended to signal to parents their sensory overload. Occupational therapists distinguish between babies who are sensitive to stimuli—that is, babies with a very low threshold for registering all sorts of sensory information, and who act in accordance with this threshold, and sensation avoiding babies—who also have low thresholds, and actually try to counteract this threshold (DeGangi, Sickel, Wiener, & Kaplan, 1996; Dunn, 1997). There is also obvious overlap here with what Kagan (1994, 2000; Kagan, Reznick, & Gibbons, 1989) conceptualized as inhibition.

We note that occupational therapists also work with *high* threshold infants, including babies who don't register information sufficiently and act in accordance with this threshold; and babies who likewise have high thresholds but counter this threshold by *seeking sensation* (Dunn, 1997).

Then there are parents who are not neurotic or preoccupied, and who don't have hypersensitive, underreactive, or dysregulated infants, but who report infant irritability because they have a colicky child (Lester, Boukydis, Garcia-Coll, & Hole, 1990; St. James-Roberts, 1993; Wessel, Cobb, Jackson, Harris & Ditweiler, 1954). As outlined in Stifter (this volume), colicky babies cry intensely and incessantly for weeks on end between the ages of 1 and 3 months, taxing even the most saintly parents. And then, just as precipitously, many stop (Stifter & Braungart, 1995)–an added headache for researchers looking for stable infant traits or charting growth curves. While the jury is still out, work by Barr and Gunnar (2000) and by Stifter (this volume), among others, suggests that infant colic may *not* be reliably related to temperament or to hypersensitivity in the long run.

Our point here is that without getting to know babies well, we may not really know who it is we're dealing with. And without knowing what babies are intending to signal, it can be pretty hard to adequately judge caregiver sensitivity. Unfortunately, most researchers have found it impractical to conduct the same thorough clinical evaluations as do pediatric psychologists, occupational therapists, and scientists with well-endowed psychophysiological laboratories. Instead, then, parent reports of temperament or, less frequently, brief structured temperament assessments serve as proxies for infant contributions.

Are such instruments able to triage with confidence different causes of infant irritability? Several certainly aspire to do so. Both parent-completed temperament inventories and structured observational assessments distinguish among different forms and manifestations of distress. Unfortunately, mother-examiner correspondence in characterizing infants' temperamental features is often rather poor (Carnicero, Perez-Lopez, Salinas, & Martinez-Fuentes, 2000; Seifer, Sameroff, Barrett, & Krafchuk, 1994). This would suggest either that parents know something that researchers don't, or that parents' own working models of their infants do not reconcile well with researchers' instruments. Reiss (this volume) captures this conundrum when he notes that the nature and extent of the gene-environment (G-E) correlations found in the reports he cites varied depending upon the source of data.

Our point is that we lack a gold standard that allows us to determine which difficult infants in studies of temperament and family systems have been reactive babies, babies with mild sensory integration problems, hypersensitive babies, colicky babies, or babies battling a combination of these or other challenges. Both the appropriate responsiveness from the caregiving environment and the actuarial pathways followed by these different groups of children differ—but this is precisely the information often lost in research reports.

POINT TWO: WITHOUT UNDERSTANDING INFANTS' SIGNALS, HOW WELL ARE WE ESTIMATING SENSITIVITY?

So who *is* a sensitive parent? The answer to this question is not as straightforward as most published studies using observational ratings of parental sensitivity would lead us to believe. In part, this is because infants with different kinds of temperaments can respond quite differently to the same styles of parenting (Collins et al., 2000). So, for sensation-seeking infants, sensitive parents would include those who help their children show more organized behavior by providing environments rich in stimulation. For infants hypersensitive to touch, they are parents who use deep pressure rather than light touch to help the baby feel comfortable. For parents of colicky infants, they are mothers and fathers who learn tricks such as carrying their babies stomach down, along the length of the forearm, with their hand supporting the baby's chest. For underreactive, avoidants and self-absorbed babies, they are parents who employ frequent "wooing" to help their children break past their self-absorption (Greenspan & Weider, 1993).

As we hope is apparent, there is a gap between how clinical practitioners and clinical researchers typically think about and gauge maternal sensitivity—one that parallels the already-highlighted discrepancy between how practitioners and researchers assess infants' signaling of their needs. When clinicians work with parent-infant dyads showing problems in homeostatic organization, they aim both to enhance the child's ability to organize increasingly complex modes of adaptation, and to strengthen the organizing quality of the maternal function (Daws, 1989; Fraiberg, 1980; Martinetti, Papini, Guerri, Stefanini et al., 1991; Stern-Buschweiler & Stern, 1989). Maternal sensitivity and responsiveness are *always* assessed with respect to the unique needs and cues of the baby, and later, in the context of the child's ego structure (Acquarone, 1992).

As such, we wish to underscore Crockenberg and Leerkes' point that brief observations of parents in non-stressful circumstances at best constrain variability and, at worst, provide none of the critical information about parental attunement to infant signals that is of real-world importance. Attempting to assess parental sensitivity in a brief contact that relies solely upon a standardized lab assessment, and does not take into account relevant information about the infant being parented, places researchers in a one-down position. Failure to understand infants well may also be at least partially responsible for the equivocal findings concerning infant difficultness and maternal sensitivity described in Crockenberg and Leerkes (this volume).

We also concur, in part, with Crockenberg and Leerkes' proposition that microanalytic techniques can be a useful tool in addressing certain issues concerning parental sensitivity to specific infant communiqués—when a parent appreciates that their distressed baby responds well to intense, deep touch, the relevant measure of sensitivity is not a decontextualized rating of the quality of touch, but rather the success of the intervention in soothing the child. Unfortunately, microanalytic methods are not without their own problems, such as variability accounted for by transient states. It is much easier for a parent to appear sensitive with a calm child than with a distressed one, regardless of the child's trait-like propensities. But this design quandary just reinforces the point that researchers are beholden to know more about any given infant's communications than could ever be gleaned from a subscale score on a parent report or a behavior count from a brief laboratory observation—and to use that knowledge to make sense of infant-caregiver-context interactions.

A few other thoughts before we move on. First, we urge clinicians and researchers, review panelists, and other judiciously-positioned professionals to strongly encourage and help foster a more widespread use of common methods than has typically been the case in our field, and journal editors to value and reward replication studies. So many of the findings described in Crockenberg and Leerkes (this volume), particularly those that emerge as unexpected results, need to be replicated at least a few times before we begin to place any enduring trust in them. For example, Crockenberg and Leerkes cites a recent report from our lab revealing greater solidarity in the early coparental alliance among families with difficult infants (Berkman et al., 2002), and also discussed findings reported by van Egeren and Lower (2001) showing high self-efficacy ratings among fathers of irritable babies. These reports can be taken as cases in point, in that they do not reconcile well with many other studies indicating *less* reciprocity in care by fathers (Hakulinen, Laippala, & Pauonen, 1998; Leerkes & Crockenberg, in press), and *later* paternal participation in infant care (Jones & Heermann, 1992) when babies are difficult. Here, before concluding that there's been a recent shift in the early coparenting zeitgeist, we'd want to see a confluence of replication studies using common methods and taking cross-time looks at both continuity and change in the relationship between infant distress and the family's co-caregiving dynamics.

Relatedly, we need to be aware of the value in examining infant signals, their correlates, and their effects across different interpersonal contexts. This is not just an intellectual exercise—context matters. Data from our ongoing longitudinal study of early coparenting dynamics during infancy and toddlerhood have been demonstrating this point rather clearly. In the Families through Time project at Clark University, we assess both child and parents in multiple interpersonal contexts and paradigms at multiple time points. For example, at 3 months postpartum, infant behavior and distress are assessed both in Garcia Coll and colleagues' (1992) temperament paradigm, and during several triadic family interaction sessions. One such triadic session is a variant of Tronick's still face paradigm, in which both parents pose a still face after a play period, and then work together to soothe the baby and re-establish emotional contact in a repair phase. This has proven to be an evocative assessment, one that provides us with a rich source of data on how well parents work together, or don't, as parenting partners.

Recently, we began testing whether early measures of infant distress or of coparenting distress at 3 months post-partum are the strongest prognosticators of coparenting difficulties at infant age one year (Berkman et al., 2001). Contrary to what we had anticipated, our initial data analyses revealed that 3-month infant distress was a better predictor of high dissonance and low warmth in the observed coparental relationship at 12 months than were measures of 3-month coparenting process. However, this was only true for infant distress as measured *in family context*, not infant distress on the Infant Behavior Questionnaire (IBQ) or in the Garcia Coll assessment. One of our colleagues in the collaborative North American-European Trilogie network recently remarked, only half jokingly, that babies appear to be better reporters of the state of the family at three months than their parents. Of course, we ourselves give these new findings the same credence as we do the other as-yet-to-be replicated findings we just commented on. Our point is that researchers studying the infant in family context need to be conscious that the babies they study, even very young ones, are already functioning within nested sets of interpersonal relationships.

A last point before we move on breaks away from the focus on temperament that has dominated the chapters comprising this subsection of the volume. Beyond temperament, babies possess many other important skills and competencies that have implications for the developing family process, and we need to be on the lookout for these. One such set of competencies concerns the infant's openness and engagement as a social partner in the family. Most work on early infant social competencies has focused narrowly on babies' social smiling during the first half year, and social referencing during the second half year. In fact, developmental scientists have been so dedicated to this timetable that seldom has anyone ever checked to see whether infants were demonstrating advanced competencies before the purported onset of intersubjectivity. This was the case until a remarkable series of studies by two independent labs—those of Tremblay-Leveau (1999; Nadel & Tremblay-Leveau, 1999) in France, and Fivaz-Depeursinge (1999; Fivaz-Depeursinge & Corboz-Warnery, 1999) in Switzerland.

Over the past few years, both scientists have uncovered robust evidence for individual differences in *3-month-old* infants' propensities to share interest, attention, and affect with two partners at once. Some infants never exhibit such affect and interest sharing, while others do so, quite literally, dozens of times within brief assessment sessions with their parents (Fivaz-Depeursinge & Frascarolo, 1999, 2000). While this astonishing finding challenges some cherished notions about intersubjectivity, equally compelling is the finding that individual differences in 3-month-olds' triangular skills (Fivaz-Depeursinge, 1998) can be linked, both concurrently (Fivaz-Depeursinge & Corboz-Warnery, 1999) and prospectively (Fivaz-Depeursinge & Frascarolo, 2000), with coordination between the coparenting partners in the family system. Infants with better triangular skills belong to family systems in which the adults neither disengage from nor oppose one another, but rather work collaboratively to help engage the baby in a sensitively-paced, warm, inclusive, and cooperative family process (McHale, Fivaz-Depeursinge, & Corboz-Warnery, 2000). Here again, attending closely to babies' particular signals in context allowed researchers to go beyond basic issues of whether aversive crying brings parents together or drives them apart.

POINT THREE: INFANT BEHAVIOR CAN EXERT ITS EFFECTS BY SERVING A REGULATORY FUNCTION IN THE FAMILY

Of course, it is quite plausible, even likely perhaps, that what Fivaz and her colleagues documented is simply that 3-month-old infants' triangular capacities *result from*, rather than prompt, well-coordinated coparenting and triadic family processes. Cross-time links seen between early triangular abilities and coordination in the family alliance could simply reflect continuity in the coparenting and triadic processes that had shaped the 3-month-olds' capacities to begin with. But this, we argue, misses the point entirely. None of the contributors to this volume really doubt that infant children are influenced by their families. The key point, pertinent here, is that once children have *been* so influenced, their behavior can then come to exert fundamental impact in the evolving family process itself by serving a regulatory function, one that helps to preserve family homeostasis.

Reiss (this volume) underscores in his discussion of gene-environment effects how it can be of great conceptual and clinical importance to know what came before what, if not how much was contributed by whom. At the same time, however, as we await findings about specific gene effects, we can step into systems at any point, taking a child rather than the adults as a starting point, and pose questions about the impact the child's behavior is having on the family. For example, Lamour and Barraco (1988) showed how young infants with psychotic parents learn to inhibit emotional expressiveness so as not to agitate the psychotic adult and hence to maintain a less tempestuous family milieu. While there is tremendous value in asking whether such infants came into their family situations genetically pre-programmed to exhibit minimal emotional expressivity or to evoke specific sorts of shaping responses from the caregiving adults, the point remains that however the children came to be this way, their behavior is now serving a homeostatic function in the family system. We advocate broadening the questions we ask about child effects in the family to accommodate the reality of reciprocal influence as operative from the very first.

We now turn to our last set of points: that infants exert their effects in families containing multiple others.

POINT FOUR: CHILD EFFECTS OCCUR IN COMPLEX FAMILY SYSTEMS CONTAINING MULTIPLE OTHERS

A review of the literature on temperament in family context conveys a sense that the field understands reasonably well what effects babies can have on mothers, and that these insights are being used to try to understand whether babies have the same effects on fathers. This tactic of approach mirrors the history of the father research movement itself, of course—mothering practices were originally taken as a metric, and fathering behavior was compared with mothering behavior. Finally, researchers began hypothesizing that perhaps fathers themselves exerted unique effects within families, because both their notions about child-rearing and the kinds of contributions that they made within families were actually quite different from those of mothers (Hawkins & Dollahite, 1997). We raise this issue here not to further ingrain the notion that has been pursued a bit too prevalently in this volume—that children actually grow up *in* families with mothers and fathers— but rather to underscore the fact that most of the world's children do grow up in families with multiple caregiving figures. To fully understand the impact of child-effects within the family, we need to come to grips with this reality (McHale, Khazan, Erera, Rotman, DeCourcey, & McConnell, 2002; McHale, Lauretti, Talbot, & Pouquette, 2002).

Most infant effects models are dyadic ones, with other-than-mothers viewed mainly as family supports or as background context. Take, for example, Papousek and Papousek's (1990) model of parents and infants as a dynamic interactional system in which 2 partners—almost always, 2 partners–possessing unequal communicative and integrative potentials form a functional unity, and reinforce one another's adaptive capacities. The Papouseks see parents as preadapted to help the infant overcome uncomfortable transitional states through intuitive parenting strategies, but also contend that *under unfavorable conditions,* infant behavioral problems can come to inhibit this intuitive supportive competence of parents.

What are these unfavorable conditions that can erode parents' intuitive competencies? Certainly, there are inconsolable infants who can create them all by themselves. But as Crockenberg and Leerkes so aptly note (this volume), family circumstances are usually far more complicated than this. Certain unfavorable conditions that can hamper intuitive parenting, such as lack of love and partnership in the adult-adult relationship, predate the baby's arrival but are further exacerbated by a difficult child. *New* interadult or family-wide dynamics not evident in the old two-person system can also be awakened by a child's arrival—triggered perhaps by the baby's gender or temperament, but also mediated by parents' conscious or unconscious enactments of long dormant coparenting and family scripts (Talbot, Pouquette, & McHale, 1999). Or, initially supportive co-parenting figures may draw away from involvement with the newborn and mother, after having met with continual frustrations with the inconsolable infant.

As we hope is apparent, the issue with there being multiple parenting adults in the family is not just whether babies affect everybody in a family system the same way—though there is certainly no reason why systemically-informed researchers should not pose and get some answers to this question. For, as Reiss notes (this volume), it certainly is possible and instructive to seek out and substantiate durable actor effects (Anderson, Lytton, & Romney, 1986). Likewise, particularly in the case of enduring and excessive infant crying, different adults often do respond to the same infant similarly—several research teams have cautioned against blindly attributing parental complaints about excessive infant crying to reporting bias in overly concerned or emotionally labile parents (Lester, Boukydis, Garcia-Coll, Peucker, et al., 1995; Papousek & von Hofacker, 1998). At the same time, however, the point we want to drive home here is that given the reality of multiple parenting figures, infant effects—which are both direct and indirect, as Crockenberg and Leerkes note—must be understood in the context of each caregiver's unique manner of thinking about, responding to, and affecting the baby. Somehow, this important multiperson point gets buried as background in so many studies of infant effects.

What are the most important adult characteristics of which to take account? Clearly, each person's beliefs about babies' needs are critical. Illustrating the organizing effect of perceptions about need, Donovan, Leavitt, and Walsh (2000) showed that cries from purportedly "difficult" infants in an experimental, signal detection task elicit more sensitive responses from mothers than do the exact same cries emanating from supposedly "easy" infants. This is an example of a transient, cognitive set effect, of course. Undoubtedly, however, more enduring individual differences also affect adults' processing of infant cues. For example, current thinking about attachment holds that infants' signaling of intense need calls forth different sets of responses from dismissing, autonomous, and preoccupied adults (Bakermans-Kranenburg, Juffer, & van Ijzendoorn, 1998; Ward & Carlson, 1995). A major contribution to the family literature would be systematic research on the over-time ministrations of parents with different states of mind with respect to attachment, as they attend to infants who signal different early levels and kinds of need—research that simultaneously takes into consideration the responsivity of other caregiving figures who would likewise vary in their own states of mind with respect to attachment. Matters would become complex quickly, of course, in family systems where co-caregiving figures were grandmothers or female relatives rather than fathers, but it is just this sort of complexity we should be dealing with anyway to advance our understandings of families and of infant effects in the family.

Beyond each person's basic beliefs about infant needs, their core beliefs about gender and potency also guide how they interpret and respond to infant signals, as Maccoby outlines (this volume). In 1976, Condry and Condry reported in a classic paper that identical infant distress signals get interpreted by naive study participants as expressions of anger when babies are thought to be boys and as expressions of fear when they are thought to be girls. While this study has sometimes been dismissed as irrelevant to parents, who fare much better than do nonparents in distinguishing among different types of infant signals (Green, Jones, & Gustafson, 1987), there is evidence that parents too reveal stereotyped gender biases. For example, Teichner, Ames, and Kerig (1997) reported that despite no overall differences in the amounts of crying by male and female infants in their study, both mothers and fathers perceived daughters, but not sons, more negatively as infant crying increased. Additionally, as infant crying increased, mothers of boys rated their sons as more powerful, while mothers of girls rated their daughters as less powerful. Girls', but not boys', crying was negatively related to mothers' self-evaluation ratings; this finding was not true of fathers. These findings indicate that infant crying may interact with the sex of the infant to differentially affect mothers' and fathers' perceptions of their infant and of themselves during the transition to parenthood.

Fascinating though any of these individual findings may be, it is also important to recognize that most articles continue to report findings only for the generic "mother" and "father", and this is unfortunate. We're going to get stuck as a field if we only continue to compare mothers' response tendencies with those of other mothers, or fathers with other fathers, or even mothers with fathers at the group level. Truly contextualizing infant effects in the family means examining the influences of infants on both mothers and fathers in the *same* family, and on the nature of the coparental relationship these individuals come to develop. Developmental research is just now beginning to catch on that different parenting adults within the same family may either compliment one another's parenting or work at cross-purposes (McHale, 1995, 1997; McHale & Cowan, 1996; McHale & Fivaz-Depeursinge, 1999). But a piece that remains terribly underdeveloped is how different caregiving adults in the same family assign meaning to, and respond to, different kinds of emotional signaling.

We suspect that there is an important developmental story to be told here. In low-risk families during the early postpartum months, mild differences in how different people respond to the baby are probably of only minor consequence in shaping the baby's developing regulatory capacities. This would be especially so when the family's mode of adaptation is for one parent to be the primary person responding to most of the infant's communications, despite fascinating findings suggesting individual differences among parents in their speed of responding to infant cries as a function of such factors as parity, degree of involvement by the parent in caretaking responsibilities, and age at which the parent believes the baby first recognizes him or her (Donate-Bartfield & Passman, 1985). At the same time, however, it does not logically follow that early infant signaling is inconsequential in the emerging family environment.

One instructive line of research has been concerned with early interparental disagreement in families where mothers suffer from postpartum depression. In such families, fathers' ratings of their babies' temperament are only moderately associated with those of the babies' mothers. The more depressed the mother is, the greater the discrepancies are between the parents' views of the baby (Whiffen, 1990). The work of Wilkie and Ames (1986), featured in Chapter 5, actually suggests that the effects of infant crying have a farther-reaching impact in the family system for fathers than for mothers, affecting not only men's own anxiety and concern about lifestyle changes, but also their views of both themselves *and* their wives as low in potency. This insidious effect on fathers' views of the babies' mothers seems especially poignant in light of Cutrona and Troutman's (1986) finding that social support can protect against depression in mothers with temperamentally difficult infants by bolstering maternal self-efficacy, and Hodapp and Young's (1992) finding that mothers with supportive spouses who had looked forward to becoming fathers (and mothers with close friends) experienced less severe emotional reactions following the birth of a premature infant. The regard of others is equally as important for mothers raising infants outside of marriages; in fact, Cohen's (1999) work indicates that such mothers are not just as, but often even *more*, sensitive to criticism from involved extended family co-caregivers than they are to criticism from the babies' fathers.

If not apparent, most of these findings still draw upon data concerning mothers and infants, though they speak to infant effects on the broader family support system. Returning to our point about the developmental picture in families, there does appear to be a normative shift in fathers' active parenting involvement as infants enter into the toddler years. At this point both their perceptions of their children's dispositions, and the impact of these perceptions on their parenting behavior, clearly *do* become a critical consideration. For example, Belsky, Putnam, and Crnic (1996) demonstrated that initially inhibited toddlers whose fathers handled them *in*sensitively actually turned out to be less inhibited at age 3 than would have been predicted on the basis of their age 2 temperament profiles. Moreover, these same children became less inhibited still when their parents clashed about parenting practices. Hence, different parental responses to the same emotional signals led to a very distinct developmental outcome. The researchers hypothesized that most fathers do not want introverted sons, and that some bristle when they believe their partners are babying the inhibited boys. Such fathers respond by behaving so as to toughen up the boys, and many also actively oppose their partners gentle handling of the boys' fear expressions. The result—bolder boys. Actually, it's not entirely clear how often the result is a courageous boy and how often it is an out of control one, but the point is that different parental responses to toddler inhibition sidetrack the expectable trajectory.

In summary, some data indicate that, especially at extreme levels, infants' communications can and do stir particular sorts of affective and behavioral responses in a variety of different adults. Be that as it may, however, the data are also clear that different people interpret infant signals in different ways, show different thresholds for responding to infants' signals, and exhibit different manners of responding once they do engage. Different patterns of responsiveness by different caregivers are likely less consequential during the early postpartum months than later on, particularly when there is one primary caregiver who responds to most of the infant's signals. However, when there are multiple caregiving others who tend regularly to the newborn or young infant, it is certainly possible that radically different sensitivities by these individuals may have a more active impact on the newborn's developing self-regulatory capacities, particularly if the infant is herself hypersensitive or physiologically immature. More commonly, infant distress in the early postpartum months is likely to affect families through its effects on coparenting solidarity, either by bringing together partners in a collaborative partnership to work with the difficult baby, as our own recent data (Berkman et al., 2002) suggest, or by driving a wedge between them when fathers disengage from parenting while criticizing mothers' handling of the infant and thereby further eroding her self-efficacy.

We'll close this chapter with a thought about infant effects in families with multiple children. Consider the case of a family in which an unplanned but otherwise normally developing and relatively well-treated first-born daughter is later followed by an attractive, wished-for infant son. Consider then the reactions of the adults when, at one month, the infant becomes colicky and screams afternoon and night. In response to their mounting frustration and irritability, what becomes of the parents' anger? Do they criticize one another, does the father disengage, or do the adults pull together? And what becomes of the first-born daughter? Do the parents thank their lucky stars that the elder child is not a problem, or do they channel their exasperation with the baby onto the older child, responding harshly to her minor transgressions and thereby instigating new and largely unforeseen problems for the first-born and the family? Do families exhibiting this not too terribly uncommon dynamic find their way into our research studies in great enough numbers that we could reliably identify the family pattern and predict the developmental trajectories of the two children? And could the complexity of the family system be picked up at all in larger-scale studies that ask questions about relative effects of different sources of contribution, be they genes and environment, child and parent, child and two parents, and so forth? As we all continue to grapple with tensions between nomothetic and idiographic, grand theory and contextual perspectives, there remains an acute need for intelligent and clinically sensitive theorizing about infant effects in family systems. In this regard, we owe a debt of thanks to Crockenberg and Leerkes for getting us started.

REFERENCES

Acquarone, S. (1992). What shall I do to stop him crying? Psychoanalytic thinking about the treatment of excessively crying infants and their mothers/parents. *Journal of Child Psychotherapy, 18,* 33–56.

Anderson, K. E., Lytton, H., & Romney, D. M. (1986). Mothers' interactions with normal and conduct-disordered boys: Who affects whom? *Developmental Psychology, 22,* 604–609.

Bakermans-Kranenburg, M. J., Juffer, F., & van Ijzendoorn, M. H. (1998). Interventions with video feedback and attachment discussions: Does type of maternal insecurity make a difference? *Infant Mental Health Journal, 19,* 202–219.

Barr, R. G., & Gunnar, M. (2000). Colic: The "transient responsivity" hypothesis. In R. G. Barr, B. Hopkins, et al. (Eds.), *Crying as a sign, a sympton, & a signal: Clinical emotional and developmental aspects of infant and toddler crying* (pp. 41–66). New York: Cambridge University Press.

Belsky, J., Putnam, S., & Crnic, K. (1996). Coparenting, parenting, and early emotional development. In J. P. McHale & P. A. Cowan (Eds.), *Understanding how family-level dynamics affect children's development: Studies of two-parent families* (pp. 45–55). San Francisco, CA: Jossey-Bass.

Belsky, J., & Rovine, M. (1987, June). Temperament and attachment security in the strange situation: An empirical rapprochement. *Child Development, 58,* 787–795.

Berkman, J. M., Alberts, A. E., Carleton, M. E., & McHale, J. P. (2002). *Are there links between infant temperament and coparenting processes at 3 months post-partum?* Paper presented at the World Association of Infant Mental Health, Amsterdam, Holland.

Berkman, J. M., Alberts, A. E., Kavanaugh, K., Carleton, M., & McHale, J. P. (2001). *Interparental coordination during 3-month still face reunions and coparenting interactions at 3 and 12 months postpartum.* Paper presented at the biennial meeting of the Society for Research in Child Development, Minneapolis, MN.

Carnicero, J. A. C., Perez-Lopez, J., Salinas, M. C. G., & Martinez-Fuentes, M. T. (2000). A longitudinal study of temperament in infancy: Stability and convergence of measures. *European Journal of Personality, 14,* 21–37.

Cohen, N. E. (1999). *Mother/co-caregiver relationships, social support, parenting, and child adjustment in single-parent African-American families.* Paper presented at the Biennial Meeting of the Society for Research in Child Development, Albuquerque, NM.

Collins, W., Maccoby, E., Steinberg, L., Hetherington, E. M., & Bornstein, M. (2000). Contemporary research on parenting: The case for nature and nurture. *American Psychologist, 55,* 218–232.

Condry, J. & Condry, S. (1976). Sex differences: A study of the eye of the beholder. *Child Development, 47*, 812-819.

Crockenberg, S. B. (1981). Infant irritability, mother responsiveness, and social support influences on the security of infant-mother attachment. *Child Development, 52*, 857–865.

Cutrona, C. E., & Troutman, B. R. (1986). Social support, infant temperament, and parenting self-efficacy: A mediational model of postpartum depression. *Child Development, 57*, 1507–1518.

Daws, D. (1989). *Through the night: Helping parents and sleepless infants.* London: Free Association Books.

DeGangi, G. A., Porges, S. W., Sickel, R. Z., & Greenspan, S. I. (1993). Four-year follow-up of a sample of regulatory disordered infants. *Infant Mental Health Journal, 14*, 330–343.

DeGangi, G. A., Sickel, R. Z., Wiener, A. S., & Kaplan, E. P. (1996). Fussy babies: To treat or not to treat? *British Journal of Occupational Therapy, 59*, 457–464.

Donate-Bartfield, E., & Passman, R. H. (1985, October-December). Attentiveness of mothers and fathers to their baby's cries. *Infant Behavior & Development, 8*, 385–393.

Donovan, W. L., Leavitt, L. A., & Walsh, R. O. (2000). Maternal illusory control predicts socialization strategies and toddler compliance. *Developmental Psychology, 36*, 402–411.

Dunn, W. (1997). The impact of sensory processing abilities on the daily lives of young children and their families: A conceptual model. *Infants and Young Children, 9*, 23–35.

Fivaz-Depeursinge, E. (1988). Infant's triangulation strategies: A new issue in development. *The Signal, 6*.

Fivaz-Depeursinge, E., & Corboz-Warnery, A. (1999). *The primary triangle: A developmental systems view of mothers, fathers, and infants.* New York: Basic Books, Inc.

Fivaz-Depeursinge, E., & Frascarolo, F. (1999). *The attentional and affective sharing abilities of 3-4 month-old infants with both parents during trilogue play.* Paper presented at the Society for Research in Child Development, Albuquerque, NM.

Fivaz-Depeursinge, E., & Frascarolo, F. (2000): *Infant's handling of triangular family interactions at four months, its relation with the family alliance.* Paper presented at the International Society on Infant Studies Conference, Brighton.

Fraiberg, S. (1980). *Clinical studies in infant mental health: The first year of life.* New York: Basic Books.

Garcia-Coll, C., Halpern, L., Vohr, B., Seifer, R., et al. (1992). Stability and correlates of change of early temperament in pre-term and full-term infants. *Infant Behavior and Development, 15*, 137–153.

Green, J., Jones, L., & Gustafson, G. (1987). Perceptions of cries by parents and non-parents: Relation to cry acoustics. *Developmental Psychology, 23,* 370–382.

Greenspan, S. (1992). *Infancy and early childhood: The practice of clinical assessment and intervention with emotional and developmental challenges.* Madison, CT: International Universities Press.

Greenspan, S., & Wieder, S. (1993). Regulatory disorders. In C. Zeanah (Ed.), *Handbook of infant mental health* (pp. 280-290). New York: Guilford.

Gustafson, G. E., Wood, R. M., & Green, J. A. (2000). Can we hear the causes of infants' crying? In R. G. Barr, B. Hopkins, et al. (Eds.), *Crying as a sign, a symptom, & a signal: Clinical emotional and developmental aspects of infant and toddler crying* (pp. 8–22). New York: Cambridge University Press.

Hakulinen, T., Laippala, P., & Paunonen, M. (1998). Relationships between infant temperament, demographic variables, and family dynamics of childrearing families. *Journal of Advanced Nursing, 27,* 458–465.

Hawkins, A. J., & Dollahite, D. C. (1997). Beyond the role-inadequacy perspective of fathering. In A. J. Hawkins & D. C. Dollahite (Eds.), *Generative fathering: Beyond deficit perspectives* (pp. 3-16). Thousand Oaks, CA: Sage.

Hodapp, R. M., & Young, K. T. (1992, January). Maternal emotional reactions to the premature infant in the context of the family. *Canadian Journal of Behavioural Science, 24,* 29–40.

Jones, L. C., & Heermann, J. A. (1992). Parental division of infant care: Contextual influences and infant characteristics. *Nursing Research, 41,* 228–234.

Kagan, J. (1994). Inhibited and uninhibited temperaments. In W. B. Carey & S. C. McDevitt (Eds.), *Prevention and early intervention: Individual differences as risk factors for the mental health of children: A festschrift for Stella Chess and Alexander Thomas* (pp. 35–41). Philadelphia, PA: Brunner/Mazel, Inc.

Kagan, J. (2000) Inhibited and uninhibited temperaments: Recent developments. In W. R. Crozier (Ed.), *Shyness: Development, consolidation and change* (pp. 22–29). New York: Routledge Falmer.

Kagan, J., Reznick, J. S., & Gibbons, J. (1989). Inhibited and uninhibited types of children. *Child Development, 60,* 838–845.

Lamour, M., & Barraco, M. (1988). Le nourrisson de mere psychotique: Une singuliere exposition. *Nouvelle Revue d'Ethnopsychiatrie, 12,* 105–118.

Leerkes, E. M., & Crockenberg, S. C. (in press). The development of maternal self-efficacy and its influence on maternal behavior. *Infancy.*

Lester, B. (1984). A biosocial model of infant crying. *Advances in Infancy Research, 3,* 167–212.

Lester, B., Boukydis, C., Garcia-Coll, C., & Hole, W. (1990). Colic for developmentalists. *Infant Mental Health Journal, 11,* 321–333.

Lester, B., Boukydis, C., Garcia-Coll, C., Peucker, M., McGrath, M., Vohr, B., Brem, F., & Oh, W. (1995). Developmental outcome as a function of the goodness of fit between the infant's cry characteristics and the mother's perception of her infant's cry. *Pediatrics, 95,* 516–521.

Martinetti, M. G., Papini, M., Guerri, S., Stefanini, M. C., et al. (1991). Psychodynamic treatment of failure in homeostatic organization in infancy. *Infant Mental Health Journal, 12,* 302–308.

McHale, J. (1995). Co-parenting and triadic interactions during infancy: The roles of marital distress and child gender. *Developmental Psychology, 31,* 985–996.

McHale, J. (1997). Overt and covert coparenting processes in the family. *Family Process, 36,* 183–210.

McHale, J., & Cowan, P. (1996). Understanding how family-level dynamics affect children's development: Studies of two-parent families. *New directions for child development* (Vol. 74). San Francisco, CA: Jossey–Bass.

McHale, J. P., & Fivaz-Depeursinge, E. (1999). Understanding triadic and family group interactions during infancy and toddlerhood. *Clinical Child & Family Psychology Review, 2,* 107–127.

McHale, J., Fivaz-Depeursinge, E., & Corboz-Warnery, A. (2000). *What do recent empirical studies of mother-father-infant triads contribute to clinicial practice?* Paper presented at the World Association for Infant Mental Health, Montreal, Canada.

McHale, J., Khazan, I., Erera, P., Rotman, T., DeCourcey, W., & McConnell, M. (2002). Coparenting in diverse family systems. In M. Bornstein (Ed.), *Handbook of parenting* (2nd ed., pp. 75–107). Hillsdale, NJ: Lawrence Erlbaum Associates.

McHale, J., Lauretti, A., Talbot, J., & Pouquette, C. (2002). Retrospect and prospect in the psychological study of coparenting and family group process. In J. McHale & W. Grolnick (Eds.), *Retrospect and prospect in the psychological study of families* (pp. 127–165). Hillsdale, NJ: Lawrence Erlbaum Associates.

Nadel, J., & Tremblay-Leveau, H. (1999). Early perception of social contingencies and interpersonal intentionality: Dyadic and triadic paradigms. In P. Rochat (Ed.), *Early social cognition: Understanding others in the first months of life* (pp. 189–212). Mahwah, NJ: Lawrence Erlbaum Associates.

Papousek, M., & Papousek, H. (1990). Excessive infant crying and intuitive parental care: Buffering support and its failures in parent/infant interaction. *Early Child Development & Care, 65,* 117–126.

Papousek, M., & von Hofacker, N. (1998, September). Persistent crying in early infancy: A non-trivial condition of risk for the developing mother-infant relationship. *Child: Care, Health & Development, 24,* 395–424.

Seifer, R., Sameroff, A. J., Barrett, L. C., & Krafchuk, E. (1994). Infant temperament measured by multiple observations and mother report. *Child Development, 65,* 1478–1490.

St. James-Roberts, I. (1993). Explanations of persistent infant crying. In I. St. James-Roberts, G. Harris, et al. (Eds.), *Infant crying, feeding, and sleeping: Development, problems, and treatments* (pp. 26–46). England: Harvester Wheatsheaf.

Stern, D. N., & Bruschweiler-Stern, N. (1998). *The birth of a mother.* New York: Basic Books.

Stifter, C. A., & Braungart, J. M. (1995, May). The regulation of negative reactivity in infancy: Function and development. *Developmental Psychology, 31,* 448-455.

Talbot, J., Pouquette, C., & McHale, J. (1999). *The second wave of transition to parenthood research in context.* Paper presented at Society for Research in Child Development, Albuquerque, NM.

Teichner, G., Ames, E. W., & Kerig, P. K. (1997). The relation of infant crying and the sex of the infant to parents' perceptions of the infant and themselves. *Psychology: A Journal of Human Behavior, 34,* 59-60.

Tremblay-Leveau, H. (1999). Avant les croyances [Before beliefs.]. *Enfance, 51,* 313-321.

van Egeren, L. A., & Lower, R. J. (2001). *Predictors of parental efficacy over the transition to parenthood.* Poster presented at the Biennial Meeting of the Society for Research in Child Development, Minneapolis, MN.

Ward, M. J., & Carlson, E. A. (1995, February). Associations among adult attachment representations, maternal sensitivity, and infant/mother attachment in a sample of adolescent mothers. *Child Development, 66,* 69-79.

Wessel, M., Cobb, J., Jackson, E., Harris, G., & Detwiler, A. (1954). Paroxysmal fussing in infancy, sometimes called "colic". *Pediatrics, 14,* 421-434.

Whiffen, V. E. (1990, September). Maternal depressed mood and perceptions of child temperament. *Journal of Genetic Psychology, 151,* 329-339.

Wilkie, C. F., & Ames, E. W. (1986, August). The relationship of infant crying to parental stress in the transition to parenthood. *Journal of Marriage & the Family, 48,* 545-550.

8

The Developmental Course From Child Effects to Child Effectiveness

Pamela M. Cole

The Pennsylvania State University

It could be said that the goal of childhood is to become an effective person. Effectiveness includes being able to get along with others and to work productively. During childhood, the development of effectiveness depends upon the acquisition of a variety of skills. Getting along with others involves, for example, being able to initiate and sustain appropriate interactions, form and maintain relationships, and know how to do this with a wide variety of people, including family members, teachers, classmates, friends, and unfamiliar persons. Effectiveness also entails being able to access, understand, and use social and academic knowledge in order to be productive in work-related activity, such as being a good student. The developmental course to such effectiveness begins very early in life and continues throughout the life course. From the moment a parent realizes a baby has been conceived, that child begins to exert an influence on the life of the parent and family. The scientific challenge for us is to understand how these child effects bear on the development course to child effectiveness.

My perspective in this discussion is that of the child clinical psychologist, trained in developmental psychopathology (Sroufe & Rutter, 1984). When children have significant difficulties in any of the component skills of effective behavior, family members or teachers often judge the child to be problematic. This judgment may lead to a professional evaluation in which the child may be classified as having clinical behavioral, emotional, or learning problems. When attempts to address these problems through ordinary home and school resources are unsuccessful, clinical intervention may be sought. The goals of such intervention are to reduce symptomatic behaviors (e.g., aggressiveness, poor grades, noncompliance) and, more importantly, to promote effective behavior (e.g., performing to one's abilities in school, having friends, getting along with the family).

The methods used by a clinician to accomplish these intervention goals depend, in large part, upon that person's model for how change occurs, including the relative degree to which development is effected by the child's own characteristics and behaviors and those of the others in the child's life. Traditionally, many clinicians work individually with the child, meeting for weekly hour-long sessions and reporting to the parents periodically. Many contemporary clinicians, however, emphasize the role of caregivers (parents at home, teachers at school) in their efforts to solve a child's problems, meeting weekly with caregivers, with and/or without the child. We can pose a general question about these two approaches and the role of child and caregiver effects in modifying a developmental trajectory that involves problematic patterns. If a clinician works individually with a child, and achieves treatment goals such that child behavior improves, how much and in what way do the caregivers in the child's life actually change? Alternatively, if intervention focuses primarily on caregiver behavior (e.g., parenting skills, classroom behavior management) and treatment goals are achieved, how much and in what way does the child actually change? This question has not been researched often but at least one study indicates that the combination of child and caregiver intervention is important, although in adolescence individual treatment may be sufficient (Barrett, Dadds, & Rapee, 1996). It may well be that in early and middle childhood, the hour a week that a clinician spends with an individual child cannot hope to compete, in effecting developmental growth and change, with the hours the child spends with caregivers at home and at school. Does this mean that caregiving effects are ultimately more influential than child effects in predicting outcomes?

Based on research on infant temperament, Crockenberg and Leerkes (this volume) present a framework for how babies and their caregivers influence each other and how these conjoint effects influence developmental outcomes, such as being emotionally effective. They contend that infant temperament, particularly in regard to its emotional quality, can effect parenting, although this is not a simple, straightforward relation. Specifically, they state that an infant's heightened and persistent angry distress can have a negative effect on parenting and family relationships, which would interfere with the child's developing emotional competence, but they conclude from a literature review that such negative effects of infant anger proneness are not consistently found. Sometimes the negative effect is shown, sometimes there are no effects, and sometimes the effects are "positive" (i.e., parents of anger prone babies have better scores on measures of sensitive parenting than parents of easier infants).

Crockenberg and Leerkes describe these child and caregiver effects as transactive and call for studies that test these mutual influences as statistical interactions. Indeed, recent longitudinal data show that a "good fit" between child temperament and parenting strategy predicts positive outcomes, both in terms of fewer child symptoms (Bates, Pettit, Dodge, & Ridge, 1998) and greater child competence (e.g., Kochanska & Murray, 2000). Crockenberg and Leerkes attribute variations in the level and direction of effect of infant temperamental anger to other risk factors in the caregiver's life (e.g., depression, economic hardship). Parenting by a caregiver who faces other stresses, in addition to raising a temperamentally angry infant, is more likely to lack sensitivity and creativity than parenting by caregivers who do not face such challenges. This point of view suggests that variation in parenting behavior is the crucial factor in the relation between child effects (infant temperament) and developmental outcomes (effective emotional self-regulation in the child).

From the clinical point of view, it is crucial to establish a scientific basis for conceptualizing and understanding how child and caregiver effects combine to yield optimal outcomes. The field of developmental psychology, however, has not firmly established this base. Crockenberg and Leerkes, and others in this volume, remind us that parenting does not create a child's development. Rather, a child *elicits* parenting. This point was articulated by Bell's seminal paper (1968) and has recurred in the literature. Lytton (1990) argued that the child "drives" the development of conduct disorder but Wahler (1990) countered that, in the end, it is parenting effects that influence outcome. Similarly, Scarr (1992) argued that a child's genotype accounts for individual differences that effect parenting, and that the effects of parenting on individual development are negligible as long as the parent provides an "average expectable environment." Baumrind (1993) responded that evidence indicates that parents play a significant role in developmental outcome through socialization processes.

Thus, the debate about how to conceptualize and understand child effects, relative to caregiver effects, continues. One solution to the debate is a transactional model of development (e.g., Sameroff, 1991), which offers the view that the child and the important persons in the child's life influence each other in reciprocal and recurring patterns. Development evolves from transactions between the person and the environment. Stable characteristics of individuals (child temperament, parental depression) and life circumstances (economic challenges) are distal influences on the developmental process. Ultimately, they have effects on outcome through the mechanism of mutually co-constructed human (not statistical) interactions. A transactional perspective argues that the interactions between individuals are greater than the sum of their parts (Minuchin, 1985). A transactional conceptualization of actual human interactions that capture process at a proximal level is most important in understanding the relative weight of child and caregiver mutual influences. Examining their co-constructed exchanges allows us to understand the mechanisms of developmental growth and change. Stable individual characteristics influence behavioral choices; human interactions are the means by which individuals influence each other. Moreover, from a clinical point of view, these social interactions are the target of intervention. They hold the most promise of ultimate therapeutic change. Clinicians cannot alter temperamental dispositions or child gender or parental personality or economic risk, but they can influence the degree to which these various factors impinge on human interaction and how they therefore influence developmental outcomes.

Let's parse the human interactions between young children and their parents. A parent comes to the parenting of a specific child with a set of potential influences. The set includes, but is not limited to, the parent's relationship history in his or her family of origin, aspirations for the child's development, general parenting knowledge and expectations, specific ideas about and practice at parenting strategies, the meaning of the child's birth, the particular stage of development for the family, and historical and current conditions (e.g., economic conditions). Each and all of these can influence the parent's behavioral choices. At the same time, the child brings his or her own set of potential influences to the interaction— appearance, phenotypic behavior, gender, temperament, talents and weaknesses, to name a few. Then, the two partners meet and the dance begins. What matters most then are not the a priori possibilities but the actualities of what happens as interactions unfold, recur, and change over time. They are not fixed by pre-existing possibilities. They are co-constructed in the moment. In addition, there are developmental points at which these child-caregiver interactions are novel and fluid—negotiations in search of a stable pattern of interaction. At other points they are stylized, even automatized (Dumas, 1997), the expected pattern until the next developmental or life event perturbation that provokes a new pattern of interaction. Thus, developmental science must examine these interactions, and do so with well-conceived transactional models, naturalistic procedures (e.g., home observations, school observations), and laboratory procedures that robustly capture usual experience. The most fascinating unit of analysis becomes, at a minimum, the dyad rather than individuals as separate influences interact (see also J. McHale, Kavanaugh, & Berkman, and S. McHale & Crouter, this volume).

In studying the role of emotional development in the etiology of competence and behavior problems, I have turned to parental socialization of children's emotional self-regulation. Emotion is an important predictor of child outcomes for several reasons. First, emotions motivate behavior. They organize (and sometime disorganize) action. Second, emotions are communications. They are often more powerful than words, conveying to others the current motivational state of each partner. Third, emotions play a salient role in the symptoms of various forms of psychopathology (e.g., Cole, Michel, & Teti, 1994) and in how clients accept or resist therapeutic change efforts. My research has focused on how young children become effective in regulating their own emotions and how risk conditions influence this aspect of the development of effective, competent emotion regulation. I will present some recent findings that portray the transactional nature of emotional interactions between children and caregivers. Then I will suggest that caregiver effects play a crucial role in paving the path from child effects to outcomes of child effectiveness.

My colleagues and I have conducted observational studies of socializing exchanges between caregivers and preschoolers when the child is angry. In moment-to-moment emotional exchanges, we witness how children drive interactions (Lytton, 1990). For example, Cohen (2001) examined the effect of maternal scaffolding on the child's ability to regulate anger effectively when alone. Scaffolding is a term introduced by Vygotsky (1962), to convey the idea that a more advanced person creates an interpersonal space that serves as a platform from which a less advanced person can achieve levels of skill that the latter could not achieve independently. We predicted this effect of parental scaffolding, over and above the influences of the child's temperament. That is, preschoolers whose mothers used scaffolding techniques when the preschoolers were frustrated would demonstrate more effective self-regulation when they were frustrated and alone than children whose mothers did not scaffold, over and above the influence of temperament. Cohen demonstrated, instead, the "positive" effect described by Crockenberg and Leerkes (this volume). In a sample of normal volunteer mothers and their 3- and 4-year-olds, greater maternal scaffolding was associated with greater child anger and less self-regulation as well as with higher scores on mother-reported temperamental anger proneness. We interpreted these findings as Crockenberg and Leerkes would. In a low-risk sample, mothers of anger-prone preschoolers anticipated how easily their children became angry and tried to help them by using a parenting behavior that ought to be effective (eventually).

The story of whether such parenting is effective in diverting a trajectory of poor emotional self-regulation in an anger-prone child cannot be told from concurrent data. It requires a longitudinal design and a sample with varying risk conditions. At the National Institute of Mental Health, my colleagues and I conducted such a study, following a group of children who varied from symptom free to clinically symptomatic as preschoolers (Time 1). Parents and teachers described the symptomatic preschoolers as "hard to manage" and parent and teacher reports revealed that these children were above the norm in externalizing symptoms (e.g., noncompliant, defiant, aggressive, angry). We examined how emotional exchanges with parents, when the children were preschoolers, predicted problem status after the children had entered and settled into elementary school (about two years later). We chose a variety of procedures, some including mothers and fathers, but here I will focus on an analysis of exchanges between the preschoolers and their mothers during a long, frustrating wait (Cole, Teti, & Zahn-Waxler, in press).

In this procedure, first developed by colleagues at University of Washington (Carmichael-Olson, Greenberg, & Slough, 1985), the mother is presented with work to do, and the child is presented with a boring toy and a gaily wrapped surprise. The mother then tells the child, "This surprise is for you but you must wait until I finish my work to open it." In our work, the wait lasted eight minutes. The beauty of this task is that all preschoolers, regardless of a child's problem status, are frustrated by the long wait. Even the asymptomatic child finds it too long. Thus, the task does not test whether a preschooler gets frustrated but how dyads handle frustration. We classified each partner's second-by-second emotional communications on the basis of facial and vocal cues. From these data, we created variables that represented each partner's initiated and contingent emotions, positive and negative. Initiated emotions were those that one partner communicated after a period of mutual neutrality. Contingent emotions were those that followed the other partner's emotion. We focused on periods when the child was dealing with the frustration of the boredom and waiting.

The first thing we noted in the emotional exchange data was a clear child effect. The preschooler took the emotional lead almost all the time. Mothers initiated speaking neutrally to their children sometimes but preschoolers led *emotionally*. Second, the transactional nature of the exchanges was evident in the high degree of mutual reciprocity. Regardless of the emotional valence of their emotions, maternal emotion was almost completely contingent upon child emotion and children reacted emotionally to parental emotion. Mothers appeared to try to remain emotionally neutral but preschoolers eventually elicited maternal emotion in almost all mothers. In addition to emotion begetting emotion in each partner, there were interesting patterns in the match between child and maternal emotional valence.

In the case of positive emotions, child-initiated positive emotion was met with positive maternal emotion and positive maternal contingent emotion was met with positive child contingent emotion. A modal dyadic exchange of this type begins with the preschooler who smiles and asks in a lilting voice, "Mom, will you be finished soon?" Mother chuckles and smiles, saying, "You know, I can't finish if you keep interrupting me." This pattern of mutual positive emotion was not predicted by mother or preschooler trait measures (e.g., temperament, hostility in the child; personality, styles of coping, depression in the mother). It seemed co-constructed in the moments. We suspect, however, that the moment-to-moment co-construction reflects an established pattern of interaction that constitutes the dyad's relationship history. Again, this pattern is not merely a product of pre-existing factors that each partner brings to the interaction. Although those distal factors can influence behavioral choices, there is still something spontaneous and new in the actual moments of the dance.

We also found that child negative emotion was reciprocated with maternal negative emotion, which was reciprocated by child negative emotion, but only in dyads in which the preschooler was identified as symptomatic. This pattern of mutual negativity has been demonstrated repeatedly in dyads that are at risk for the development of stable child behavior problems (e.g., Patterson, Capaldi, & Bank, 1991). Again, maternal personality questionnaires were not predictive of maternal negative emotion; child temperament ratings did slightly better in predicting child negative emotion but most of the variance seemed to relate to the interaction itself and presumably its history as a pattern of interaction. Thus, examining statistical interactions between child and mother traits may fall short of capturing the full nature of their human interactions and the processes that underlie the eventual developmental outcomes.

An important question for this project was the clinically relevant one of how these early preschooler-mother emotional exchanges predicted child outcomes approximately two years later. The children were seen again after they had completed at least one semester of first grade. We showed that the emotions of each partner elicit emotional reactions in the other partner and that there is a natural tendency for those to be reciprocal. But we assumed that parents have a greater degree of behavioral flexibility, as well as a greater imperative to be flexible, and that this would make an important difference in child outcomes. Their flexibility allows them to anticipate their child's particular needs, to regulate their own emotions and therefore the organization of their own behavior, and to strategize in how to respond to prevent child's dispositions from becoming problems and to promote the development of effective skills.

At the risk of redundancy, I'll note again that child clinicians like myself rely completely on this premise. The hour a week that a clinician could spend in the office with an individual child client cannot have the same influence as the hours a week that a parent has to spend with a child. We assume that there is something special about the side of the transaction with the arrow pointing from parent to child. Nonetheless, the dyad is the crucial unit of analysis. In clinical work, we believe we must help the parent, who cannot do so, tailor his or her caregiving to the particular needs of the child. We try to help parents understand that they cannot change a child's disposition and then we work to find parenting strategies that will help that child of that type become an effective person. But again, the arrows of mutual influence are not to be forgotten. Our strategy requires that we appreciate the effects of the child on the parent's emotions, behavior, hopes, and plans, and on other relationships within the family.

Let me provide an example of a real-life emotional exchange, which a valued colleague offered me as we discussed the paper by Crockenberg and Leerkes (this volume). In this scenario, Mom wanted to work out at the health club. Her temperamentally anxious school-age daughter, however, did not want her mother to go and communicated this in a fussy, demanding way. Mom really wanted to go (and may have felt some guilt about it) so she held her ground, but found herself getting more and more exasperated by her daughter's whining insistence and feeling more and more ineffective at calming her daughter. Daughter and mother soon found themselves in a spiraling, reciprocal, unhappy dance. Then, the phone rang. After a brief chat, the interaction changed. The phone call may have broken the power of the emotional reciprocity, helping Mom distance herself from her aggravation with her temperamental child, who was always anxious about separating with her mother despite maternal attempts to reduce the anxiety (not to mention the countless reunions). At this point, Mom found herself able to interact differently with her daughter and in a way that helped the temperamentally anxious child cope with the reality of her anxiety in an effective way. There is the transactional path from child effects to child effectiveness!

Let us step away from this anecdote and return to the emotional exchange data. In our study, we hoped that the emotional exchanges during an eight-minute, frustrating wait would capture the real-life experiences of these dyads and therefore predict the developmental trajectories of behavior problems between preschool and school age. This seems a large task to place on an eight-minute social interaction and yet we believed that human interactions, properly assessed, capture the dynamic flow of family relationships. First, we examined the degree to which each partner's contributions to the emotional exchanges predicted the level of Time 2 behavior problems based on teacher reports. In a hierarchical regression, we first entered the child's Time 1 externalizing score and child gender because of the well-established clinical finding that behavior problems tend to be persistent. Indeed, Time 1 child behavior problems accounted for a significant degree of Time 2 child behavior problems. The second step, child-initiated emotions, was nonsignificant. The third step, maternal contingent emotional reactions, predicted additional, significant variance in child behavior problems two years later. Child contingent emotions, the fourth step, was nonsignificant. (The interaction terms were also nonsignificant.) Thus, the interesting finding was the influence of maternal emotional reactions in accounting for the level of children's later behavior problems. Specifically, if a mother responded angrily to her child's emotions during the wait, her child had even higher levels of behavior problems two years later than were predicted by the fact of the child's problems at Time 1. Maternal angry distress seemed to exacerbate existing child behavior problems.

Another approach to the question was to classify children into three groups on the basis of their problem status at two points in time. This yielded three patterns: a stable problem pattern, an improved pattern, and a stable nonproblem pattern. We used discriminant function analysis to examine whether each partner's emotions, considered as initiations and reactions, predicted the child's group membership. In an initial analysis, we again found that child emotion failed to contribute. We ran the analysis then using only maternal emotions (adding maternal self-reported emotion from the wait to the observational data). Maternal emotion significantly predicted the child's group. The specific function reflected maternal negative and positive contingent emotion and maternal self-reported antagonistic emotion (anger, contempt, disgust). What was particularly interesting about the classification results was that we had good rates of prediction for the stable nonproblem (73%) and stable problem (74%) groups but completely missed with the improved group (0%). In fact, the improved group was not distinguished from the stable nonproblem group. That is, the analysis suggested that mothers of improved children were emotionally like the mothers of the nonproblem children.

We returned to the examination of the dyadic emotions for the final set of analyses. There were a number of fascinating differences in these groups. In the nonproblem group, children generated positive emotion even as they interacted with their mothers about the wait being difficult and their mothers reacted in emotionally positive, sympathetic ways. In the stable problem group, there were two distinct qualities. The first was the mutual negativity, already described. The second was dyadic emotional insensitivity. Stable problem children laughed when their mothers got angry with them and their mothers often found it funny when their children became frustrated.

Most interesting of all was the improved group. Here we found that mothers of children who improved engaged in mutual positive exchanges with their difficult preschoolers but they were also the least angry mothers, compared to the other two groups. It appeared that these mothers understood that to convey any anger to their oppositional preschoolers was to engage in a battle they would not win. They appeared to have the ability to avoid responding to growing frustration with their own frustration. As in the anecdote, these mothers may have modulated their own concern and frustration, providing an interpersonal context that avoided the escalation or continuation of the child's angry distress and that provided calmness and empathic understanding. All tests of whether improved and problematic children were different as preschoolers (level of behavior problems, quality of their contributions to the emotional exchange, temperament, trait hostility) were not significant.

These data provided support for a transactional model in which child and caregiver are simultaneously and mutually effecting each other in their social interactions. In predicting outcome, it is evident that the arrows from child to parent are powerful but the arrows from parent to child may, in the end, be most important in redirecting developmental trajectories toward greater child effectiveness. There is no question that children are active co-creators of their experiences and relationships. They elicit parenting. Perhaps the reason child effects have tended to be neglected despite the periodic reminders that they must be considered is that we ultimately cling to the belief that caregivers have the capacity to be flexible and mindful in their parenting and not simply reactive. We believe that caregivers can and will play the most crucial role in the path from child effects to child effectiveness. Adults have the greater burden. They have to manage themselves and their children, trying to disentangle themselves from the influences that will interfere with their parenting and yet remain sensitive to the child in the moment. The call for attention to child effects can be addressed by a transactional model that focuses on human interactions between children and others that inform us of how children make parents feel (Dix, 1991), how parents come to juggle successfully the multiple factors that could bear on their interactions with their different children, and how parents interact with each other and their child in ways that promote that child's ability to harness his or her temperament into the service of a happy, productive life. Ultimately, caregiving is crucial in harnessing child effects, particularly when the child is at risk, into child effectiveness.

REFERENCES

Barrett, P. M., Dadds, M. R., & Rapee, R. M. (1996). Family treatment of childhood anxiety: A controlled trial. *Journal of Consulting and Clinical Psychology, 64,* 333–342.

Bates, J. E., Pettit, G. S., Dodge, K. A., & Ridge, B. (1998). Interaction of temperamental resistance to control and restrictive parenting in the development of externalizing behavior. *Developmental Psychology, 34,* 982–995.

Baumrind, D. (1993). The average expectable environment is not good enough: A response to Scarr. *Child Development, 64,* 1299–1317.

Bell, R. Q. (1968). A reinterpretation of the direction of effects in studies of socialization. *Psychological Review, 75,* 81–95.

Carmichael-Olson, H., Greenberg, M. T., & Slough, N. (1985). *Manual for the waiting task.* Unpublished manuscript, University of Washington.

Cohen, L. (2001). *Scaffolding as a form of parental socialization of preschooler's self-regulatory skill.* Unpublished master's thesis, The Pennsylvania State University, University Park, PA.

Cole, P. M., Michel, M. K., & Teti, L. O. (1994). The development of emotion regulation and dysregulation: A clinical perspective. *Monographs of the Society for Research in Child Development, 59,* 73–100.

Cole, P. M., Teti, L. O., & Zahn-Waxler, C. (in press). Mutual emotion regulation and the stability of conduct problems between preschool and early school age. *Development and Psychopathology.*

Dix, T. (1991). The affective organization of parenting: Adaptive and maladaptive processes. *Psychological Bulletin, 110,* 3–25.

Dumas, J. E. (1997). Home and school correlates of early at-risk status. In R. F. Kronick (Ed.), *At-risk youth. Theory, practice, reform* (pp. 97–117). New York: Garland.

Kochanska, G., & Murray, K. T. (2000). Mother–child mutually responsive orientation and conscience development: From toddler to early school age. *Child Development, 71,* 417–431.

Lytton, H. (1990). Child and parent effects in boys' conduct disorder: A reinterpretation. *Developmental Psychology, 26,* 683–697.

Minuchin, P. (1985). Families and individual development: Provocations from the field of family therapy. *Child Development, 56,* 289–302.

Patterson, G. R., Capaldi, D., & Bank, L. (1991). An early starter model for predicting delinquency. In D. J. Pepler & K. H. Rubin (Eds.), *The development and treatment of childhood aggression* (pp. 139–168). Hillsdale, NJ: Lawrence Erlbaum Associates.

Sameroff, A. J. (1991). The social context of development. In M. Woodhead & R. Carr (Eds.), *Becoming a person. Child development in social contact, Vol. 1* (pp. 167–289). Florence, KY: Taylor & Francis/Routledge.

Scarr, S. (1992). Developmental theories for the 1990s: Development and individual differences. *Child Development, 63,* 1–19.

Sroufe, L. A., & Rutter, M. (1984). The domain of developmental psychopathology. *Child Development, 55,* 17–29.

Vygotsky, L. S. (1962). *Thought and language.* New York: Wiley.

Wahler, R. G. (1990). Who is driving the interactions? A commentary on "Child and parent effects in boys' conduct disorder." *Developmental Psychology, 26,* 702–704.

III

What Roles Do Adolescents Play in Actively Shaping Relationships With Parents, Siblings, and Peers?

9
Parenting of Adolescents: Action or Reaction?

Margaret Kerr
Håkan Stattin
Örebro University

The other papers in this volume have grappled with whether and how researchers can tease apart the child's role in shaping family interactions and their own development from the parents' role. They have cited diverse empirical findings to illustrate the conceptual and empirical problems in asking, and the complexity of the answers to the question regarding, whether parents affect children or children affect parents. In this paper, we take a different approach. First, we limit our focus to adolescence. We start with a robust set of correlational findings that researchers have virtually *always* attributed to parent effects, and we present empirical evidence that those particular findings might have been child effects. We make a circumscribed argument; we do not make the larger argument that parents have no effect on children or that they have played no active role in creating the relationship within which these findings appear. But we argue that directionality in these findings is important in current perspective—regardless of what has led up to them—because researchers have used these findings as a basis for handing out practical advice to parents about how they should parent their adolescents.

PARENTING AND ADOLESCENT DELINQUENCY

Delinquency in a child is one of the most salient indicators that parents have been doing something seriously wrong. This seems to be a natural way to think. When people hear about an adolescent who has committed a crime, they often wonder out loud what the parents were like and comment that they must not have been paying attention or controlling what their adolescent was doing. The everyday assumption seems to be that parents, through their actions or failures to act, have, at worst, produced a delinquent adolescent or, at best, allowed the delinquency to develop.

Parents as Active Agents

This same assumption appears in adolescent research. The major views of parenting that have dominated research on adolescence during the past 20 years are consistent with the assumption that failures in parenting are causes of adolescent problems such as delinquency. They point the finger at two broad classes of parenting behaviors. One concerns the relational side of parenting—emotional warmth and responsiveness to the youth's needs. The other concerns the regulatory-supervisory side of parenting—active regulation of the youth's activities and associations.

In research on delinquency, in particular, both these classes of parenting behaviors have appeared in theory and research about the role of parents. On the relational side, one idea is that delinquency results from poor attachment to the family (Hirschi, 1969). The reasoning is that if youths are strongly attached to their parents, they will not want to engage in delinquency because doing so would embarrass or hurt their parents. This is supported by findings that delinquents tend to have weak emotional bonds to others (Benda & Whiteside, 1995; Farrington & Hawkins, 1991; Loeber, Farrington, Stouthamer-Loeber, & van Kammen, 1998; Sokol-Katz, Dunham, & Zimmerman, 1997). On the regulatory side, the idea is that parents of delinquents have failed to provide the kind of structure in the home that would help a child develop internal controls by internalizing the externally imposed structure (Hawkins, Herrenkohl, Farrington, Brewer, Catalano, & Harachi, 1998). This is supported by findings that delinquents tend to come from homes with poor structure, more disorganization, and conflict (Eron, Huesmann, & Zelli, 1991; Henry, Moffitt, Robins, Earls, & Silva, 1993; West & Farrington, 1973). A third idea rests mainly on the regulatory side of parenting; it is that parents of delinquents have failed to directly control their youths' activities and associations (Dishion & McMahon, 1998; Loeber, Farrington, Stouthamer-Loeber, & van Kammen, 1998; Weintraub & Gold, 1991). This idea appears in two large, influential literatures—the parental monitoring literature and the parenting styles literature. Both these literatures bring in the relational side of parenting as well, but they both make parents' direct regulation of the youth's activities and associations the primary causal factor in the development of adjustment problems such as delinquency.

In the parental monitoring literature, it is thought that if parents fail to monitor disruptive children, they will be free to hang out on the streets with deviant peers who will draw them into delinquency and other problem behaviors (Patterson, Reid, & Dishion, 1992). On the other hand, parents who are vigilant monitors of their children's behavior can steer them away from bad influences, thus preventing the development of delinquency. Hence, in this view, poor parental monitoring is a link in a causal chain of events that can produce delinquency. In support of this idea, scores of studies have shown that the more parents know about their youths' everyday activities and associations, the less likely youths are to engage in delinquency, have deviant friends, become delinquent because of peer pressure (for a review, see Patterson & Stouthamer-Loeber, 1984; for empirical examples, see Cernkovich & Giordano, 1987; Crouter, MacDermid, McHale, & Perry-Jenkins, 1990; Dishion, Capaldi, Spracklen, & Li, 1995; Fridrich & Flannery, 1995;

McCord, 1986, Sampson & Laub, 1994; Weintraub & Gold, 1991), or engage in other problem behaviors such as drug use or risky sexual activity (Chassin, Pillow, Curran, Molina, & Barrera, 1993; Flannery, Vazsonyi, Torquati, & Fridrich, 1994; Fletcher, Darling, & Steinberg, 1995; Metzler, Noell, Biglan, Ary, et al., 1994; Romer, Black, Ricardo, Feigelman, Kaljee, Galbraith, Nesbit, Hornik, & Stanton, 1994). The conclusions that are drawn from this assume that causality rests with parents:

> ...parental monitoring *is* an appropriate strategy for parents attempting to deter adolescents from engaging in substance use. Strong parental monitoring helps to deter adolescents from using alcohol and drugs themselves and, as a consequence, prevents nonusing adolescents from associating with drug-using peers (Fletcher, Darling, & Steinberg, 1995, p. 270).

> ... supervision fosters appropriate parental reaction to antisocial and delinquent behaviors (Snyder & Patterson, 1987, p. 227).

> ... monitoring affects boys' delinquency by preventing them from associating with [other delinquents] (Weintraub & Gold, 1991, p. 279).

In the parenting styles literature, similar conclusions appear. When samples are divided into groups according to parents' characteristics, youths of "authoritative" parents, or those who score high on measures of the relational *and* regulatory sides of parenting, are less likely to be delinquent, and those of "neglecting" parents, who score low on both measures, are more likely to be delinquent (e.g., Steinberg, Lamborn, Darling, Mounts, & Dornbusch, 1994). As in the monitoring literature, the conclusions from these correlational findings assume that causality resides with parents. This is evident in both titles and text, as revealed in the following examples:

> *The influence of parenting style on adolescent competence and substance use* (title of Baumrind, 1991)

> The success of authoritative parents in protecting their adolescents from problem drug use and in generating competence should be emphasized...authoritative upbringing...consistently generated competence and deterred problem behavior (Baumrind, 1991, p. 91).

Hence, these literatures have been clear and consistent on one point: Parents' active supervisory or regulatory efforts work protectively by keeping youths away from deviant peer contexts and out of trouble, and adolescent adjustment indicators such as delinquency and school achievement are *outcomes* of parents' actions or failures to act.

Reasons to Doubt

Although it may be natural to think of parents as causal agents in their youths' adjustment, is it valid to infer causality from findings such as these that are mainly correlational? On general principles, the answer is no, of course, but in addition to that, there are reasons to question (1) the idea that parents can and should closely supervise their adolescents and (2) the validity of the findings in both the parenting styles and monitoring literatures.

Can parents closely supervise adolescents, and should they?

For parents who want to directly supervise their adolescents' activities and associations, a logistical problem arises: they are not usually where the adolescents are. Adolescents spend much of their time away from home (Csikszentmihalyi & Larsen, 1984, Hirschi, 1969; Nye, 1958), so direct supervision and control of behavior are difficult, if not impossible. It is questionable, then, whether parents' direct supervision and control of adolescents' behavior *can* be effective. In addition, the psychological literature, more broadly, raises questions about whether direct control *should* be effective. There is much evidence that people react badly to being controlled by others (Hiroto, 1974; Langer & Rodin, 1976; Rodin & Langer, 1977; Seligman 1975) and why would this not be true for adolescents? Some have even argued that, based on the social psychological literature, there is no reason to believe that children would internalize the values of firmly controlling parents (Lewis, 1981). In fact, the opposite should be true. Internalization should take place if children comply with parents' wishes by choice but not if firmly controlling parents compel them to comply.

Construct validity problems in measures of parents' regulatory-supervisory efforts

In addition, there are problems with the way that control or supervision have been operationalized and measured, and they leave open the possibility that parental supervisory or control efforts have not really been responsible for the findings that link these parenting behaviors with lower rates of adolescent delinquency and other adjustment problems. This issue was raised 20 years ago in a critique of, among other things, Baumrind's parenting styles research (Lewis, 1981). In Baumrind's studies, parents were considered controlling if the child followed their wishes during in-home observations. Lewis argued that this measure could have been tapping parent-child harmony or the child's willingness to comply with parents' authority rather than parental control. She argued, further, that the good adjustment in families who scored high on this control measure could have come about through a process that had nothing to do with control—perhaps a process in which children were encouraged to negotiate solutions to disagreements, and through which the *child* would actually develop a sense of control (Lewis, 1981). To support this suggestion, Lewis cited Baumrind's own findings. She pointed out that the parents of Baumrind's highly competent children were more likely to encourage verbal communication, respect the child, and even withdraw demands after being convinced by the child's arguments. Baumrind (1991) later agreed with Lewis' position, stating,

> Lewis...suggested that neither demanding practices nor authoritative child rearing is necessary to the development of optimal competence. She is correct...Authoritative child rearing was the only pattern that consistently produced optimally competent children and failed to produce incompetent children...However, most of the optimally competent children did not come from authoritative homes (Baumrind, 1989, p. 364).

Hence, although it is widely believed that Baumrind's parenting styles research has provided clear evidence that parents should firmly control their adolescents, the evidence is not clear, even to Baumrind herself.

The construct validity of parental monitoring measures is also in doubt (see Crouter & Head, 2001; Kerr & Stattin, 2000; Stattin & Kerr, 2000) and, for reasons that will become apparent below, this has consequences for some of the most highly respected, recent parenting styles studies, as well. Parental monitoring is conceptualized as parents' active tracking and surveillance efforts, and monitoring studies claim to have shown that parents can control adolescents' opportunities for deviance by keeping track of, or monitoring, what they are doing from day to day (Snyder & Patterson, 1987). But monitoring has been operationalized with questions such as, "How much do your parents REALLY know about...where you go at night, who your friends are," etc. (Fletcher, Darling, & Steinberg, 1995, p. 262), the assumption being that parents know these things if and only if they have been monitoring the youth's activities. In a recent study, we questioned that assumption and tested an alternative interpretation: that parents' knowledge comes through the free, willing disclosure of the youths themselves (Stattin & Kerr, 2000). Our results supported the alternative interpretation. Parents' monitoring and controlling actions contributed little to their knowledge of their youths' activities and were only weakly related to delinquency and other measures of personal and social adjustment (Kerr & Stattin, 2000; Stattin & Kerr, 2000). In contrast, the youth's free, willing disclosure of information was strongly linked to both parental knowledge and youth adjustment, suggesting that the measures that have been used to capture parents' monitoring are not construct valid. They seem to capture youths' more than parents' actions. Hence, these studies show that the monitoring literature is vulnerable to the same criticism that Lewis raised about Baumrind's parenting styles studies: the results that have been attributed to parents' active regulatory efforts might actually represent some other process.

These findings also have implications for the interpretation of some of the more recent parenting styles literature. The same monitoring scale, "How much do your parents REALLY know ...," has been part of the operationalization of parenting styles in the most highly respected and widely cited parenting styles studies of the last decade (e.g., Brown, Mounts, Lamborn, & Steinberg 1993; Gray & Steinberg, 1999; Lamborn, Mounts, Steinberg, & Dornbusch, 1991; Steinberg, Lamborn, Darling, Mounts, & Dornbusch, 1994). In these studies, parenting styles are defined by scores on two scales: strictness/supervision and acceptance/involvement. However, almost half of the strictness/supervision scale consists of measures of parental knowledge. The scale taps the 9 issues shown below and 4 of those (shown in bold) deal with parental knowledge.

1. child can't stay out late on school nights
2. child can't stay out late on weekends
3. **parents try to know a lot about where child goes at night**
4. **parents try to know a lot about what child does with free time**
5. **parents try to know a lot about where child is most afternoons after school**
6. parents know exactly where child is most afternoons after school
7. parents really know a lot about where child goes at night
8. parents really know a lot about what child does with free time
9. parents really know a lot about where child is most afternoons after school

If parents' knowledge comes mainly from the child's free, willing disclosure, it is highly questionable whether this scale really taps parents' supervisory or regulatory efforts. Children's willingness to share their everyday experiences with their parents are heavily represented here.

PARENTING: ACTION OR REACTION?

The possibility of reverse causality—that parents' behaviors could be reactions to adolescent adjustment—has rarely received more than lip service. Many Discussion sections in the monitoring and parenting styles literatures contain a few sentences noting that the findings are correlational and that causality cannot be determined. Sometimes plausible arguments are even raised for how and why the correlations could represent child effects rather than parenting effects. These comments, however, are overshadowed by the ubiquitous assumption that it is, indeed, parenting effects that are being studied.

But suppose that we take the possibility of reverse causality seriously. Is it reasonable to think that parents would lessen their supervision or monitoring efforts *in response to* a youth's delinquency? Why should they lessen their efforts, rather than increasing them? One possible reason involves the delinquent child's behavior at home. Delinquent youths might be defiant or threatening at home, or they might be secretive and deceptive, particularly when their parents question them about, or try to control, who their friends are and what they are doing when they are away from home. This behavior might discourage parents from attempting to supervise them or control their activities and associations. Hence, it is plausible that parents might lessen their supervision or monitoring efforts in response to a youth's delinquency. In a cross-sectional perspective, then, higher delinquency could be linked to less regulatory effort on parents' parts, but correlational results would not permit one to distinguish this reactive effect from what has always been assumed: that parents actively contribute to their child's problems through their actions or failures to act.

In this study, we take seriously and test the possibility that parenting behaviors might be *re*actions to youths' delinquency. We use data from a short-term longitudinal study of youths in mid-adolescence (ages 14 and 16). Using cross-lagged regression models, we look first at predictors of changes over time. If parenting practices act protectively in a causal way, then parenting at Time 1 should predict delinquency at Time 2, controlling for delinquency at Time 1. If parenting behaviors are reactions to the youth's delinquency, then delinquency should predict parenting at Time 2, controlling for parenting at Time 1. We consider several parenting behaviors that have been linked to delinquency in the literature and/or that might, theoretically, be instigators of or reactions to the youth's delinquency— parental control, parental solicitation of information, parental support, and bad reactions to the child's communication.

Method

Participants

Participants were 14-year-old youths and their parents in a mid-sized Swedish city. Students in all 8th-grade classes in the city ($N = 1,283$) composed the target sample for the study, which was the first wave of a longitudinal investigation. They took part in the study unless their parents returned a form stating that they did not want their child to participate (12 parents returned this form). Neither parents nor children were paid for their participation. Of the 1,283 students, 1,186 (92.4%) were present on the day of the data collection and answered the questionnaires.

A questionnaire was sent to the home in which the child lived during the school week. It was addressed to the child's biological parent or legal guardian. Parents were asked to return the completed questionnaire by mail; 1,077 (83.9%) did so. In 73.4% of cases, mothers filled out the questionnaire alone, in 18% of cases fathers filled it out alone, in 7.6% of cases, mothers and fathers worked together, and in 0.9% of cases, a guardian other than a parent filled out the questionnaire.

Almost two years later, in the Spring of 2000, the same youths and parents participated in a second data collection. Youths and parents answered about the same questions as earlier.

Measures

Delinquency. Youths answered 15 questions about whether they had engaged in certain behaviors during the past year. The response scale was a 5-point scale ranging from "never" (1) to "more than 10 times" (5). The questions were about: shoplifting; being caught by the police for something they had done; vandalizing public or private property; taking money from home; creating graffiti; breaking into a building; stealing from someone's pocket or bag; buying or selling stolen goods; stealing a bike; being in a physical fight in public; carrying a weapon; stealing a car; stealing a moped or motorcycle; using marijuana or hashish; and using other drugs. Parents answered the same questions about what their youths had done, according to their knowledge.

Child disclosure. This measure comprised 5 items. The children's questions were: "Do you talk at home about how you are doing in the different subjects in school?", "Do you usually tell how school was when you get home (how you did on different exams, your relationships with teachers, etc.)?", "Do you keep a lot of secrets from your parents about what you do during your free time?", "Do you hide a lot from your parents about what you do during nights and weekends?", and "If you are out at night, when you get home, do you tell what you have done that evening?" Parents answered the same questions, with only minor changes in wording where necessary. Five-point response scales were used. Alpha reliabilities were .80 for parents' reports and .78 for youths' reports at Time 1 and .78 for parents' reports and .79 for youths' reports at Time 2.

Parental solicitation. Five items were averaged to form the parental solicitation measure. The children's items were: "In the last month, have your parents talked with the parents of your friends?", "How often do your parents talk with your friends when they come to your home (ask what they do or what they think and feel about different things)?", "During the past month, how often have your parents started a conversation with you about your free time?", "How often do your parents initiate a conversation about things that happened during a normal day at school?", and "Do your parents usually ask you to talk about things that happened during your free time (whom you met when you were out in the city, free time activities, etc.)?" Parents answered the same questions, with slight changes in wording where necessary. The alpha reliabilities were .70 and .69 for youth-reported and parent-reported solicitation, respectively, at Time 1 and .70 and .76 for youth- and parent-reported solicitation at Time 2.

Parental control. This construct was measured with 5 items. Youths answered: "Do you need to have your parents' permission to stay out late on a weekday evening?", "Do you need to ask your parents before you can decide with your friends what you will do on a Saturday evening?", "If you have been out very late one night, do your parents require that you explain what you did and whom you were with?", "Do your parents always require that you tell them where you are at night, who you are with, and what you do together?", and "Before you go out on a Saturday night, do your parents require you to tell them where you are going and with whom?" The 5-point scale ranged from "yes, always" to "no, never." Parents answered the same questions, with minor changes in wording. The alpha reliabilities were .78 and .75 for youths' reports and parents' reports at Time 1 and .82 and .77 for youths' and parents' reports at Time 2.

Parental support. Youths answered the following question about their mothers and fathers, separately: "Does your mother(father) usually support and encourage you?" The correlation between these two variables was $r = .67$ at Time 1 and $r = .69$ at Time 2. The means of the two were used as the measures of parental support in this study.

Parents' bad reactions to disclosure. Youths answered the following questions about their parents' responses to their past disclosure of information: "Have you told your parents things and later regretted it?", "How often have you regretted that you told your parents too much about yourself, your friends, and your free time?", "Have you ever been punished for something that you spontaneously told your parents?", "Have your parents ever used what you told them against you?", "Do your parents bring up things that you have confided again and again?", and "Have your parents ever made fun of things you happened to tell them about yourself and your life?" The alpha reliabilities for this scale were .81 at Time 1 and .83 at Time 2.

Results and Implications

Are parenting behaviors in middle adolescence antecedents of delinquency or reactions to it? The answer seems to be that they are reactions to it. The significant slopes from the cross-lagged models appear in Table 9.1. In every case where there was a cross-lagged link between delinquency and a parenting behavior, earlier delinquency was linked to a change over time in the parenting behavior. Specifically, youth delinquency was linked to less parental control over time, less emotional support and encouragement from parents over time, and more bad reactions to the youths' communication over time. However, contrary to what much of the developmental literature would lead us to expect, there were no instances in which a parenting behavior predicted a change in delinquency over time. Hence, parenting behaviors seem to be reactions to youth's delinquency, but they do not seem to produce it.

Table 9.1.
Significant Cross-Lagged Slopes From Regression Models Using Youth-
Reported Delinquency and Various Parenting Behaviors at Two Time Points

	Youth effect[a]	Parent effect[b]
Youth's ratings		
Control	-.12 ***	
Support	-.12 ***	
Bad reactions to disclosure	.08 *	
Solicitation		
Parents' ratings		
Control	-.05 *	
Solicitation		

[a]Cross-lagged slope in which the youth's delinquency predicts a change in parenting
[b]Cross-lagged slope in which parents' behavior predicts a change in the youth's delinquency
*p < .05; ***p < .001

What is particularly interesting in these results is that delinquency seemed to prompt parents to be less controlling and less supportive. This is precisely the pattern that has been thought of as "neglectful parenting," but neglectful parenting has been considered as a cause, not a consequence, of poor adolescent adjustment: "It is in the case of neglectfully reared adolescents…where we see the clearest evidence of the *impact* of parenting on adjustment during the high school years" (Steinberg, Lamborn, Darling, Mounts, & Dornbusch, 1994, p. 765; italics in original). Parenting models have typically assumed that parents affect adolescent adjustment in unidirectional fashion. These results offer enough justification for questioning that assumption and trying to understand how parents react to adolescents' behavior.

MODELING AND EXPLAINING PARENTS' REACTIONS

Parents might be reacting to the knowledge of the child's delinquency, or they might not even know about the delinquency and be reacting, instead, to the youth's behavior at home that accompanies delinquency. Either way, it is relatively easy to imagine how parents might react to a delinquent youth by withdrawing support and encouragement and by reacting badly to the youth's communication. For example, personality characteristics such as manipulativeness, dishonesty, and pathological lying have all been linked to serious criminality in adults (e.g., Cleckley,

1972; Hare, 1996, 1999) and adolescents (e.g., Forth, 1995), and to delinquency in community samples such as this one (Andershed, Kerr, & Stattin, in press). Delinquency has also been linked to hiding information from parents about everyday activities (Kerr & Stattin, 2000; Stattin & Kerr, 2000). If parents are aware that the delinquent youth is lying to them, trying to manipulate them, or being secretive, then they might very well withdraw their support and encouragement and reflexively react to the youth's communication with bitterness, sarcasm, or ridicule. In addition, certain outward behaviors that tend to accompany delinquency might evoke parents' disapproval and cause them to withdraw support and react badly to the youth's communication. For instance, failing to concentrate on difficult tasks such as schoolwork and engaging instead in off-task, irrelevant behaviors has been linked to delinquency (Nurmi, 1993, 1997), as has characteristically failing to take responsibility for one's own actions (e.g., Forth, 1995). These behaviors and characteristics might earn parents' disapproval and cause them to withdraw support and react badly to the youth's communication. Hence, there are a number of possible explanations for our findings that involve parents' emotional reactions to the youth's delinquency.

It is relatively more difficult to imagine why parents would react to delinquency by lessening their control attempts rather than increasing them. One possible scenario is that the youth's attempts to hide delinquent behavior are successful, and parents actually do not know about the youth's delinquency. If so, then even if they do not like the youth's behavior, they might not see the need to step up their control attempts or attempts to gain information. Of course, this does not explain why they would go the next step and actually reduce their monitoring attempts. An alternative explanation is that knowledge of a child's misbehavior, particularly serious misbehavior such as delinquency, is so anxiety-provoking for parents that their natural self-protective instinct is to try to avoid that kind of information. Our measures of control focused on required information giving—telling of Saturday night plans, getting permission to be out, telling where and with whom, explaining if out past curfew. If parents have reasons to suspect that they would not like what they would hear if given truthful answers to these question, then they might, without even being consciously aware of it, lessen their control attempts in order to avoid getting this anxiety- and worry-provoking information. A third explanation involves futility. Perhaps some parents believe that parents are powerless to handle an adolescent's misbehavior. This might go hand-in-hand with a belief that some degree of delinquency is a normative and normal part of adolescence. The need to reduce dissonance about a youth's delinquency might drive parents' beliefs that delinquency is normal and that the youth will outgrow it in time. Hence, parents' slackening of control in response to delinquency might reflect their beliefs that they cannot and need not try to stop it. A final explanation rests on the possibility that parents are intimidated by delinquent youths. These youths might act defiantly toward parents at home and this might make parents reticent to ask questions about what the youth is doing away from

home or to enforce rules and restrictions that require the youth to give them information and get their permission before going out. Asking might intensify conflicts
in the home and silence might keep peace. Hence, parents' silence or passivity
might be negatively reinforced because it is followed by a temporary cessation of
the youth's defiant behaviors. Their control attempts might be punished if they
provoke those behaviors. Hence, delinquency could decrease parents' control or
monitoring attempts in several possible ways. For some of these explanations,
parents are reacting to the youth's behavior at home as much as to the delinquency
itself, thus making the youth's behavior at home a mediator in the process.

With these ideas as a conceptual background, we test a model that includes
delinquency measures at two points in time. The earlier delinquency measure is
considered as the possible impetus for parenting behaviors that traditionally have
been considered as causes of delinquency (e.g., parental support and control or
monitoring attempts), and, consistent with the traditional view, the later delinquency measure is considered as a possible result of these same parenting behaviors. Concerning parents' reactions, we consider the possibilities that parents might
react to the delinquency itself or to the youth's behaviors at home that correlate
with delinquency. We divide parents' (re)actions into two categories: one that we
think of as "gut-level," or automatic, emotion-linked reactions, and another that
we think of as active monitoring efforts. In this model, we also examine the possibility that parenting behaviors might affect future delinquency by including delinquency at Time 2 as the ultimate outcome of the model.

Measures

Problem behavior

Delinquency measures, as described above, were used.

School adjustment. Youths answered 5 questions using 5-point Likert scales,
the end points of which are given in parentheses: "Do you enjoy school?" ("a lot"
to "not at all"), "Do you try to do the best that you can in school?" ("mostly" to
"almost never"), "Do you feel that you are forced to be at school against your
will?" ("almost never" to "very often"), "How would you describe the relationship between you and school?" ("like best friends" to "like enemies"), "Are you
satisfied with your school work?" ("mostly" to "almost never"). Some items were
reversed so that higher scores indicated more problems. The alpha reliabilities for
this scale were .80 and .82 at Times 1 and 2, respectively. Parents answered similar questions about their children (e.g., "Does your child enjoy school?", "Does
you child try to do his or her best at school?"). The alpha reliabilities for this scale
were .83 and .82 for Times 1 and 2, respectively.

Bad peers. Parents were asked, "Lately, has your child spent time with friends
that you do not think are appropriate?" ("No, it has not happened" to "Yes, it has
happened many times"), and "Are there friends that you do not let your son/daughter

spend time with?" ("No" to "Yes, many"). The correlation between these two measures was .44 (p<.001) at time 1 and .33 (p<.33) at Time 2.

Loitering. Children were asked, "Do you usually hang out in the city at night without doing anything special?" ("Seldom or never" to "Almost every night").

Youth's behavior in the family

Different informants are able to observe and give information about different behaviors in the family—their own and other family members'. Hence, this composite measure comprises different elements for youths' and parents' reports (see Table 9.2).

Table 9.2.
Scales Included in Composite Youth- and Parent-Report Measures of the
Youths' Behavior in the Family and Parents' "Gut-Level" Reactions

Youths' reports	Parents' reports
Youth's behavior in the family	
Manipulativeness	
Hiding information	Defiance
Off-task behavior	Hiding information
Dishonest charm	Off-task behavior
Lying	
Failure to accept responsibility	
Parents' "gut-level" reactions	
Worry	Worry
Distrust	Distrust
Bad reactions	
Lack of support	
Lack of warmth	

Youths' reports. For youths' reports, the mean of several scale scores was used: manipulativeness, hiding information from parents, off-task behavior, dishonest charm, lying, and failure to accept responsibility for own actions. *Manipulativeness* was from an 11-item scale that included items such as, "I can usually talk my way out of anything" and "I think I could 'beat' a lie detector." (The alpha reliabilities were .82 at Time 1 and .86 at Time 2.), *Hiding information* from parents comprised five items such as: "Do you keep a lot of secrets from your parents about what you do during your free time?", "Do you hide a lot from your parents about what you do during nights and weekends?" (The alpha reliabilities were .78 at Time 1 and .79 at Time 2.), *Off-task behavior* was an 8-item scale that included items such as: "It is very easy for me to think about other things about other things, daydream or get lost in my own thoughts when I really should be concentrating on more important things"; "I often find other things to do when I should be solving a difficult problem;" and "I am a person that chooses to do something else if a problem is not quickly solved" (the alphas were .81 at Time 1 and .84 at Time 2) (Nurmi, 1993, 1997). *Lying and dishonest charm* were 5-item subscales of the Youth Psychopathic traits Inventory (Andershed, Kerr, Stattin, & Levander, 2001). They included items such as: "Sometimes I lie for no reason, other than because it's fun" and "I've often gotten into trouble because I've lied too much" (lying); "When I need to, I use my smile and my charm to use others" and "When someone asks me something, I usually have a quick answer that sounds believable, even if I've just made it up" (dishonest charm). Finally, *failure to accept responsibility* for own actions consisted of five items such as these: "When I've done something that's hurt someone, they usually exaggerate and make it seem worse that it really was", "I'm always getting blamed for things that aren't my fault", and "When I've done something that my parents thought was wrong, they have often overreacted" (failure to accept responsibility). The alphas for these scales at Time 2 were .83, .82, and .80 for lying, dishonest charm, and failure to accept responsibility, respectively.

Parents' reports. The parent-reported composite measure was made up of three scales: two were parent-reported *hiding information* from parents and *off-task behavior* (as above, except for slight changes in wording; alphas were .80 and .88 at Time 1 and .78 and .90 at Time 2) and the third was a 7-item measure of the youths' *defiance* of parents' authority, which included items such as: "What does the child usually do when you as parents tell him/her to stop doing something that you don't like?" (response options ranged from "Stops immediately" to "Doesn't listen at all"), "What happens if you as parents tell the child that he/she isn't allowed to go out a particular night – but the child has already promised his/her friends to come out?" (responses ranged from "The child listens to you and stays home" to "The child doesn't listen to you and goes out anyway"), and "During the present school semester, how has the child reacted when you have asked about homework or about what have happened during a regular day in school" (responses ranged from "Is glad you asked and tells a lot" to "Becomes angry and won't answer") (alpha at Time 2 was .76).

Parents' reactions to youth's behavior

"Gut-level" reactions. Youths' reports of parents' "gut-level" reactions at Time 1 were a composite of four scales: worry, distrust, bad reactions to commu-

nication, and lack of support. At Time 2 they were a composite of five scales: worry, distrust, bad reactions to communication, lack of support, and lack of warmth. The alpha reliability for the composite of 4 scales at Time 1 was .70 and for the 5 scales at Time 2 it was .75. We have described the lack of support and the scale bad reactions to communications above. The *worry* scale included items such as: "Are your parents worried that you will: start using narcotics, not finish school, get in trouble with the police, get into bad company, or begin to abuse alcohol," and "Are your parents worried about what you do together with your friends at night and on weekends?" The 5-point response options ranged from "No, not at all" to "Yes, a lot." Alpha reliabilities were .90 at Time 1 and .87 at Time 2. The *trust* scale included 6 items: "Do your parents trust that you will not hang out with bad people?", "Do your parents trust that you will be careful with your money?", "Do your parents completely trust you to take responsibility for your life?", "Do your parents trust that you will try to do your best in school?", "Do your parents trust that you will not do anything dumb during your free time?", and "Do your parents trust that what you say that you are going to do on a Saturday night is true?" There were 5 response options, ranging from: "Yes, completely" to "No, absolutely not." The alpha reliability for this measure was .82 at Time 1 and .84 at Time 2. Finally, at Time 2, a measure of parental warmth was used. It contained six items, which we reversed to represent lack of warmth: "They always show their love for me without a reason – almost independent of what I do," "They always show how proud they are of me," "They praise me for no special reason," "They do small things that make me feel special (wink, smile)," "They always take up the positive and seldom the negative things that I do," and "They show with words and gestures that they like me." Responses ranged from "Not at all" to "Very much." The alpha reliability for the scale was .82.

For the *parent-reported* measure of "gut-level" reactions, a mean of the *worry* and *trust* scales was used. The wordings of the scales were similar to the child reports except for exchanging "your parents" with "you". The alpha reliabilities were .81 at Time 1 and .83 at Time 2 for the worry scale, and .80 and .86, respectively, for the trust scale.

Monitoring strategies. For both parents' and youths' reports, monitoring strategies were measured by 10 items that made up the control and solicitation scales described above. These items tapped parents' active efforts to keep track of the youth's whereabouts and associations by requiring the youth to do things such as check with parents before making plans to be out with friends and by asking for information from the youth, the youth's friends, and the friends' parents. For the monitoring-efforts measure, a mean of the 10 individual items was used. The reliabilities for these scales were .78 and .81 for youths' reports at Times 1 and 2, respectively, and .72 and .73 for parents' reports at Times 1 and 2, respectively.

ANALYTICAL STRATEGY

In a series of multiple regression path analyses, we examined a conceptual model of parents' reactions to the youths' problem behavior. In this model, we assume that the youth's problem behavior is reflected in certain behaviors in the family and that it is these, as well as the delinquency itself, to which parents react. Parents react to delinquency and/or the youth's behavior on an emotional, or "gut," level. Their emotional reactions can then prompt active monitoring attempts, and this can influence the youth's problem behavior. As informants, we use parents and the youths themselves, and as measures of problem behaviors we use delinquency, loitering, having deviant friends, and poor school adjustment. We use data from two time points. First, we look at models in which the initial problem behavior measures are from Time 1 and all other variables are from Time 2. Then, we look at models in which problem behavior at Time 2 is the final end point of the path and all other measures are from Time 1.

Results

Parents' reactions to the youth's behavior: The youth's point of view

Figure 9.1 shows the results of path analyses using delinquency as the problem behavior measure and youth reports of all variables. As the model shows, delinquency is, indeed, strongly linked to behavior that the youth might exhibit at home, and that behavior does seem to be important in understanding parents' reactions to the youth's delinquency. Parents' "gut-level" reactions are weakly linked to delinquency, but strongly linked to the youth's behavior—manipulativeness, lying, hiding information, and shirking responsibility. But, despite the fact that parents seem to react emotionally to this behavior by, for instance, withdrawing warmth, support, and trust, these emotional reactions do not correspond to any active monitoring efforts. The youth's behavior, on the other hand, is directly linked to monitoring efforts in that the more the youth is lying, manipulating, and shirking responsibility, the less parents are engaged in active monitoring attempts. Note, also, that in this model parents' "gut-level" reactions and monitoring strategies are both weakly linked, concurrently, to delinquency.

When, in the lower half of Figure 9.1, Time-2 delinquency is predicted from Time-1 measures of all other variables, the model remains the same in many respects, except that there are no across-time links between the parenting variables and delinquency. Monitoring strategies are not linked to later delinquency and parents' "gut-level" reactions are not linked to later delinquency. It is also true that "gut-level" reactions tend to be weakly linked to monitoring strategies in this model.

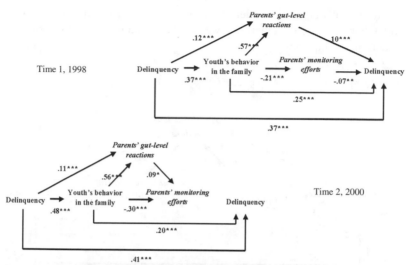

FIG. 9.1.   Path models depicting parenting behaviors as reactions to the youth's delinquency and behavior in the family. All measures are youth-reported.

We tested the same models that appear in Figure 9.1 using measures of poor school adjustment and loitering as the problem-behavior measures in place of delinquency. These models were strikingly similar to the delinquency models. Problem behavior was always strongly linked to behavior in the family, which in turn was always strongly positively linked to parents' "gut-level" reactions and negatively linked to parents' monitoring efforts. Monitoring efforts were typically unrelated to the later problem-behavior measures. In one out of these four models, there was a weak, concurrent link between monitoring and problem behavior similar to that which appears in the delinquency model. Taken together, then, these analyses offer a wealth of evidence that parenting behaviors are reactions to adolescent delinquency, but only weak, spotty evidence that they are causal factors in the youth's delinquency.

Parents' reactions to the youth's behavior: The parents' points of view

Parents' reports yield models that are highly consistent with those from the youths' reports. The top panel of Figure 9.2 shows the results of the same conceptual path model using delinquency as the problem behavior measure and using parents' reports of all variables. The core relations are much the same as in the youth-report models. Youths' behaviors in the family are strongly positively linked to parents' "gut-level" reactions and negatively linked to their active monitoring attempts. The more secretive youths are about their daily activities and the more they defy their parents' wishes and requests, the more worried and distrustful parents are, but the less they actively try to keep track of their youths' activities and associations. Paradoxically, "gut-level" reactions are positively linked to

monitoring efforts in this model. Also, in this model as in the first youth-report
model that we presented, there is a weak link between monitoring strategies and
concurrent delinquency.

Time 1, 1998   Time 2, 2000

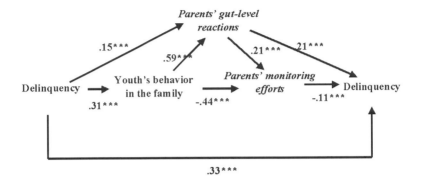

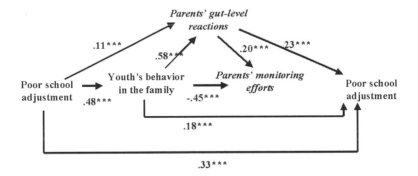

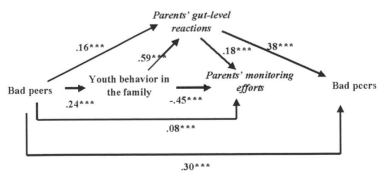

FIG. 9.2.   Path models depicting parenting behaviors as reactions to the youth's
delinquency and behavior in the family. All measures are parent-reported.

The second and third panels of Figure 9.2 show the results for two other measures of problem behavior—poor school adjustment and deviant peer association. These results are strikingly similar to the results for delinquency. Again, they suggest that youths' problem behaviors are reflected in secretiveness and defiance in the family setting. Parents react to that emotionally and their emotional reactions are somewhat related to increased monitoring, but they also respond to the youth's secretiveness and defiance by slackening their monitoring efforts. In these models, however, parents' monitoring efforts are unrelated to concurrent problem behavior. As with the youths' reports, we also tested these models using Time-2 problem behavior as the final end point of the path and Time 1, concurrent measures of everything else. As with the youth-report models, there were no across-time links between parents' monitoring efforts and later youth problem behaviors. Hence, the unmistakable conclusion from these youth- and parent-report models is that in middle adolescence, when parenting behaviors are correlated with delinquency and other problem behaviors, they might be better interpreted as reactions to the problem behavior than as causes of it.

Another look at directions of effects

We have been talking about parents' reactions to the youth's behavior in the family in directional terms. Largely, this is justified by the cross-lagged relations with which we began (see Table 9.1). They showed that delinquency is linked to reductions in parental warmth and control over time and more bad reactions to communication over time, whereas these parenting behaviors are not linked to changes in delinquency over time. In these models, we have shown that the youth's behavior in the family context seems to mediate those relations. However, to be able to infer the directions of effects between the youth's behavior in the family and the composite measures of parents' gut-level reactions and monitoring efforts, we used a series of cross-lagged models, including two variables at a time and measures of each from two time points. The significant cross-lagged slopes appear in Table 9.3.

Table 9.3.
Significant Slopes From Cross-Lagged Models Used to Infer Directionality

	Youth effect[a]		Parent effect[b]	
Youth's reports of all variables				
Comparing youth's behavior in the family with:				
Parents' "gut-level" reactions	.17	***	.09	**
Parents' monitoring efforts	-.08	**		
Parents' reports of all variables				
Comparing youth's behavior in the family with:				
Parents' "gut-level" reactions	.23	***		
Parents' monitoring efforts	-.06	*	.07	***

As shown in the table, the lion's share of the evidence suggests that parenting behaviors are reactions to the youth's behavior in the family. For youth's reports, there is a bi-directional relation between the youth's behavior in the family and parents' "gut-level" reactions, but the youth effect is by far the stronger. The youth's behavior in the family also predicts lower monitoring efforts over time, whereas monitoring efforts do not predict changes in the youth's behavior over time. Using parents' reports of all variables, the youths' behavior predicts an increase in parents' "gut-level" reactions and a decrease in their monitoring efforts over time. "Gut-level" reactions do not predict changes in the youth's behavior, however, and parents' monitoring efforts are linked to *increases* in secretiveness and defiance toward parents over time rather than decreases. Hence, taken together, these analyses suggest that parents' emotional reactions are more responses to the youth's behavior at home than causes of that behavior, although there is some evidence for that effect, as well. However, all the evidence suggests that the negative relation between the youth's behavior at home and parents' monitoring efforts is solely a youth effect. Secretive, defiant youth behavior predicts a decrease in monitoring over time, according to both youths' and parents' reports. There is a link in the opposite direction for parents' reports, but it is positive rather than negative, so it does not show bi-directional effects in the same process. Rather, it suggests that another process is at work in which higher parental monitoring is associated with an increase in secretive, defiant youth behavior over time.

What do parents react to and what is their reaction?

The evidence that we have presented suggests that many parenting behaviors at these ages (14–16) are reactions to youth's problem behavior rather than producers of it. To some extent, this makes sense. It is easy to imagine why parents would react on an emotional level to secretiveness or defiance by worrying and distrusting the youth more or showing less support and encouragement. It is not so easy to imagine why parents would respond to these behaviors by lessening their monitoring efforts. Above, we suggested four potential reasons why parents would reduce their monitoring efforts in response to the youth's delinquency. One is *ignorance*—youths might successfully hide what they are doing so parents just do not realize the need to monitor or control. Another is *intimidation*—the idea that youth's defiant, secretive behavior at home discourages parents from asking for information because they know that asking will just bring conflicts. *Denial* is a third explanation. Perhaps parents want to avoid getting anxiety-provoking information. And *futility* is a final explanation. Parents might think that delinquent behavior is such a normal part of adolescence that they cannot do anything to change it.

To get some clues about which, if any, of these might be responsible, we first divided the composite monitoring-efforts measure into two scales that we have used separately in previous research: solicitation and control (see Stattin & Kerr,

2000). Solicitation refers to parents' efforts to get information by talking to the youth, the youth's friends, and the friends' parents, and control refers to the items that tap parents' regulation of the youth's activities and associations by requiring the youth to get permission and inform them before going out in the evening or on weekends and to explain curfew violations. Then we used youth-reported delinquency, parent-reported youth delinquency, and the youth's behavior at home to predict solicitation and control. If *intimidation* is driving the negative link between the youth's behavior at home and parents' monitoring efforts, then the youth's behavior at home, independent of delinquency itself or parents' knowledge of delinquency, should be linked to solicitation and control. On the other hand, if parents' ignorance is driving the link between delinquency and lessened monitoring, then youth-reported delinquency, not parent-reported delinquency or the youth's behavior at home, should be linked to lessened control because it should be behavior of which parents are *not* aware that should be linked to a slackening of rules and restrictions. If *denial* is the explanation, then parents' knowledge of delinquency should be uniquely linked to a slackening of solicitation because knowledge of delinquency should prompt parents to stop asking for information that might be anxiety-provoking. Finally, if *futility* is the explanation, then knowledge of delinquency should be uniquely linked to a slackening of control attempts, because parents should feel that there is no use in trying to control delinquency.

Results

The results, which appear in Table 9.3, show more evidence for intimidation than any other explanation. The strongest relations are between youth behavior at home and solicitation, suggesting that the more defiant and secretive youths are at home, the less parents ask about their activities and associations. This is also somewhat true for control. Hence, these findings suggest that parents might lessen their monitoring efforts in order to avoid conflicts or defiant reactions from their youths. The other significant relations in Table 9.4 are between control and parent-reported delinquency, which provides some evidence, albeit weaker, for a futility explanation. The more parents know about the youths' delinquency, apart from any behavior at home or actual delinquency, the less they try to control the youth.

Table 9.4.
Multiple Regression Analyses Predicting Solicitation and Control,
Respectively, From Delinquency and Youths' Behavior at Home

	Solicitation		Control	
Time 1				
Delinquency (youth report)	.07		.03	
Delinquency (parent report)	-.01		-.10	**
Youth behavior at home	-.33	***	-.09	*
Time 2				
Delinquency (youth report)	-.01		.01	
Delinquency (parent report)	-.01		-.15	***
Youth behavior at home	-.34	***	-.09	*

GENERAL DISCUSSION

Two influential literatures—the parental monitoring literature and the parenting styles literature—have concluded that parents' direct control of adolescents' activities and associations works protectively to keep youths away from bad friends and out of trouble. In this study, we have found strong evidence that the direction of effects is the opposite—parents' behaviors are reactions to the youth's problem behavior rather than causes of it. What is even more interesting and somewhat counterintuitive is that when parents know about the youth's delinquency, they slacken their control efforts rather than increasing them; and when youths are defiant and secretive at home, parents really stop asking what they are doing away from home.

Why do these findings contradict so much previous literature? We believe that there are two likely reasons. One is that the measures of parents' active regulation used in the present study were more construct-valid than many measures previously used in the monitoring and parenting styles literatures. For instance, in Baumrind's classic parenting styles studies (Baumrind & Black, 1967), observers rated parental control while parents and children were doing a task. The child's compliance during this activity *and* the successful completion of the task were both taken as evidence of firm parental control, but it is unclear whether those observational measures tapped parental control, the child's willingness to comply, or just harmony in the relationship (Lewis, 1981). In a number of more recent, widely cited parenting styles studies, active parental regulation was represented by a scale entitled, "strictness/supervision" (e.g., Lamborn et al., 1991; Steinberg et al., 1994). Almost half of this strictness/supervision measure dealt with parents' knowledge of the youth's daily activities (i.e., "How much do your parents REALLY know...?"). Once again, it is questionable how much parental strictness/supervision was actually being measured and, consequently, how construct valid this scale is as a measure of parents' active regulation (see Kerr & Stattin, 2000; Stattin & Kerr, 2000). If parents' active regulatory efforts have not been validly operationalized and measured in these literatures, then the conclusions that emerge from them are likely to be different from those that emerge when regulatory efforts *are* validly measured.

A second reason why our findings contradict research in the monitoring and parenting styles traditions is that these bodies of research have not looked for child-to-parent effects. The assumption that parents are the causal agents has been so strong that reverse causality has not been considered seriously. This can be seen in Baumrind's original identification of parenting styles. She identified parenting behaviors and child characteristics that covaried and then gave explanations that implicitly and explicitly made parents the causal agents (e.g., Baumrind, 1966; Baumrind & Black, 1967). Perhaps this was a reflection of her behaviorist leanings or perhaps it was a reflection of the assumptions of the broader culture, as has been suggested before (Bell, 1968). But this tradition has continued.

Although longitudinal studies of parenting styles have been conducted, rarely have the data been used to try to rule out reverse causality, and when they have, the designs have typically been inadequate. For example, cross-lagged designs can be used as we have done in this study to offer some evidence of the direction of effects. However, when the only cross-lagged slope that is calculated is for parenting as a predictor of changes in the child's behavior, and the child's behavior is not considered as a predictor of changes in parenting (e.g., Steinberg, Lamborn, Darling, Mounts, & Dornbusch, 1994), then the results should not be taken as support for directionality.

Although our findings contradict the conclusions that have been drawn from the parenting styles and monitoring literatures, they are consistent with other studies showing that parents and other adults change their behavior in response to children's actions. This literature goes back as far as parenting styles research. At about the same time that Baumrind published her first parenting styles study, Bell (1968) published a review paper questioning the unidirectional interpretations that had been made in socialization studies in general. He cited many examples of experimental findings in which parents' and other adults' behaviors had changed in response to certain children's behaviors, and he argued that, because of these findings, parent-child correlations should not be interpreted as only parent-to-child effects. Later, Lewis (1981) questioned the directionality assumption in Baumrind's published studies, particularly Baumrind's claim that parental control produced well-adjusted children. She pointed out that in Baumrind's published studies the variables that really distinguished the parents of competent children from all other groups of parents had nothing to do with the use of control: "respect the child's decision," "use reason to obtain compliance," "encourage verbal give and take," and "satisfy child" (Lewis, 1981, p. 562), and that this left open the possibility that competence had developed through some process that had nothing to do with parental control. More recently, Harris (1995; 1998) offered a controversial critique of the assumption that parents influence children in unidirectional fashion. Her critique was broader than parenting styles, as were Bell's and Lewis'. But, concerning the parenting styles findings, she offered a reverse-causality explanation for the correlations between authoritative parenting and good child adjustment. She argued that most parents in Western cultures try to be authoritative because they know that is what parents "should" be. If the child behaves well (i.e., is well-adjusted), then they have no reason to change their strategy. However, if the child is difficult to manage (i.e., not well-adjusted), then they have to become more controlling and less democratic (i.e., more authoritarian). According to this reinterpretation, then, parents adjust to the child's behavior rather than producing it, and this adjustment explains the correlation between parenting styles and children's behavior. In addition, numerous experimental and longitudinal studies have shown that parents and other adults react to children's characteristics and adjust their behavior accordingly (e.g., Anderson, Lytton, & Romney, 1986; Bell & Chapman, 1986, for a review; Buss, 1981; Dix, Ruble, Grusec, & Nixon, 1986; Mulhern & Passman, 1981; Passman & Blackwelder, 1981) or have shown good evidence for bidirectional effects (e.g., Hastings & Rubin, 1999; Kochanska, 1998; Lytton, 1990, 2000; Mink & Nihira, 1986; Stice & Barrera, 1995). Hence, even though a view of the child as an active, causal agent has not been part of the most influential parenting literatures, it has appeared in numerous studies published in the most visible journals.

A particular strength of the present study was the use of both youths' and parents' points of view. These different informants provided different kinds of information. Hence, the measures were not identical in the youths' and parents' models. Nonetheless, the results were essentially identical. This, we believe, offers strong evidence for the robustness of the findings. The findings are not dependent upon the exact measures or the exact informants. They show a general phenomenon.

Should we conclude that parents can do nothing to keep their adolescents out of trouble? We believe that the answer is no. There are two reasons for this. First, we should keep in mind that this study focused solely on middle adolescence. Much of the research concerning parenting of adolescents rests upon ideas developed and tested in younger samples (Baumrind, 1968, 1971; 1991; Coopersmith, 1967; Maccoby & Martin, 1983). But, parenting behaviors that are appropriate at one developmental period may not be at another (McNally, Eisenberg, & Harris, 1991). Snyder, Dishion, and Patterson (1986) reported that parental monitoring did not have the same importance from middle childhood to adolescence. Similarly, Baumrind (1991) reported different parenting findings for children aged 4, 9, and 15 years than for preschoolers (Baumrind, 1973). In short, it is questionable whether a parenting pattern in one developmental period is appropriate for a later period or should logically be associated with similar outcomes during a later period. This is one good reason to be cautious about generalizing the findings of this study to parenting in general. Our findings might very well only apply to middle and later adolescence. This remains an empirical question.

A second reason why we should not conclude that parents are powerless to prevent their adolescents from becoming delinquent is that there is still much that researchers have to learn about parenting. For instance, it has become obvious to us over the past two years that the relational side of parenting is an underdeveloped, but promising, line of research. Indeed, as we have argued above, part of the reason why the regulatory side of parenting has been considered so important is because the measures have actually been tapping the relational side. We believe that parents' daily interactions with children are highly important. For instance, in our studies, the youths' willingness to tell parents about their daily activities has been a strong marker for good adjustment, broadly defined (Kerr & Stattin, 2000; Kerr, Stattin, & Trost, 1999). What is more, youths who tell their parents the most are overrepresented among those who claim that their family operates as a democracy, "where people respect each other, and people discuss and make decisions together" (Trost, Stattin, & Kerr, 2001). Obviously, this type of family system is not possible without well-adjusted adolescents *and* well-adjusted parents, but perhaps developing these kinds of family interactions is an important, active step that parents can take early in the child's life to prevent problems in adolescence.

As researchers we typically forge ahead, confidently building upon previous findings and conclusions. However, sometimes we can forge ahead by questioning our confidence in previous findings, and this might be one of those times. To begin, we should probably rethink the research questions in the literature on parenting adolescents. What we know is limited to what we have tried to know, and, for the most part, that has been how parents *influence* adolescent adjustment—a unidirectional question. A challenge for future research, then, is to figure out how to pose research questions that can give us the largest set of possible answers. Second, we should reexamine the measures that have been used in the literature on parenting adolescents, because they may not be measuring what we have been assuming they were measuring. An assumption that parents are the active agents affecting children can spur us to use as indicators of parenting measures that could actually be tapping qualities of children rather than parents. This was the crux of Lewis' (1981) critique of Baumrind's parental control measures, and that critique was never adequately answered. The same problem arises in the large literatures in which "How much do your parents REALLY know?" is used as an operationalization of both parental monitoring and strictness/supervision. Our studies suggest that this measure taps qualities of youths more than parents. Presently, much of our belief that parents should strictly control their adolescents, and much of the advice given to parents to do just that, rests on these measures with questionable construct validity. The chances are that these are not the only examples of this in the literature. In short, future research on parenting adolescents should, at least for a time, test the validity and question the conclusions of past research.

For most of us, it is quite natural to think that parents, through their efforts, produce children with certain qualities. Some of the most visible, influential parenting research of the past few decades has seemed to support this natural way of thinking, but this is largely because alternatives have not been considered and studied. Alternative views have emerged, but they have not been able to penetrate the mainstream thinking. At best, this could represent premature enthusiasm among parenting researchers. At worst, it could represent a lack of scientific rigor. Either way, parenting research has been driven by the assumption that the direction of causality is known in correlational studies, and it has been a very long trip. Perhaps it is time to switch drivers.

ACKNOWLEDGMENTS

This research was supported by grants from the Swedish Research Council and The Bank of Sweden Tercentenary Foundation.

REFERENCES

Anderson, K. E., Lytton, H., & Romney, D. M. (1986). Mothers' interactions with normal and conduct-disordered boys: Who affects whom? *Developmental Psychology, 22*, 604–609.

Andershed, H., Kerr, M., & Stattin, H. (in press). Understanding the abnormal by studying the normal. *Acta Psychiatrica Scandinavica.*

Andershed, H., Kerr, M., Stattin, H., & Levander, S. (2001). Psychopathic traits in non-referred youths: Initial test of a new assessment tool. Under editorial review.

Baumrind, D. (1968). Authoritarian vs. authoritative parental control. *Adolescence, 3*, 255–272.

Baumrind, D. (1971). Current Patterns of Parental Authority. *Developmental Psychology Monographs, 4*, 1–103.

Baumrind, D. (1973). The development of instrumental competence through socialization. In A. D. Pick (Ed.), *Minnesota symposium on child psychology* (vol. 7). Minneapolis: University of Minnesota Press.

Baumrind, D. (1983). Rejoinder to Lewis's reinterpretation of parental firm control effects: Are authoritative families really harmonious? *Psychological Bulletin, 94*, 132–142.

Baumrind, D. (1989). Rearing competent children. In W. Damon (Ed.), *Child Development: Today and tomorrow.* The Jossey-Bass social and behavioral science series (pp. 349-378). San Francisco: Jossey-Bass.

Baumrind, D. (1991). The influence of parenting style on adolescent competence and substance abuse. *Journal of Early Adolescence, 1*, 56–95.

Baumrind, D., & Black, A. E. (1967). Socialization practices associated with dimensions of competence in preschool boys and girls. *Child Development, 38,* 291–327.

Bell, R. Q. (1968). A reinterpretation of the direction of effects in studies of socialization. *Psychological Review, 75,* 81–95.

Bell, R. Q., & Chapman, M. (1986). Child effects in studies using experimental or brief longitudinal approaches to socialization. *Developmental Psychology, 22,* 595–603.

Benda, B. B., & Whiteside, L. (1995). Testing an integrated model of delinquency using LISREL. *Journal of Social Science Research, 21,* 1–32.

Brown, B., Mounts, N., Lamborn, S. D., & Steinberg, L. (1993). Parenting practices and peer group affiliation in adolescence. *Child Development, 64,* 467–482.

Buss, D. M. (1981). Predicting parent-child interactions from children's activity level. *Developmental Psychology, 17,* 59–65.

Cernkovich, S. A., & Giordano, P. C. (1987). Family relationships and delinquency. *Criminology, 24,* 295–321.

Chassin, L., Pillow, D. R., Curran, P. J., Molina, B. S. G., & Barrera, M. Jr. (1993). Relation of parental alcoholism to early adolescent substance use: A test of three mediating mechanisms. *Journal of Abnormal Psychology, 102,* 3–19.

Cleckley, H. (1976). *The mask of sanity* (5th ed.). St. Louis, MO: Mosby.

Coopersmith, S. (1967). *The antecedents of self-esteem.* San Francisco: Freeman.

Crouter, A. C., & Head, M. R. (2001). Parental monitoring: What are we really measuring and what does it mean? To appear in M. Borstein (Ed.), *The handbook on parenting* (2nd ed.).

Crouter, A. C., MacDermid, S. M., McHale, S. M., & Perry-Jenkins, M. (1990). Parental monitoring and perceptions of children's school performance and conduct in dual- and single-carner families. *Developmental Psychology, 26,* 649–657.

Csikszentmihalyi, M., & Larsen, R. (1984). *Being adolescent.* New York: Basic Books.

Dishion, T. J., Capaldi, D., Spracklen, K. M., & Li, F. (1995). Peer ecology of male adolescent drug use. Special Issue: Developmental processes in peer relations and psychopathology. *Development and Psychopathology, 7,* 803–824.

Dishion, T. J., & McMahon, R. J. (1998). Parental monitoring and the prevention of child and adolescent problem behavior: A conceptual and empirical formulation. *Clinical Child and Family Psychology Review, 1,* 61–75.

Dix, T., Ruble, D. N., Grusec, J. E., & Nixon, S. (1986). Social cognition in parents: Inferential and affective reactions to children of three age levels. *Child Development, 57,* 879–894.

Eron, L. D., Huesmann, L. R., & Zelli, A. (1991). The role of parental variables in the learning of aggression. In D. J. Pepler & K. H. Rubin (Eds.), *The developmental and treatment of childhood aggression* (pp. 169–188). Hillsdale, NJ: Laurence Erlbaum Associates.

Farrington, D. P., & Hawkins, J. D. (1991). Predicting participation, early onset, and later persistence in officially recorded offending. *Criminal Behaviour and Mental Health, 1*, 1–33.

Flannery, D. J., Vazsonyi, A. T., Torquati, J., & Fridrich, A. (1994). Ethnic and gender differences in risk for early adolescent substance use. *Journal of Youth and Adolescence, 23*, 195–213.

Fletcher, A. C., Darling, N., & Steinberg, L. (1995). Parental monitoring and peer influences on adolescent substance use. In J. McCord (Ed.), *Coercion and punishment in long-term perspectives* (pp. 259–271). Cambridge, MA: Cambridge University Press.

Forth, A. E. (1995). Psychopathy in adolescent offenders: Assessment, family background, and violence. *Issues in Criminological and Legal Psychology, 24*, 42–44.

Fridrich, A. H., & Flannery, D. J. (1995). The effects of ethnicity and acculturation on early adolescent delinquency. *Journal of Child and Family Studies, 4*, 69–87.

Gray, M. R., & Steinberg, L. (1999). Unpacking authoritative parenting: Reassessing a multidimensional construct. *Journal of Marriage and the Family, 61*, 574–587.

Hare, R. D. (1996). Psychopathy: A clinical construct whose time has come. *Criminal Justice and Behavior, 23*, 25–54.

Hare, R. D. (1999). Psychopathy as a risk factor for violence. *Psychiatric Quarterly, 70*, 181–197.

Harris, J. R. (1995). Where is the child's environment? A group socialization theory of development. *Psychological Review, 102*, 458–489.

Harris, J. R. (1998). *The nurture assumption: Why children turn out the way they do*. New York: The Free Press.

Hastings, P. D., & Rubin, K. H. (1999). Predicting mothers' beliefs about preschool-aged children's social behavior: Evidence for maternal attitudes moderating child effects. *Child Development, 70*, 722–741.

Harkins, J. D., Herrenkohl, T., Farrington, D. P., Brewer, D., Catalano, R. F., & Harachi, T. W. (1998). A review of predictors of youth violence. In R. Loeber & D. P. Farrington (Eds.), *Serious & violent juvenile offenders: Risk factors and successful interventions* (pp. 106–146). Thousand Oaks, CA: Sage.

Henry, B., Moffitt, T. E., Robins, L., Earls, F., & Silva, P. A. (1993). Early family predictors of child and adolescent antisocial behaviour: Who are the mothers of delinquents? *Criminal Behavior and Mental Health, 3*, 97–118.

Hiroto, D. (1974). Locus of control and learned helplessness. *Journal of Experimental Psychology, 102*, 187–193.

Hirschi, T. (1969). *Causes of delinquency*. Berkeley: University of California Press.

Kerr, M., & Stattin, H. (2000). What parents know, how they know it, and several forms of adolescent adjustment: Further support for a reinterpretation of monitoring. *Developmental Psychology, 36*, 366–380.

Kerr, M., Stattin, H., & Trost, K. (1999). To know you is to trust you: Parents' trust is rooted in child disclosure of information. *Journal of Adolescence, 22*, 737–752.

Kochanska, G. (1998). Mother-child relationship, child fearfulness, and emerging attachment: A short-term longitudinal study. *Developmental Psychology, 34*, 480–490.

Lamborn, S. D., Mounts, N. S., Steinberg, L., & Dornbusch, S. M. (1991). Patterns of competence and adjustment among adolescents from authoritative, authoritarian, indulgent and neglectful families. *Child Development, 62*, 1049–1065.

Langer, E., & Rodin, J. (1976). The effects of choice and enhanced personal responsibility for the aged: A field experiment in an institutional setting. *Journal of Personality and Social Psychology, 34*, 191–198.

Lewis, C. (1981). The effects of parental firm control: A reinterpretation of findings. *Psychological Bulletin, 90*, 547–563.

Loeber, R., Farrington, D. P., Stouthamer-Loeber, M., & van Kammen, W. B. (1998). *Antisocial behavior and mental health problems: Explanatory factors in childhood and adolescence*. Mahwah, NJ: Laurance Erlbaum Associates.

Lytton, H. (1990). Child and parent effects in boys' conduct disorder: A reinterpretation. *Developmental Psychology, 26*, 683–697.

Lytton, H. (2000). Toward a model of family-environmental and child-biological influences on development. *Developmental Review, 20*, 150–179.

Maccoby, E. E., & Martin, J. A. (1983). Socialization in the context of the family: parent-child interaction. In P. Mussen & E. M. Hetherington (Eds.), *Handbook of child psychology, Vol. 4* (pp. 1–101). New York: Wiley & Sons.

McCord, J. (1986). Instigation and insulation: How families affect antisocial aggression. In J. Block, D. Olweus, & M. R. Yarrow (Eds.), *Development of antisocial and prosocial behavior* (pp. 343–357). New York: Academic Press.

McNally, S., Eisenberg, N., & Harris, J. D. (1991). Consistency and change in maternal child-rearing practices and values: A longitudinal study. *Child Development, 62*, 190–198.

Metzler, C. W., Noell, J., Biglan, A., Ary, D., & Smolkowski, K. (1994). The social context for risky sexual behavior among adolescents. *Journal of Behavioral Medicine, 17*, 419–438.

Mink, I. T., & Nihira, K. (1986). Family life-styles and child behaviors: A study of direction of effects. *Developmental Psychology, 22*, 610–616.

Mulhern, R. K. Jr., & Passman, R. H. (1981). Parental discipline as affected by the sex of the parent, the sex of the child, and the child's apparent responsiveness to discipline. *Developmental Psychology, 17*, 604–613.

Nurmi, J.-E. (1993). Self-handicapping and a failure-trap strategy: A cognitive approach to problem behaviour and delinquency. *Psychiatria Fennica, 24*, 75–85.

Nurmi, J.-E. (1997). Self-definition and mental health during adolescence and young adulthood. In J. Schulenberg, J. L. Maggs, & K. Hurrelmann (Eds.), *Health risks and developmental transitions during adolescence* (pp. 395–417). New York: Cambridge University Press.

Nye, F. I. (1958). *Family relationships and delinquent behavior.* New York: Wiley.

Passman, R. H., & Blackwelder, D. E. (1981). Rewarding and punishing by mothers: The influence of progressive changes in the quality of their sons' apparent behavior. *Developmental Psychology, 17*, 614–619.

Patterson, G. R., Reid, J. B., & Dishion, T. J. (1992). *Antisocial boys: A social interactional approach.* Eugene, OR: Castalia.

Patterson, G. R., & Stouthamer-Loeber, M. (1984). The correlation of family management practices and delinquency. *Child Development, 55*, 1299–1307.

Rodin, J., & Langer, E. J. (1977). Long-term effects of a control-relevant intervention with the institutionalized aged. *Journal of Personality and Social Psychology, 35*, 897–902.

Romer, D., Black, M., Ricardo, I., Feigelman, S., Kaljee, L., Galbraith, J., Nesbit, R., Hornik, R. C., & Stanton, B. (1994). Social influences on the sexual behavior of youth at risk for HIV exposure. *American Journal of Public Health, 84*, 977–985.

Sampson, R. J., & Laub, J. H. (1994). Urban poverty and the family context of delinquency: A new look at structure and process in a classic study. Special Issue: Children and poverty. *Child Development, 65*, 523–540.

Seligman, M. E. P. (1975). *Helplessness: On depression, development, and death.* San Francisco: W. H. Freeman.

Snyder, J., Dishion, T. J., & Patterson, G. (1986). Determinants and consequences of associating with deviant peers during preadolescence and adolescence. *Journal of Early Adolescence, 6*, 29–43.

Snyder, J., & Patterson, G. (1987). Family interaction and delinquent behavior. In H. C. Quay (Ed.), *Handbook of juvenile delinquency. Wiley series on personality processes* (pp. 216–243). New York: Wiley.

Sokol-Katz, J., Dunham, R., & Zimmerman, R. (1997). Family structure versus attachment in controlling adolescent deviant behavior: A social control model. *Adolescence, 32*, 199–215.

Stattin, H., & Kerr, M. (2000). Parental monitoring: A reinterpretation. *Child Development, 71*, 1070–1083.

Steinberg, L., Lamborn, S. D., Darling, N., Mounts, N. S., & Dornbusch, S. M. (1994). Over-time changes in adjustment and competence among adolescents from authoritative, authoritarian, indulgent, and neglectful families. *Child Development, 65*, 754–770.

Stice, E., & Barrera, M. Jr. (1995). A longitudinal examination of the reciprocal relations between perceived parenting and adolescents' substance use and externalizing behaviors. *Developmental Psychology, 31*, 322–334.

Trost, K., Stattin, H., & Kerr, M. (2001). Parental control of adolescents: A new look at an old issue. Under editorial review.

Weintraub, K. J., & Gold, M. (1991). Monitoring and delinquency. *Criminal Behavior and Mental Health, 1*, 268–281.

West, D. J., & Farrington, D. P. (1973). *Who becomes delinquent?* London: Heinemann.

10

On the Brink: Stability and Change in Parent-Child Relations in Adolescence

Elizabeth G. Menaghan

The Ohio State University

As Crockenberg and Leerkes (this volume) make clear, babies can drive their parents to tears, and the research reported by Margaret Kerr and Håkan Stattin (this volume) certainly suggests that adolescents can do the same.

As we think about parents and adolescents and their interaction, it's important to recall that the children we glimpse here at ages 14 and 16 were once those babies, and come trailing a very long history of interaction during which, we think, both parents and children have sought to shape each other's responses. In concert, they have developed a relationship that is now close or distant, harmonious or conflictual. Their family life may be high in verbal interaction and discussion or marked by mutual avoidance. They may have many explicit family rules or relatively few. These rules may have been handed down by the parents or negotiated between parents and children. In short, by age 14 much has already happened, which likely sets the stage for what is to come. This history, unfortunately, remains unknown, as it does in most studies of parents and their adolescent children.

Kerr and Stattin make three important contributions. First, they provide some fresh thinking regarding dimensions of parent-child interaction. Second, they offer new data that tests specific hypotheses elaborating the direction of influence and the mechanisms by which parents and children affect one another. Finally, they suggest new questions regarding the causal processes surrounding parent-child interaction and factors moderating those processes.

DIMENSIONS OF PARENT-CHILD RELATIONSHIPS

First, the authors re-visit the key dimensions of parent-child relations—both the affective quality of the relationship, as tapped by warmth, support, and emotional ties, and what they call the regulatory-supervisory side. Regarding the latter, they note two somewhat competing ideas—one stressing conditions under which children come to adopt and internalize norms regarding appropriate behavior, and the second emphasizing direct controls.

The relative importance of these two aspects should vary by child age. Both theory and research suggest that direct parental supervision and control must gradually yield to co-regulation of behavior and eventual self-regulation. Both too-early relinquishment of parental authority and granting of autonomy, and too-rigid and persistent insistence on direct control are likely to backfire (Steinberg, Lamborn, Dornbusch, & Darling, 1992). Steinberg and his colleagues emphasize the importance of older children's participation in rule-making (Lamborn, Mounts, & Steinberg, 1991; Steinberg et al., 1992), rather than feeling powerless to affect them. And Kerr and Stattin remind us that feelings of mutual respect, verbal give and take, and reasoning may distinguish Baumrind's competent children more than firm control, and that in any case Baumrind's measure did not directly assess parental efforts to exercise control or obtain children's compliance (see Baumrind, 1991, and discussion in Kerr and Stattin (this volume). Measures of parental monitoring currently in use are also an uncertain mix of parental rules and parental knowledge—and parental knowledge may be as likely to come from adolescent casual disclosure in informal interaction as from parental cross-examinations. In short, the match between our concepts and our measures is problematic.

In their own study, Kerr and Stattin directly assess children's self-disclosure versus tendency to hide information. And they distinguish parents' initiative to solicit information about their children's everyday experiences from other approaches to control. Importantly, Kerr and Stattin also directly ask parents about the outcome of their efforts to seek information or to exercise authority.

Interestingly, even in their own 5-item measure of control, there is a mix of dimensions: two items tap parental veto power over child actions—needing parental permission for certain things—and three other items tap parental requirements for information and accounts—the child being expected to explain their past and planned whereabouts, activities, and companions. These seem closely related but not quite the same thing. Families may have shared, and mutual, norms about communication and information that do not imply requirements for approval of all actions.

Finally, and most crucially, Kerr and Stattin suggest that by early- to mid-adolescence, parents are at least as likely to be responding to child behavior as they are to be influencing it. To test these ideas, Kerr and Stattin collect a wide range of data from both parents and children over two time periods, and they provide a complex set of analytic models. My own wishes are for more basic information about these data; more discussion of change; and then, of course, for still more complications to their already complex models.

WHAT DO PARENT-CHILD RELATIONS ON THE BRINK OF ADULTHOOD LOOK LIKE?

First, the basic information that I still wanted, before knowing what to make of the various multivariate models, includes the actual distribution of their key variables, the extent of stability and change in each over time that occurs in a two-year window, and the extent of agreement or disagreement between parents and children as they report on parallel constructs.

For example, the key measure of delinquency asks about fifteen different transgressions, including six different thefts. My guess is that a large majority of adolescents pile up near the zero-point on this measure at both time points, and this produces a high time one-time two correlation. What is the average response? What is the magnitude and direction of change on this measure over a two-year period? Fuller description would provide a better grasp of how much change is occurring and the nature of that change. Some increases in delinquency are produced by a child who moves from a zero score to a single incident of shoplifting; others may now be fencing stolen property and regularly stealing cars. Which should we be picturing as we think about observed increases in delinquent behavior? More generally, if there is relatively little variation on delinquency at a single time point, and high stability over time, then it will be hard to link other variables, including parenting variables, to delinquency levels or to increases or decreases in delinquency over time.

Similarly, I was curious to see, on average and at any point in time, how much self-disclosure is occurring, how prevalent is "dishonest charm," and so on. And, while the authors' major models in Figures 9.1 and 9.2 rely either on all youth reports or all parent reports, I was interested to learn the extent to which parents and children are agreeing, especially in their views of three things: (1) youth behaviors at home; (2) parent solicitation and control, where presumably they are both observing and reporting on the same behavior; and (3) youth delinquency, where some parents may be aware of substantially less delinquency than is actually occurring as the youth report it.

These questions are interesting because they may help to flesh out what this "two-year window" of parent-child relationships is like. Are child tendencies like "dishonest charm" or the tendency to drift off-task in the face of difficulties already highly stable at these ages, and resistant to change? Are parents' approaches similarly established? Or, as many developmental arguments would suggest, is this a time when, independent of the level of delinquent acts, some or most parents are re-negotiating family routines and beginning to think of their adolescents as moving to the brink of adulthood?

This information might also provide some insights into methodological decisions to model lagged versus concurrent effects, and whether a two-year window in which to observe changes seems adequate. Where there IS extensive change occurring, it may be reasonable to examine how *change* in one variable, say youth behavior at home, is linked to *change* in another variable, say parents' warmth or trust, rather than expecting earlier (or in some models later) levels of a variable to be linked to change.

How else would I complicate Kerr and Stattin's already complex models? I would suggest two things: inclusion of plausible moderators, and greater situation of family interaction within a larger social context.

CONDITIONS UNDER WHICH PARENT-CHILD RELATIONS MAY VARY

I begin by discussing some moderators. Here we are essentially asking whether an additive model suffices, or whether the strength or direction of effects of any one variable varies for some subgroups or under some conditions.

It seems to me that one very plausible moderator is gender. We talk about generic "youth" behaviors, but these youths are either girls or boys. We know that parents often treat boys and girls differently (see, for example, Bronfenbrenner, Alvarez, & Henderson, 1984; Mott, 1994), and studies of behavior problems also reveal differences in the levels and manifestations of problems by gender, with boys on average showing more externalizing, aggressive behavior, and girls more prone to social withdrawal and depressed mood. The same parental actions may have differing effects on boys and girls, and such interactive effects may importantly qualify general conclusions or recommendations regarding appropriate child socialization. Conversely, the same youth behavior may elicit different parental responses to daughters than to sons. In the present study, it will be important to document how the distributions of delinquency and other problems vary for boys and girls, and to also examine how the links among them vary.

Parents of course also vary by gender—they are mothers or fathers, and in this study nearly three-quarters of the reporting "parents" are mothers. Does this matter? To what extent is the emerging story about "delinquent youth intimidating parents" being dominated by responses of mothers to their sons?

A second plausible moderator in these processes is socioeconomic position. Parents vary in educational attainment and economic resources. These variables may be linked to both parents' and children's ideas about the age of independence or adulthood, as well as to parents' perceptions of their own efficacy in the face of difficult or challenging circumstances. They may also proxy for community and school conditions that may amplify or dampen some behavior tendencies.

Finally, family composition may also affect both youths' responses to parental concerns, demands, and expectations, and parents' responses to new or persistent challenges from their children. Some studies by Steinberg and his colleagues (Steinberg et al., 1992) suggest that mothers who are sole parents may be more ready to relinquish parental authority and grant autonomy than mothers with partners, who at least potentially could provide reinforcement of family expectations and generational boundaries. The interactive questions would be whether single mothers are *especially* likely to do so when faced with more troubling child behaviors. Testing such interactions would help to specify the circumstances under which the general patterns Kerr and Stattin describe are more or less powerful.

PARENTS AND CHILDREN IN SOCIAL CONTEXT

I would also like to complicate an already complex story by thinking more about the social context of these families. Kerr and Stattin begin by observing associations between parent and child variables, which we can call X and Y, and utilize data from two time points to establish the temporal order between X (which, depending on the model, can be either parent or child variables) and Y (the other one). They seek to evaluate the causal direction between them by estimating the association between the Time 1 level of X and the Time 2 level of Y, controlling for the correlations between Time 1 and 2 levels of Y. It is always possible, however, that some third variable (or set of variables) is affecting both X and Y, and this third variable is responsible for all or a large part of the observed association. By failing to take such factors into account, we may be misled in our causal conclusions.

I sometimes summarize my concern about the way we think about and try to explain family processes and child outcomes by pointing out that if one had to imagine people's lives by looking at the variables that are considered, one would get the impression that no one ever leaves the house—except possibly the child, and then only to commit delinquent acts. Of course this is an exaggeration, but it does seem that we too often neglect social circumstances outside the family that are nevertheless affecting family members. Yet we know that most parents have jobs, most children and adolescents attend school (and many of them have jobs, too). It seems important to consider how the quality of experiences in these and other major social settings may be affecting both parents and children.

Research analyzing the connection between social contexts and stress outcomes for individuals and families has examined several key links. First, research has examined how stressors originating outside the family—especially work and economic stressors—can affect individual family members' emotional well-being (see, for example, Windell & Dumenci, 1999; and for a more general introduction, Pearlin, 1999). Second, research has investigated how each individual's emotional well-being may in turn affect family interactions. These studies suggest that individuals who are already struggling with emotional turmoil or depression are less available for satisfying interaction and are more prone to become aggressive and argumentative (Downey & Coyne, 1990; Elder, 1974). Third, studies also examine how and whether one family member's emotional state can be transmitted to other family members (Larson & Almeida, 1999); some results from these latter studies suggest that the work-family boundary may be more permeable for fathers than for mothers, with fathers' negative emotions aroused in the work place more apt to spill over and affect both their wives and their children, but mothers' work-linked emotions less apt to adversely affect other family members. It remains to be examined whether this difference is due to mothers' greater active efforts to manage those emotions or shield other family members from their effects. For youth as well, we would expect that negative emotions aroused elsewhere—including school—should similarly affect interaction.

Let me briefly discuss two major contextual factors—economic pressures and work place experiences. Clearly, a major contextual factor is family income. For both parents and children, economic pressures may take their toll. Both persistence of low overall economic levels and the experience of economic losses can lead to parental demoralization and depression and disrupt skillful parenting (Conger, Conger, Elder, Lorenz, Simons, & Whitbeck, 1992; Elder, Nguyen, & Caspi, 1985; McLoyd, 1989, 1990; Pearlin, Lieberman, Menaghan, & Mullan, 1981).

Economic factors also affect youth in other ways. First, family income constrains the community, neighborhood, and school conditions that children and youth experience. Second, as Eleanor Maccoby (1984) suggested some time ago, it is likely that by the pre-adolescent years, children have begun to understand their own family's position in a highly stratified social system, and to develop attitudes about what this position implies about their own opportunities and probabilities for success. These understandings and attitudes will affect children independent of income-linked family interaction patterns.

A second major social context is linked to employment. Many aspects of the work place may be stressful—including low control over scheduling, having to work very long hours, or being limited to fewer hours than desired. The substantive demands of the job also seem to matter. Some work is repetitive, straightforward, and closely supervised, providing little opportunity for the worker to innovate, solve problems, or exercise self-direction. Work stress research suggests that conditions at work such as routinization, low autonomy, heavy supervision, and little opportunity for substantively complex work, have adverse effects on emotional well-being, self-esteem, and a sense of personal mastery (Kohn & Schooler, 1983; Miller, Schooler, Kohn, & Miller, 1979; and for a more general argument, Schooler, 1987). Work socialization arguments (Kohn, 1977: Kohn, Slomczynski, & Schoenbach, 1986) also suggest that occupational experiences shape parents' goals for their children, with parents with little leeway for independent judgment at work putting more emphasis on children's obedience and conformity to convention. Research, including my own work with colleagues, suggests that when work experiences leave parents feeling uncertain of their own worth and emotionally distressed, they are less able to be emotionally available to their children or to provide them with responsive, stimulating environments (Belsky & Eggebeen, 1991a, 1991b; McLoyd, 1989; Menaghan, 1991). These work conditions affect both level and change in children's home environments (Menaghan & Parcel, 1995). In this study, we assessed changes in the overall quality of the home environment over a two-year period, for children initially aged 3 through 6 years old. We found that changes in mothers' employment status shaped changes in home environments, and that these effects varied depending on the quality of the employment that mothers obtained. Mothers' working conditions are also linked to children's behavior difficulties at the beginning of the middle childhood period (Cooksey, Menaghan, & Jekielek, 1997) and to both academic and social outcomes at later ages (Menaghan, Kowaleski-Jones, & Mott, 1997). In the latter study, we focused on children aged 10 through 14, and found that the quality of both mothers' employment and their marital/partner relationships affected both family interaction and child outcomes, even when earlier levels of behavior problems and cognitive achievement were statistically taken into account.

These studies used the rich longitudinal data from the National Longitudinal Survey of Youth (NLSY), and its associated Child-Mother data set (for further information about these data sets, see Center for Human Resource Research, 1999, 2000). Begun in 1979 when the initial respondents were aged 14 through 21, by 2000 these respondents were 35 through 42 years of age, and the female respondents had completed most of their childbearing. Beginning in 1986, and continuing every other year through 2000, age-varying data on all of the children born to the female NLSY respondents have been collected via maternal report and direct child assessments.

Once the children are 10, they begin more extensive self-reports, and beginning at age 15 they complete an increasingly more adult interview reporting on schooling, employment, sexual activity, and childbearing, as well as delinquency and other nonnormative behaviors. These data contain oversamples of African-American and Hispanic respondents, and researchers can use data from multiple waves of data to construct synthetic cohorts of children that overcome the associations between child and maternal age that hold for individual data waves (see, for example, Cooksey, Menaghan, & Jekielek, 1997).

The data also permit interesting studies of genetically related individuals, since some of the initial NLSY respondents were sisters and so some of the NLSY children are cousins. Among children of the same mother, Frank Mott, the intellectual leader for the Child-Mother data collection, has done extensive work to estimate which children also have the same father; and Joseph Rodgers at the University of Oklahoma has coded the full set of children in terms of their relationships as full siblings, half-siblings, and so on. Thus, these data have enormous potential for addressing many of the research questions raised at this conference.

The work socialization and work stress literatures suggest that, for both men and women, work circumstances such as repetitiveness and substantive complexity are likely to be shaping both their own well-being, their goals for their children, and the way they interact with them. Interestingly, at least one study, by Karen Miller and her colleagues (Miller, Kohn, & Schooler, 1985) suggests that schools can be described in somewhat parallel ways, with some schools offering more opportunities for choice and independence and others emphasizing repetition and conformity; and these same factors influence students' attitudes and well-being. Presumably, these impact family interaction as well; this hypothesis is richly deserving of additional attention as we consider how youth may affect their parents and their family lives.

More broadly, I am suggesting that in addition to considering how parents may be affecting their children and also being affected by them, we see both parents and children as actors and reactors in a larger social world that includes stressful circumstances beyond the family, circumstances that may have direct, indirect, and interactive effects on their interaction.

REFERENCES

Baumrind, D. (1991). The influence of parenting style on adolescent competence and substance abuse. *Journal of Early Adolescence, 1*, 56–95.

Belsky, J., & Eggebeen, D. (1991a). Early and extensive maternal employment and young children's socioemotional development: Children of the National Longitudinal Survey of Youth. *Journal of Marriage and the Family, 53*, 1083–1098.

Belsky, J., & Eggebeen, D. (1991b). Scientific criticism and the study of early and extensive maternal employment. *Journal of Marriage and the Family, 53*, 1107–1110.

Bronfenbrenner, U., Alvarez, W. F., & Henderson, C. R. Jr. (1984). Working and watching: Maternal employment status and parents' perceptions of their three-year-old children. *Child Development, 55*, 1362–1378.

Center for Human Resource Research, The Ohio State University. (1999). *NLSY79 user's guide: A guide to the 1979-1998 National Longitudinal Survey of Youth Data*. Columbus, OH: The Ohio State University.

Center for Human Resource Research, The Ohio State University. (2000). *1998 NLSY79 Child and Young Adult Data users guide*. Columbus, OH: The Ohio State University.

Conger, R. D, Conger, K. J., Elder, G. H. Jr., Lorenz, F. O., Simons, R. L., & Whitbeck, L. B. (1992). A family process model of economic hardship and adjustment of early adolescent boys. *Child Development, 63*, 526–541.

Cooksey, E. C., Menaghan, E. G., & Jekielek, S. M. (1997). The intergenerational costs of parental social stressors: Academic and social difficulties in early adolescence for children of young mothers. *Journal of Health and Social Behavior, 38*, 72–86.

Downey, G., & Coyne, J. C. (1990). Children of depressed parents: An integrative review. *Psychological Bulletin, 108*, 50–76.

Elder, G. H. Jr. (1974). *Children of the Great Depression*. Chicago: University of Chicago Press.

Elder, G. H. Jr., Nguyen, T. V., & Caspi, A. (1985). Linking family hardship to children's lives. *Child Development, 56*, 361–375.

Kohn, M. L. (1977). *Class and conformity, A study in values* (2nd ed.). Chicago: University of Chicago Press.

Kohn, M. L., & Schooler, C. (1983). *Work and personality.* Norwood, NJ: Ablex.

Kohn, M .L., Slomczynski, K. M., & Schoenbach, C. (1986). Social stratification and the transmission of values in the family: A cross-national assessment. *Sociological Forum, 1,* 73–102.

Lamborn, S. D., Mounts, N. S., Steinberg, L., & Dornbusch, S. M. (1991). Patterns of competence and adjustment among adolescents from authoritative, authoritarian, indulgent and neglectful families. *Child Development, 62,* 1049–1065.

Larson, R. W., & Almeida, D. M. (1999). Emotional transmission in the daily lives of families: A new paradigm for studying family process. *Journal of Marriage and the Family, 61,* 5–20.

Maccoby, E. E. (1984). Middle childhood in the context of the family. In A. W. Collins (Ed.), *Development during middle childhood: The years from six to twelve* (pp. 184-239). Washington, DC: National Academy Press.

McLoyd, V. C. (1989). Socialization and development in a changing economy. *American Psychologist, 44,* 293–302.

McLoyd, V. C. (1990). The impact of economic hardship on Black families and children: Psychological distress, parenting, and socioemotional Development. *Child Development, 61,* 311–346.

Menaghan, E. G. (1991). Work experiences and family interaction processes: The long reach of the job? *Annual Review of Sociology, 17,* 419–444.

Menaghan, E. G., Kowaleski-Jones, L., & Mott, F .L. (1997). The intergenerational costs of parental social stressors: Academic and social difficulties in early adolescence for children of young mothers. *Journal of Health and Social Behavior, 38,* 72–86.

Menaghan, E. G., & Parcel, T. L. (1995). Social sources of change in children's home environments: Effects of parental occupational experiences and family conditions over time. *Journal of Marriage and the Family, 57,* 69–84.

Miller, J., Schooler, C., Kohn, M. L., & Miller, K. A. (1979). Women and work: The psychological effects of occupational conditions. *American Journal of Sociology, 85,* 66–94.

Miller, K. A., Kohn, M. L., & Schooler, C. (1985). Educational self-direction and the cognitive functioning of students. *Social Forces, 63,* 923–944.

Mott, F. L. (1994). Sons, daughters, and fathers' absence: Differentials in father-leaving probabilities and in home environments. *Journal of Family Issues, 15,* 97–128.

Pearlin, L. I. (1999). The stress process revisited: Reflections on concepts and their interrelationships. In C. S. Aneshensel & J. C. Phelan (Eds.), *Handbook of the sociology of mental health* (pp. 395–415). New York: Kluwer Academic/ Plenum.

Pearlin, L. I., Lieberman, M. A., Menaghan, E. G., & Mullan, J. T. (1981). The stress process. *Journal of Health and Social Behavior, 22,* 337–356.

Schooler, C. (1987). Psychological effects of complex environments during the life span: A review and theory. In C. Schooler & W. W. Schaie (Eds.), *Cognitive functioning and social structure over the life course* (pp. 24–49). Norwood, NJ: Ablex.

Steinberg, L., Lamborn, S. D., Dornbusch, S. M., & Darling, N. (1992). Impact of parenting practices on adolescent achievement: Authoritative parenting, school involvement, and encouragement to succeed. *Child Development, 63*, 1266–1281.

Windell, M., & Dumenci, L. (1999). Parental and occupational stress as predictors of depressive symptoms among dual-earner couples: A multilevel modeling approach. *Journal of Marriage and the Family, 59*, 625–634.

11

Parental Monitoring: Action and Reaction

Gene H. Brody
University of Georgia

Kerr and Stattin (this volume) focus on two main issues. First, they make the crucial point that the direction of causality in parental monitoring processes is unclear; hence, it is necessary to determine whether these processes are a cause of variations in child externalizing behaviors or a consequence of them. Is inadequate parental monitoring a risk factor for the development of aggressive and delinquent behaviors, or do aggressive and delinquent behaviors evoke or suppress parental monitoring processes? Second, Kerr and Stattin note the importance of moving beyond the statistical association between parental monitoring and children's externalizing behaviors to the rigorous testing of the hypothesis that this association represents a causal mechanism by which parental monitoring reduces children's risk of developing externalizing behaviors. They emphasize the need to consider causal chains over time and to examine the role of individual differences in parental monitoring together with the mechanisms involved.

In exploring the role that children's characteristics play in determining the care that they receive, which in turn may influence their functioning, Kerr and Stattin conclude that parental monitoring is actually epiphenomenal or unimportant in the development of delinquent behavior. Instead, they consider the effects attributed to parental monitoring to be best explained by children's willingness to disclose information to their parents rather than by active parental monitoring efforts. These conclusions are based upon data gathered from a sample of 14- to 16-year-olds in mid-sized cities in Sweden. The findings, however, could be specific to the youths' age group, the context in which they live, the measures used in the study, or the authors' conceptualization of the operation of child effects with respect to parental monitoring. Although they are complex, these dynamics can be examined empirically. Rather than considering these issues from a conceptual standpoint, I will offer an empirical commentary using data from a three-wave longitudinal study of African American youths living in single-parent households in small towns and cities in rural Georgia. The children were an average of 11 years old at the first wave of data collection and 13 years old at the third wave. Although 75% of the mothers in the sample are employed, 68% of the families live below federal poverty standards and the remaining 32% live within 150% of the poverty threshold. In all, 156 families participated; 93% were retained across the three waves of data collection.

163

As part of this research, focus groups of rural African American community members were convened to provide feedback about the study's conceptualization and methodology. The focus groups consistently indicated that "knowing what children are up to and who they are hanging with" is an important part of guiding them toward success and away from problems. These prescriptions, as well as several advanced in the literature (Dishion & McMahon, 1998), attest to the contributions that monitoring may make to youths' development. Accordingly, I formulated three questions to clarify the associations among child effects, parental monitoring, and children's development of externalizing behaviors. First, is maternal monitoring linked to changes in children's externalizing behavior or vice versa? Second, does maternal monitoring serve a protective function by moderating the longitudinal links between difficult child temperament and externalizing behaviors? Third, through what processes are child temperaments directly and indirectly linked over time with maternal monitoring? My commentary will focus on these issues.

IS MATERNAL MONITORING LINKED TO CHANGES IN CHILDREN'S EXTERNALIZING BEHAVIOR OR VICE VERSA?

Data from the first and third waves of collection are used to address this question. Because data were collected at 1-year intervals, wave 1 and wave 3 are separated by 2 years. Maternal monitoring was assessed at both times using a 17-item measure developed by Patterson and Stouthamer-Loeber (1984) and modified for this study. It assesses mothers' knowledge about various aspects of their children's lives. Items are rated on a 4-point Likert scale ranging from 1 ("never") to 4 ("always"). Sample items include: "How often do you know where [your child] is and what she/he is doing when away from home?" "How often do you know about [your child's] use of alcohol?" and "How often do you know what [your child's] grades are?" For this sample, the instrument's alpha coefficients exceeded .90 at each wave of data collection. Children's externalizing behavior was assessed using the Aggressive Behavior and Delinquent Behavior subscales of the Teacher Report Form (TRF; Achenbach, 1999). Because the children progressed through the grades of school during the study, the teachers who assessed the children's adjustment at wave 3 were different from those who assessed their externalizing behavior at wave 1.

We conducted a cross-lagged panel analysis using structural equation modeling (SEM) with maximum likelihood estimation procedures in LISREL 8 (Jöreskog & Sörbom, 1996). The model provided an excellent fit to the data. Maternal monitoring ($\beta = .12$, $p < .01$) and children's externalizing behavior ($\beta = .41$, $p < .01$) were stable from wave 1 to wave 3. Mothers who evinced high levels of monitoring at wave 1 were likely to continue to do so at wave 3. Children whose teachers rated them high in externalizing behaviors at wave 1 were likely to be rated high in externalizing behaviors by a different teacher at wave 2. Even after accounting for the stability in externalizing behavior, maternal monitoring at wave 1 was significantly and negatively associated with children's externalizing behaviors at wave 3 ($\beta = -.20$, $p < .05$). This indicates that maternal monitoring at wave 1 was associated with a decrease in children's externalizing behavior over time. Children's externalizing behaviors at wave 1 were not associated with changes in maternal monitoring over time. Thus, single African American mothers' monitoring appears to be an influence over time on their children's levels of externalizing behaviors rather than a reaction to them.

DOES MATERNAL MONITORING MODERATE THE LINK BETWEEN CHILD TEMPERAMENT AND CHILDREN'S EXTERNALIZING BEHAVIORS?

If maternal monitoring served a protective function by reducing the contribution of a risk factor to the development of children's externalizing behavior, this would constitute further evidence that monitoring contributes unique variation to children's levels of externalizing behaviors. We tested the hypothesis that children's temperaments at wave 1 would be linked to their externalizing behaviors at wave 3, and that this association would be stronger for children whose mothers monitored their behavior less. In assessing child temperament, we focused on activity and emotionality because they have been theoretically and empirically tied to the development of externalizing behavior (Buss & Plomin, 1975; Cummings, Davies, & Campbell, 2000; Rothbart & Ahadi, 1994). From a transactional perspective, risk factors such as temperamental characteristics transact with contextual processes such as maternal monitoring to create different developmental trajectories. To determine whether maternal monitoring functioned this way, we obtained measures of children's temperaments at wave 1 from teachers' reports on the Temperament Assessment Battery (TAB; Martin, 1984). The Activity and Emotional Intensity subscales were used in this analysis; Cronbach's alpha exceeded .70 for each subscale. At wave 3, different teachers rated the children on the Aggressive Behavior and Delinquent Behavior Subscales of the TRF (Achenbach, 1999). The wave 3 assessment of maternal monitoring served as a moderator in this analysis; Cronbach's alpha exceeded .90. A SEM analysis indicated that children's activity and emotionality at wave 1 were longitudinally associated with teachers' ratings of externalizing behavior at wave 3. These data fit the model well. We also conducted a moderational analysis using multigroup comparison procedures from LISREL 8. We first estimated a two-group invariance model by imposing equality constraints on every coefficient estimate. We then relaxed one equality constraint for the specific coefficient under investigation and re-estimated the model. If the coefficients differed across groups, relaxing the equality constraint would yield a significant improvement in fit. A change in chi-square between the invariance model and the re-estimated model indicates a significant group difference. Consistent with the transactional hypothesis, the re-estimated multigroup model that allowed the effect of temperament to vary resulted in a significant reduction in chi-square ($\Delta\chi^2 = 4.02$, $\Delta df = 1$, $p = .045$). This indicates that the link between children's active/emotional temperaments and their externalizing behaviors was significantly stronger when mothers monitored children less.

THROUGH WHAT PROCESSES ARE CHILD TEMPERAMENTS LINKED DIRECTLY AND INDIRECTLY WITH MATERNAL MONITORING?

Kerr and Stattin (this volume) propose that the confusion surrounding parental monitoring is partially due to misplaced causal attributions: Effects attributed to parental monitoring efforts actually arise from children's willingness to share information with their parents. Testing this hypothesis involves identification of the conditions under which parents are likely to know about their children's friends, whereabouts, and activities in and out of school, as well as the implications of child effects for this process.

In keeping with the purpose of this volume, this issue creates an opportunity to illustrate the direct and indirect links of child effects, such as the impact of an active/emotional temperament, with parent-child relationships and parents' knowledge of their children's activities and behavior. Accordingly, we tested a theoretical model in which active/emotional child temperament placed mothers at risk for compromised psychological functioning. Children with active/emotional temperaments place stress on their mothers above and beyond the normal demands of child rearing. Over time, this added stress can occasion a decline in maternal self-esteem and an increase in depressive symptoms. These decrements in psychological functioning can combine with the evocative behavior styles that active and emotional children display in ways that undermine mother-child relationship quality. Under these circumstances, mothers and children are hampered in developing involved, supportive relationships that seldom include repetitive arguing, the kind of relationship that we hypothesized would be positively associated with maternal monitoring. Active/emotional child temperament, therefore, was hypothesized to exert both a direct effect on mother-child relationship quality and an indirect effect through its impact over time on maternal psychological functioning. We used data from all three waves of our study to test this model. At waves 1 and 2, different teachers assessed children's temperaments and mothers reported their own psychological functioning; at wave 3, mothers and children assessed their relationships with each other and mothers reported their knowledge about their children's lives. The use of teachers' reports of child temperament provided an independent assessment unaffected by ongoing family dynamics. The methods used to assess maternal monitoring and child temperament have already been described. Mothers' psychological functioning at waves 1 and 2 was indexed using Rosenberg's (1965) 10-item Self-Esteem Scale and the Center for Epidemiological Studies Depression Scale (Radloff, 1977). Cronbach's alphas for these instruments exceeded .70 at both waves. At wave 3, supportive/involved parenting was indexed by combining mothers' and children's reports on the Interaction Behavior Questionnaire (Prinz, Foster, Kent, & O'Leary, 1979). Mothers and children also completed the Ineffective Arguing Inventory (Kurdek, 1994), which measures a pattern of repetitive arguing over the same issues, and their reports were aggregated.

After determining that the measurement model fit the data as specified, we tested the structural model, which also fit the data well. As hypothesized, active/ emotional child temperament and maternal psychological functioning were stable across waves 1 and 2. Even after accounting for the stability in maternal psychological functioning, active/emotional child temperament at wave 1 was significantly and negatively associated with maternal psychological functioning at wave 2. This finding is consistent with the hypothesis that children's active/emotional temperaments can erode mothers' psychological functioning over time. Active/ emotional child temperament and maternal psychological functioning at wave 2 forecast parent-child relationship quality one year later at wave 3. Active/emotional temperament was negatively linked, and maternal psychological functioning was positively linked, with parent-child relationship quality at wave 3. Supportive/involved parenting, in turn, was positively linked with maternal monitoring. Taken together, these results suggest that children's temperaments are linked both directly and indirectly to variations in parent-child relationship quality and mothers' monitoring of their children's behavior. Parent-child relationships characterized by high levels of involvement, emotional support, and instrumental support along with low levels of repetitive arguing were hypothesized to create a context in which children would be likely to share information with their mothers. These results both support and extend some of Kerr and Stattin's conjectures. They support the notion that variations in monitoring may mirror variations in parent-child relationship quality. The analysis extends Kerr and Stattin's proposals by illustrating that variation in parent child relationships is multiply influenced by the direct and indirect effects of child temperament. At the least, these results indicate that careful theoretical and empirical analyses are required to understand variations in parental monitoring.

We then tested an alternative model, reversing the order of parent-child relationships and maternal monitoring from their positions in the previous structural model. This analysis was designed to determine whether maternal monitoring, like the parent-child relationship, would be linked directly with active/emotional child temperaments and maternal psychological functioning. Because parent-child relationships and maternal monitoring were assessed at the same point in time, I expected the link between monitoring and parent-child relationship quality to remain the same. The results of this analysis revealed that difficult child temperament at wave 2 was *not* linked to maternal monitoring at wave 3, although a link did emerge between mothers' psychological resources and monitoring. These results are similar to those of the cross-lagged panel analysis of the link between children's externalizing behavior and subsequent levels of maternal monitoring. Neither child characteristic was associated with maternal monitoring over time.

CONCLUSION

The data analyses presented in this commentary answered the three questions around which it was structured. The results suggest that: (a) maternal monitoring contributes over time to children's development of externalizing behavior rather than vice versa; (b) maternal monitoring moderates the longitudinal association between active/emotional child temperament and children's externalizing behavior; and (c) variations in maternal monitoring can be traced to the links among child temperament, maternal psychological functioning, and mother-child relationship quality.

The divergence of these findings from those reported by Kerr and Stattin (this volume) can be attributed to several factors. Our sample consists of single African American mothers and their late childhood to early adolescent-aged offspring living in small communities in rural Georgia. Perhaps at the age of the children in our sample, monitoring processes function as an influence on externalizing behaviors rather than a reaction to them. At these ages American children are still in elementary school and typically are not as peer-oriented as are older adolescents, such as those who participated in Kerr and Stattin's study. Monitoring during the elementary school years may inhibit the development of externalizing behaviors during adolescence, so that parents' need for vigilance about their children's activities, whereabouts, and friends decreases.

The present findings suggest that context must be considered in analyses of pivotal processes in child and adolescent development. This awareness is essential because processes such as monitoring are more than mere academic curiosities. They carry important implications for policy, practice, and theory concerning the development of child competence or psychopathology. Progress on issues regarding the unique importance of parenting processes in general, and monitoring in particular, will come from a clear conceptualization of child effects and parenting processes, along with research designs and measurement approaches that rigorously test causal hypotheses.

REFERENCES

Achenbach, T. M. (1999). The Child Behavior Checklist and related instruments. In M. E. Maruish (Ed.), *The use of psychological testing for treatment planning and outcomes assessment* (2nd ed., pp. 429–466). Mahwah, NJ: Lawrence Erlbaum Associates.

Buss, A. H., & Plomin, R. (1975). *A temperament theory of personality development.* New York: Wiley-Interscience.

Cummings, E. M., Davies, P. T., & Campbell, S. B. (2000). *Developmental psychopathology and family process: Theory, research, and clinical implications.* New York: Guilford Press.

Dishion, T. J., & McMahon, R. J. (1998). Parental monitoring and the prevention of child and adolescent problem behavior: A conceptual and empirical formulation. *Clinical Child and Family Psychology Review, 1,* 61–75.

Jöreskog, K. G., & Sörbom, D. (1996). *LISREL 8 user's reference guide.* Chicago: Scientific Software International.

Kurdek, L. A. (1994). Conflict resolution styles in gay, lesbian, heterosexual nonparent, and heterosexual parent couples. *Journal of Marriage and the Family, 56,* 705–722.

Martin, R. P. (1984). *Manual for the Temperament Assessment Battery.* Unpublished monograph, University of Georgia, Athens.

Patterson, G. R., & Stouthamer-Loeber, M. (1984). The correlation of family management practices and delinquency. *Child Development, 55,* 1299–1307.

Prinz, R. J., Foster, S., Kent, R. N., & O'Leary, K. D. (1979). Multivariate assessment of conflict in distressed and nondistressed mother-adolescent dyads. *Journal of Applied Behavior Analysis, 12,* 691–700.

Radloff, L. S. (1977). The CES-D Scale: A self-report depression scale for research in the general population. *Applied Psychological Measurement, 1,* 385–401.

Rosenberg, M. (1965). *Society and the adolescent self-image.* Princeton, NJ: Princeton University Press.

Rothbart, M. K., & Ahadi, S. A. (1994). Temperament and the development of personality. *Journal of Abnormal Psychology, 103,* 55–66.

12

Parental Monitoring: A Person-Environment Interaction Perspective on This Key Parenting Skill

Deborah M. Capaldi
Oregon Social Learning Center

Kerr and Stattin (this volume) address the issue of parental monitoring and adolescent delinquent behavior. A better understanding of the key dimensions and behaviors within the realm of parental monitoring is certainly a worthy research pursuit, given the strong association of monitoring with delinquency and substance use. For example, Friedman, Lichtenstein, and Biglan (1985) found that over 80% of smoking initiation episodes occurred in friends' houses with no supervising adult present.

Further evidence for the necessity of understanding this construct is found in recent work of our own, showing a significant association between parental monitoring assessed every other year across an 11-year period, from ages 11–12 to 21–22 years, with lifetime average sexual risk behavior assessed annually across a 10-year period from ages 13–14 to 22–23 years, and with contraction of a sexually-transmitted disease (STD; Capaldi, Stoolmiller, Clark, & Owen, in press). Parental monitoring was assessed by awareness of the youth's activities, including tracking their whereabouts and also time spent with the child. Monitoring showed a significant association with both lifetime average sexual risk behavior (-.39, $p <$ .001), which comprised the mean of frequency of intercourse, number of sexual partners, and condom use, as well as with contraction of an STD (-.22, $p < .01$). Dishion and McMahon (1998) identified physical safety (including injury risk), antisocial behavior, substance use, and academic achievement as key areas of child and adolescent adjustment in which monitoring is thought to play an important role. Clearly then, parents would be grateful if we could increase understanding of this key parenting skill so that they could assist their child in healthier and more successful development.

Kerr and Stattin emphasize a very important point at the heart of this volume—that parenting of children, in this case monitoring of adolescents, is not just a passive interaction between the child and the family environment, whereby the child has only a very limited ability to affect the environment. Unfortunately, their swing from a theoretical stance, where the effect is all from the parent, to the stance where the effect is all from the child, is one that replaces one overly narrow view with another.

Kerr and Stattin (2000) have posited that children's disclosure of information is spontaneous rather than reliant on the parent's behavior. This seems totally at odds with what we know about dyadic interactions from observation of behavior in many kinds of dyads. Do the authors really believe that an adolescent will keep disclosing regardless of the parental reaction? A dyadic or person-environment interaction model is a much better starting place for conceptualizing parenting and adolescent behavior.

A DEVELOPMENTAL-CONTEXTUAL APPROACH

We have argued that the most fruitful approach to examining parenting and the development of problem behavior in children is that of a developmental-contextual model or a person-environment interaction approach (Capaldi & Shortt, in press). Scarr and McCartney (1983) described individual-environment interaction effects that shape the environment and the individual's behaviors. In addition to the *passive* effect described above, *evocative* interactions involve responses elicited from others. Thus, sullen hostility or explosive temper outbursts by an adolescent may lead a parent to back down from asking them about their activities with peers or outside the home. Evidence of evocative effects of child behaviors include the findings that explosive temper tantrums by a child may predict harsh parental discipline (Ge, Conger, Cadoret, & Neiderhiser, 1996), and aggression toward peers may lead to peer rejection (Coie & Dodge, 1988). Buss (1987) distinguished evocation from *manipulation* (i.e., more active attempts to change environments) that may be either positive or negative. Adolescents may use negative manipulation with their parents in order to continue doing the activities they choose, rather than to face parental restrictions or sanctions (e.g., lying about whereabouts or use of substances). Individuals may also *react* to environmental events (e.g., an adolescent chatting about their friends to a parent who shows positive interest in their activities).

The final type of environmental effect described by Scarr and McCartney (1983) is the *active* type or through selection of environments by the individual. Individuals may select environments that suit their dispositions and goals. Thus, adolescents generally have some degree of latitude, often considerable, regarding how much time they spend with family, how much time they spend with peers, and in selection of friends. We have posited that a further person-environment interaction effect is due to *restriction of environmental options* that can occur as a result of prior developmental failures and problem behaviors (Capaldi & Shortt, in press; Capaldi & Stoolmiller, 1999). Thus, an adolescent who drops out of high school may not go to college, and a teen who smokes may find that nonsmoking peers do not want to date him.

Parental monitoring plays an important role from infancy into young adulthood, and should be developmentally as well as contextually appropriate (Dishion

& McMahon, 1998, 1999). It is important to remember that examining parent-adolescent behavior across a relatively short window (e.g., 1 or 2 years) represents a brief look at a process that has been developing for the child's entire life. Indeed, adjustment across the developmental span is encompassed within a dynamic person-environment or developmental-contextual framework.

Kerr and Stattin posit that the association between lower levels of monitoring and youth problem behavior is not due to the former causing the latter, as has frequently been argued. Rather, they draw the conclusion that "In this study, we have found strong evidence that the direction of effects is the opposite – parents' behaviors are reactions to the youth's problem behavior rather than causes of it" (p. 142). An examination of their models can only lead to some surprise that they would make such a strong claim. Other than monitoring, each of the variables in the tested models in Figures 9.1 and 9.2 appears to be based on reports from a single agent. Increased error or bias resulting from such designs has frequently been discussed (e.g., Patterson & Bank, 1986, 1987). Kerr and Stattin run separate models for parent and youth report. The reasons for doing this, rather than running stronger models using both parent and youth indicators for the constructs, are unclear. Furthermore, all but one of the variables in each model is from a single time point. Thus, these models are a very weak test of their hypotheses, and alternative models do not appear to have been tested. It would have been helpful if the authors had presented a correlation matrix.

MONITORING AS A MULTIDIMENSIONAL CONSTRUCT

Kerr and Stattin increase our awareness of the fact that monitoring is not a unidimensional construct. In the study reported on in this volume, they assessed child disclosure, parental solicitation, parental control, parental support, and parental bad reactions to disclosure. Dishion and McMahon (1998, 1999) also emphasized the importance of the concept of monitoring as encompassing a larger set of critical parental activities than supervision. They proposed a broad definition of monitoring, including both *structuring* the child or adolescent's home, school, and community environments and *tracking* the child's behavior in these environments.

It seems that the foundation of parental monitoring is parental awareness of all aspects of their adolescent's life and development, including activities in and outside the home, friendships and other relationships, progress in school, and health-related behaviors. This awareness is based in a true interest in the youth, and in the welfare of the youth being a high priority to the parent. Such awareness involves a great deal of positive and regular communication. Parents must track the signs of normal development and signals of potential problems and adjust their behaviors accordingly. Parents who are more interested in their own lives or other concerns, who are too busy or stressed, whose capacity for such skilled parenting is diminished by substance use or other psychopathology, or who have cognitive deficits and lower problem-solving abilities are unlikely to maintain full awareness. Without such awareness, parents are likely to do a poor job of choosing a response to their adolescent's behavior.

A further key factor in parental monitoring is the ability to detect the difference between behaviors that are over or under a level of acceptability for family comfort and for the risk for developmental failure, including outcomes such as arrest and health risk. To achieve this, parents need to know how their adolescent's behavior compares to the behavior and daily routines of other youth. Dishion and Kavanaugh (in press) have developed the Family Check-Up, an intervention involving concepts of motivational interviewing designed to increase parents' motivation to monitor their adolescent. First, an intense, ecologically oriented assessment of the child and family is conducted, using measures with normative comparisons. In a second session, feedback is provided to the family. An interventionist discusses strengths and weaknesses within the family, supports the parent's confidence to change, and helps the family to set realistic goals. The Family Check-Up serves as a method for enhancing parental motivation to engage in monitoring practices appropriate for their youth's behavior and developmental stage. Parental motivation to monitor has also been the target of universal, communitywide interventions (Biglan, 1995).

A life-span perspective helps us to understand the importance of parental monitoring at all stages of the child's life. Parental discipline becomes inappropriate as a child reaches late adolescence. However, monitoring in the form of parental awareness as a basis for timely provision of support is a form of parenting that may be particularly important through the young-adult transition to independence, and frequently continues throughout the adulthood of offspring.

A THREE-GENERATIONAL PARENTING MODEL

Presented in Figure 12.1 is the conceptual model that we are using to test the interactive association of child characteristics and behavior, parenting, and the development of antisocial behavior across three generations (Capaldi, Pears, Patterson, & Owen, 2002). This model is based on a dynamic person-environment perspective, and illustrates that the interactive association of child behavior and parenting is ongoing throughout development, beginning with temperamental risk factors of the child and unskilled parenting in infancy. We must also remember the critical importance of the familial and neighborhood contextual factors in which these interactions take place, including risk characteristics of the parent (e.g., antisocial behavior, substance use) and the interplay of parenting and child behavior with peer associations.

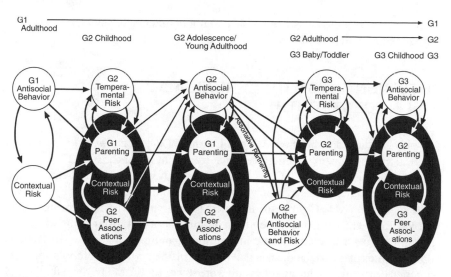

FIG. 12.1.   Interactive association of child characteristics and behavior, parenting, and the development of antisocial behavior across three generations.

In our first test of the intergenerational association of parenting behaviors (Capaldi, Pears et al., 2002), we found a significant direct association between poor parenting practices of parents (Generation 1, G1) and those of their sons (Generation 2, G2) approximately 12 years later. Parenting was assessed by multimethod, multiagent indicators: For G1 of monitoring, discipline and parent-child relationship when the son was 9–10 and 11–12 years of age, and for G2 of discipline and pleasure in parenting when the Generation 3 child was 16–20 months old. The correlation of parenting across G1 and G2 was .46 ($p < .01, N = 99$). This certainly suggests (though does not prove) the importance of learned parenting skills, and that the effects do not all come from the child (of course, this was not specifically addressing adolescent monitoring).

MONITORING ACROSS A RANGE OF ADOLESCENT PROBLEM BEHAVIORS

The greatest concern I have with Kerr and Stattin is that they seem to conclude that parents should not be advised to monitor their adolescents by using rules and structure. A very critical issue here is the difference between parenting an adolescent whose behavior is in the normal range and an adolescent whose behavior is much higher in levels of conduct problems. Within the normal range, much awareness and some deft parental steering when necessary may be the best approach, along with some rules in areas such as curfew and safe transportation. With an adolescent who is engaging in more than minor delinquent behavior, a much more structured and rule-based approach may be needed.

INTERVENTIONS WITH CHRONICALLY DELINQUENT YOUTH

A study conducted at the Oregon Social Learning Center employed a randomized clinical trial contrasting multidimensional treatment foster care (MTFC) and services-as-usual group care (GC) for male adolescents with histories of chronic and serious juvenile delinquency who were mandated into residential care by the juvenile court. The MTFC program included highly structured monitoring of the adolescent's day, particularly their time out of school in a foster home where the parents had been specially trained in parenting a delinquent adolescent. The initial outcomes of the trial indicated that rates of official criminal referrals and self-reported criminal acts during follow up were lower for the MTFC than for the GC youth (Chamberlain & Reid, 1998). Eddy and Chamberlain (2000) then conducted the first known study of factors mediating the effect of treatment on youth delinquency.

The influence of family management skills (i.e., supervision, discipline, and positive adult-youth relationship) and deviant peer association on youth delinquent behavior was examined (Eddy & Chamberlain, 2000). Supervision was significantly and negatively associated with arrests during the time between placement and one year after exit from placement. All four of Baron and Kenny's (1986) conditions for mediation were successfully met. Shown in Figure 12.2 is a test of the mediational model. The three parenting/guardian skills employed by the foster parents in MTFC or in GC formed a strong construct along with reduced association with deviant peers. These mediators were found to account for the association between group assignment and the lower levels of antisocial behavior at outcome. Thus, the improvement in antisocial behavior for the MTFC group was best described as mediated by improvements in supervision and other aspects of parenting and by associated reductions in deviant peer association. This indicates that, if employed successfully, supervision can be part of a multidimensional intervention that results in reductions in offending for chronically delinquent youth.

There has been additional work involving interventions on monitoring that has shown improvements in antisocial behaviors. Martinez and Forgatch (2001) found that a parent training intervention for divorcing mothers that included monitoring practices resulted in lower levels of noncompliance for the intervention compared with the control group for boys 6–9 years of age.

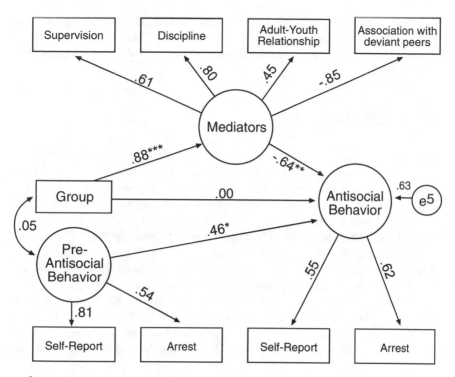

$\chi^2_{(22)}$= 21.802, p = .472, goodness-of-fit index = .920, adjusted goodness-of-fit index = .837, N = 53

*p < .05, **p < .01, ***p < .001

FIG. 12.2.   Test of the mediational model.

In summary, Kerr and Stattin have made a good contribution to the field by facilitating a greater focus on monitoring and its role in adolescent delinquent behavior. Future work in the field will hopefully address the issue of parent-youth interaction effects in monitoring so that we may assist parents with empirically grounded advice regarding supervision strategies suited to their youths' needs.

ACKNOWLEDGMENTS

Support for the Oregon Youth Study was provided by the Prevention, Early Intervention, and Epidemiology Branch, National Institute of Mental Health (NIMH), U.S. Public Health Service (Grant R37 MH 37940). Additional support was provided by the Prevention, Early Intervention, and Epidemiology Branch, National Institute for Mental Health, and Office of Research on Minority Health, U.S. Public Health Service (Grant MH P30 46690); the Prevention, Early Intervention, and Epidemiology Branch, NIMH, U.S. Public Health Service (Grant RO1 MH 50259); and the Center for Research for Mothers and Children, National Institute of Child Health and Human Development, U.S. Public Health Service (Grant R01 HD 34511).

REFERENCES

Baron, R. M., & Kenny, D. A. (1986). The moderator-mediator variable distinction in social psychological research: Conceptual, strategic, and statistical considerations. *Journal of Personality and Social Psychology, 51*, 1173–1182.

Biglan, A. (1995). *A contextual framework for changing cultural practices.* Reno: Context Press.

Buss, D. M. (1987). Selection, evocation, and manipulation. *Journal of Personality and Social Psychology, 53*, 1214–1221.

Capaldi, D. M., Pears, K. C., Patterson, G. R., & Owen, L. D. (2002). *The association of parenting and antisocial behavior in an at-risk sample: A prospective three-generational study.* Manuscript submitted for publication.

Capaldi, D. M., & Shortt, J. W. (in press). Understanding conduct problems in adolescence from a life-span perspective. In G. R. Adams & M. Berzonsky (Eds.), *Handbook of adolescence.* United Kingdom: Blackwell Publishers Ltd.

Capaldi, D. M., & Stoolmiller, M. (1999). Co-occurrence of conduct problems and depressive symptoms in early adolescent boys: III. Prediction to young-adult adjustment. *Development and Psychopathology, 11*, 59–84.

Capaldi, D. M., Stoolmiller, M., Clark, S., & Owen, L. D. (in press). Heterosexual risk behaviors in at-risk young men from early adolescence to young adulthood: Prevalence, prediction, and STD contraction. *Developmental Psychology.*

Chamberlain, P., & Reid, J. (1998). Comparison of two community alternatives to incarceration for chronic juvenile offenders. *Journal of Consulting and Clinical Psychology, 6*, 624–633.

Coie, J. D., & Dodge, K. (1988). Multiple sources of data on social behavior and social status in the school: A cross-age comparison. *Child Development, 59*, 815–829.

Dishion, T. J., & Kavanaugh, K. (in press). *Adolescent problem behavior: An intervention and assessment sourcebook for working with families in schools.* New York: Guilford.

Dishion, T. J., & McMahon, R. J. (1998). Parental monitoring and the prevention of child and adolescent problem behavior: A conceptual and empirical formulation. *Clinical Child and Family Psychology Review, 1*, 61–75.

Dishion, T. J., & McMahon, R. J. (1999). Parental monitoring and the prevention of problem behavior: A conceptual and empirical reformulation. In R. S. Ashery (Ed.), *Research meeting on drug abuse prevention through family interventions. NIDA Research Monogram 177* (pp. 229–259). Rockville, MD: U.S. Department of Health and Human Services, National Institutes of Health, National Institute on Drug Abuse.

Eddy, J. M., & Chamberlain, P. (2000). Family management and deviant peer association as mediators of the impact of treatment condition on youth antisocial behavior. *Journal of Consulting and Clinical Psychology, 5,* 857–863.

Friedman, L. S., Lichtenstein, E., & Biglan, A. (1985). Smoking onset among teens: An empirical analysis of initial situations. *Addictive Behaviors, 10,* 1–13.

Ge, X., Conger, R. D., Cadoret, R. J., & Neiderhiser, J. M. (1996). The developmental interface between nature and nurture: A mutual influence model of child antisocial behavior and parent behaviors. *Developmental Psychology, 32,* 574–589.

Kerr, M., & Stattin, H. (2000). What parents know, how they know it, and several forms of adolescent adjustment: Further support for a reinterpretation of monitoring. *Developmental Psychology, 36,* 366–380.

Martinez, C. R. Jr., & Forgatch, M. S. (2001). Preventing problems with boys' noncompliance: Effects of a parent training intervention for divorcing mothers. *Journal of Consulting and Clinical Psychology, 69,* 416–428.

Patterson, G. R., & Bank, L. (1986). Bootstrapping your way in the nomological thicket. *Behavioral Assessment, 8,* 49–73.

Patterson, G. R., & Bank, L. (1987). When is a nomological network a construct? In D. R. Peterson & D. B. Fishman (Eds.), *Assessment for decision* (pp. 249–279). New Brunswick, NJ: Rutgers University Press.

Scarr, S., & McCartney, K. (1983). How people make their own environments: A theory of genotype leading to environment effects. *Child Development, 54,* 424–435.

13

Straw Men, Untested Assumptions, and Bi-directional Models: A Response to Capaldi and Brody

Margaret Kerr
Håkan Stattin
Örebro University

What do we know about middle and late adolescence? We know that youths spend more time with their friends than their parents, and that they develop their own, independent identities that include philosophies of life, values, and so forth. In short, they become more and more autonomous and independent as they move closer to adulthood. All of this suggests that parents' direct influence should decrease as youths move through adolescence. But, for the most part, research on parenting of adolescents does not reflect this knowledge. In most of the literature, assumptions about the roles parents play in the adjustment of adolescents are essentially similar to assumptions about their roles in the adjustment of younger children. The adolescent's development is not taken into account. This reveals the unidirectional theoretical stance that most parenting research takes. Parenting is generally considered something that parents do *to* children and adolescents.

Our view is different. We assume that parenting behaviors are partly action and partly reaction to the child or adolescent, because all parenting behaviors are part of the ongoing, bi-directional interactions that make up family dynamics. There might be individual differences in the balance between action and reaction, but on the whole that balance should shift over childhood and adolescence. As youths become more independent, parents have less direct influence on their behavior, and correlations between parents' and youths' behaviors might be better explained as parents' reactions to the youths' behaviors than as causes of them. These are the theoretical ideas that spurred us to consider the possibility that parenting factors that correlate with delinquency in middle and late adolescence might be reactions to the youth's delinquency rather than causes of it, because it is specifically in mid-to-late adolescence that youths should be less directly influenced by their parents. For this age period, then, we thought that a child-to-parent direction in the correlations was reasonable, but for younger children we would not have expected it because parents should have more direct influence.

Straw men—what we have *not* argued

In their discussions, Capaldi and Brody have made straw men of our arguments by stating them in such extreme ways that anyone—even we ourselves—would disagree with them. Capaldi claims that we have "[swung] from a theoretical stance that the effect is all from the parent to the stance that the effect is all from the child ...[thus replacing] one overly narrow view with another" (p. 171). Brody says, "Kerr and Stattin (2000) conclude that parental monitoring is actually epiphenomenal or unimportant in the development of delinquent behavior" (p. 163). These misstatements suggest that we have made a blanket argument that parents have no effect on children, irrespective of age or domain. We have not. In fact, we drew the boundaries for our argument in the first paragraph of our paper when we said: "We make a circumscribed argument; we do not make the larger argument that parents have no effect on children or that they have played no active role in creating the relationship within which these findings appear" (p. 122). Later, we were careful to say that our findings should not be indiscriminately generalized to other ages:

> ... we should keep in mind that this study focused solely on middle adolescence ... parenting behaviors that are appropriate at one developmental period may not be at another ... This is one good reason to be cautious about generalizing the findings of this study to parenting in general. Our findings might very well only apply to middle and later adolescence (pp. 144–145).

This was, however, a symposium on the child's influence on family dynamics, and our task was to talk about the child's active role. Therefore, we did not focus on the whole socialization history that might have contributed to the development of delinquent behavior. Instead, we concentrated our efforts on a particular middle-and-late adolescent finding that has virtually always been interpreted as a parent-to-child effect—the correlation between neglectful parenting and adolescent delinquency—and which we thought might be better interpreted as an instance of the child's influence on family dynamics. The results suggested that it should be.

WHY DO THEY CALL IT "MONITORING"? (UNTESTED ASSUMPTIONS)

We are troubled by both discussants' use of the term "monitoring." Parental monitoring is conceptualized as "... attention to and tracking of the child's whereabouts, activities, and adaptations" (Dishion & McMahon, 1998, p. 61). The verb "to monitor" means "to keep watch over or check as a means of control" (Read et al., 1995, p. 822). Monitoring is an action verb and parental monitoring is something that parents actively do. Both discussants describe their own research as examples of results that contradict ours by showing that parental monitoring *is* important to adolescent adjustment. Brody offers evidence from his study of adolescents in rural Georgia that good parental monitoring deters adolescents from delinquency. Capaldi cites some of her own work in which parental monitoring is related to risky sexual behavior and other problems. Brody describes his measures very clearly (see p. 165), and from our perspective, he did not measure monitoring. Capaldi's descriptions were less clear (see p. 171), but based on them and what we know of previous research from her group, we would argue that she has not measured monitoring either.

In fact, both discussants have measured parental knowledge of the youth's activities, associations, and whereabouts. By calling it monitoring, they are implicitly assuming that parents did monitoring, or active tracking and surveillance, to get their knowledge, but this is an untested assumption. It requires a demonstration of validity. In the studies described by Brody and Capaldi, did parents actually do monitoring to get their information? We suspect that they did not, based on our own investigations of the same issue (Kerr & Stattin, 2000; Stattin & Kerr, 2000). In our studies, we tested the assumption that if parents have knowledge it is because they did tracking and surveillance to get it. We found little support for that assumption. On the contrary, we found more support for the notion that parents' knowledge mainly comes through the youth's free, willing disclosure, independent of parents' asking. Therefore, we question both discussants' claims. We think that it is misleading to claim that they have studied monitoring, and even more misleading to use the term "parental" to label a variable that might represent something about youths more than something about parents.

On the other hand, both discussants have made the important point that parental knowledge measures are robustly linked to adolescent adjustment. Thus, even if knowledge measures do not represent parental monitoring, they represent something that is critical to understand if we want to understand adolescent adjustment. This is something that we have been working on. Below, we describe our own recent efforts to understand parents' knowledge and where it comes from.

THE ISSUE OF A BI-DIRECTIONAL MODEL

In her discussion, Capaldi describes a three-generation study that looks at interactions between parent and child variables in the development of antisocial behavior (Capaldi, Pears, Patterson, & Owen, 2001). Behind the model that she presents is an enormous, sustained research effort that is truly impressive. The model itself, however, does little to address the present question: What is the direction of effects in correlations between parenting behaviors and child behaviors? The example that Capaldi cites, "a direct association between poor parenting practices of parents and those of their sons approximately 12 years later" (p. 175), could be interpreted different ways. It might, as Capaldi suggests, show that children learn poor parenting skills from their parents (a parent-to-child effect). On the other hand, perhaps the "poor parenting practices" of the first generation were partly reactions to their children's bad behavior, and perhaps those same misbehaving youths turn out to be bad parents 12 years later. It appears that Capaldi has a rich, longitudinal dataset that would allow her to test for the possibility of bi-directional effects (parent-to-child *and* child-to-parent) and changes in these directions over time and development. Such a study would be a great contribution to the literature.

In addition, the model that Capaldi presents cannot reveal *what* is going on between parents and children and *how* those interactions result in the development of antisocial behavior. To answer these important questions, one needs measures of specific parent and child actions and reactions. What are these poor parenting practices? Could they be reactions to the child's behavior? How does the child react to what parents are doing? How do parents respond to the child's reactions? These are the kinds of questions that we are dealing with in our efforts to understand how parents get knowledge about their youths' activities, whereabouts, and associations and why this knowledge is so robustly linked to antisocial behavior and other forms of adjustment.

We have been developing a working model of some of the core features of the ongoing, bi-directional interactions in the family that ultimately end in parents having much or little information about their child's activities and associations (Kerr, Stattin, Biesecker, & Ferrer-Wreder, in press). This model appears in Figure 13.1.

It shows parent-child interactions during a slice in time. Theoretically, however, we view this process as ongoing—with parents and children acting and reacting to each other. Beginning at one point in time at the bottom of the figure, parents act (and/or react to the child's past behavior) in certain ways that evoke reactions from the child that will ultimately make the child more or less willing to disclose information. They can be warm, exercise firm control, ask for information, or react badly (with sarcasm, ridicule, or criticism) to the child's communication. These influence the child's feelings of being controlled and general good or bad feelings about the relationship. These feelings, in part, determine whether the child feels free to disclose information to parents, which, in turn, determines how much information parents get. Parents' trust is largely based on how much they know about the child's activities and associations (Kerr, Stattin, & Trost, 1999), and, in the model, their trust or lack thereof should influence the warmth that they express, the degree of control they try to exercise, how much they ask, and how they react to what the child tells them. Of course, this is not a complete model. There are other factors that come into play such as information that parents get through other means, the child's temperament and personality, peer associations, and so forth. But this model helps us to understand how parents get information and how and why the information they get is so dependent upon what the child is willing to tell.

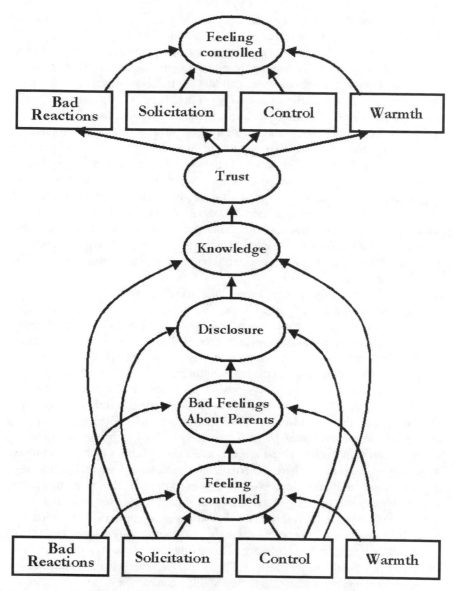

FIG. 13.1.   A working model of the ongoing, bi-directional parent-child interactions that underlie parental knowledge.

We should stress that we would not label this "the monitoring process," even though it is a model of the processes underlying parents' knowledge. To use that label would be to imply that this is the process through which *parents* track their youths' activities—a process in which youths do not play an active role. It is far

from that. Another point to be made is that we do not expect the pattern of associations in this model to be identical for children of different ages. For instance,
we know from our studies that in middle adolescence parental control is linked to
feelings of being overly controlled, negative emotions, and lack of disclosure.
Earlier in childhood, however, when children are less autonomous and independent, control might not be linked to feelings of being overly controlled, and might
not set up the negative emotional state that inhibits disclosure. In short, we expect
the character of these interactions to change with the child's developmental
progress. A final issue is how and why these processes that underlie parental
knowledge should be linked to antisocial behavior. Based on knowledge we have
gained from our studies, we do not accept the simple explanation in the monitoring literature that if parents know a lot they can step in with direct control and
steer their youths away from undesirable peers and activities. It is clear to us that
such direct control processes do not explain the link between knowledge and
antisocial behavior. A more nuanced explanation is needed. Although it is beyond
the scope of this response, we have offered one such explanation elsewhere (Kerr
et al., in press).

Like Capaldi and most developmental researchers, we are concerned about
giving good, empirically grounded advice to parents. Some of the current advice
is based on a monitoring literature in which monitoring has not been validly measured. To us, that is not good, empirically grounded advice. We should, as Capaldi
suggests, develop the basis to give empirically grounded advice, but we should
keep open minds about what that advice might be.

Imagine that this had been a symposium on parents' active roles in influencing their children. We think that we could have presented correlational findings
and interpreted them as parent-to-child effects without challenge. We suspect
that people would have accepted that interpretation just as people have for decades accepted similar interpretations of correlational findings in the literature on
parenting of adolescents. There is inertia among adolescence researchers for staying with a parent-effects view, even though everything we know about adolescence suggests that parents' direct influence should wane over time. A parent-
effects view seems to be comfortable. In our paper, we presented evidence that
some findings that adolescence researchers have comfortably assumed to be parent effects *can* actually be child effects. Some interpreted this as a shift to a radi-
cal child-effects-only position. But, we think that the study we presented did look
at both parent and child effects, and that in other contexts or at different ages we
might have been telling a different story. Overall, we believe that bi-directional
thinking is needed in mainstream parenting research to replace the static, unidirectional ideas that currently exist (e.g., parenting styles, parental monitoring).
Perhaps the field needs the antithesis that is provided by evidence of child effects
in order to bring the mainstream view away from an extreme parent-effects view
to a more realistic bi-directional position.

REFERENCES

Capaldi, D. M., Pears, K. C., Patterson, G. R., & Owen, L. D. (2001). The association of parenting and antisocial behavior in an at-risk sample: A prospective three-generational study. Manuscript submitted.

Dishion, T. J., & McMahon, R. J. (1998). Parental monitoring and the prevention of child and adolescent problem behavior: A conceptual and empirical formulation. *Clinical Child and Family Psychology Review, 1*, 61–75.

Kerr, M., & Stattin, H. (2000). What parents know, how they know it, and several forms of adolescent adjustment: Further evidence for a reinterpretation of monitoring. *Developmental Psychology, 36*, 366–380.

Kerr, M., Stattin, H., Biesecker, G., & Ferrer-Wreder, L. (in press). Parents and peers as developmental context. In R. M. Lerner, M. A. Easterbrooks, & J. Mistry (Eds.), *Comprehensive handbook of psychology: Vol. 6. Developmental psychology*. New York: Wiley.

Kerr, M., Stattin, H., & Trost, K. (1999). To know you is to trust you: Parents' trust is rooted in child disclosure of information. *Journal of Adolescence, 22*, 737–752.

Read, A. W., et al. (Eds.) (1995). *The new international Webster's comprehensive dictionary of the English language* (encyclopedic edition). Chicago, IL: Trident Press International.

Stattin, H., & Kerr, M. (2000). Parental monitoring: A Reinterpretation. *Child Development, 71*, 1070–1083.

IV

How Do Children Affect Parents' Marriage and Other Family Relationships?

14

The Gender of Child and Parent as Factors in Family Dynamics

Eleanor E. Maccoby
Stanford University

HISTORICAL OVERVIEW

That children do indeed influence family dynamics is no longer in doubt, if it ever was. The papers by my colleagues in this symposium amply attest to the importance of child effects. Now I wish to introduce some complications arising from the fact that children are either male or female. This aspect of a child's current persona must surely affect many things about the role of a child in the family and the kind of interaction that occurs between the child and other family members.

Early Emphasis on Socialization

Our task in this volume is not only descriptive. Mainly, we are concerned with trying to work out who is influencing whom between parent and child. As my colleagues have noted, early theories of socialization were top-down theories that embodied the assumption that children were highly malleable, and parents highly influential. We should note, though, that the thinking of those days was not actually as top-down as it is being depicted today. In 1955, Alfred Baldwin wrote:

> There is one extreme position . . . which holds that criminality is inevitable in some people . . . inherited, and essentially unchangeable. At the other extreme are those . . . who maintain that criminality is completely a result of learning. One need not adopt either point of view. Few do, in fact... Sometimes a mixture is formulated—so much heredity plus so much environmental influence. A more likely view is that the two interact...An (inborn) love for adventure and high courage might predispose a person to become a criminal in some environments but predispose him to become a war hero in other environments or a successful competitor in certain lines of business . . .We cannot add up heredity and environment or ask what percentage is due to one and what percentage is due to the other (Baldwin, 1955, pp. 364–365).

I believe Baldwin was right to reject the notion that influence is a zero-sum game—that in any dyad, if one person's influence is large, the other's must be small. But my point now is that the early twin and adoption studies were already well known and widely accepted in the 1930s, 1940s and 1950s. So were the studies of maturation, pointing to an inborn developmental time-table around which socialization inputs had to be organized. But the idea that our genetic makeup is important was not taken to mean that environment is unimportant. People did elect to study mainly the environmental inputs embodied in within-family socialization of children, perhaps because they wanted to understand more about what could be done to improve the outcomes for children via improving their environments, rather than emphasizing what was inevitable. In other words, the mid-20th century was a time of optimistic social activism. One of the major weaknesses of this early work, though, was the readiness to accept a correlation between parenting and child outcomes as indicating evidence for a parent effect. Yes, there was a nurture assumption with regard to the direction of effects.

Emphasis on Children's Influence (Via Their Genetics)

Since that time, this assumption has been widely challenged. From Bell's early (1968) writing on the subject, to the recent popular summary by Harris (1998), new information has accumulated. Some excellent experimental work had demonstrated child effects. For example, Bugenthal and colleagues (Bugenthal, Caporeal, & Shennum, 1980) trained child confederates to be either compliant or resistive while working with an unfamiliar woman on a difficult task. When the confederate child was compliant, the adults were generally calm and kindly. When the child was noncompliant, however, many of the women became increasingly firm and assertive. But a subgroup of women backed off and became less assertive. I will return to the issue of child compliance below.

During the 1980s and early 1990s, a large body of research was generated by behavior geneticists who used quantitative twin and adoption studies to study the individual variation in a given characteristic in a population of children (or adults), and estimate its heritability. They reported substantial heritabilities for many of children's characteristics. The variance remaining after genetic variance had been accounted for, they reasoned, could be attributed to environmental factors. But *which* environmental factors? Behavior geneticists used statistical procedures to distinguish what they called shared from unshared environmental factors. Their reasoning was that if two children were growing up in the same household, with the same parents and the same family constellation, they ought to be more alike than children growing up in different households. As things turned out, they often were not (Plomin & Daniels, 1987). When correlations were found between the parenting a child received and the child's characteristics, the absence of shared environmental effects must mean that the correlation reflected evocative effects of children's behavior on parental responses, rather than effects of parents on children. And, the absence of shared environmental effects was also sometimes interpreted as meaning that variations in such family characteristics as poverty, parental education, parental conflict or harmony, or parenting style, had little impact on children growing up together in a given household.

SOME CURRENT VIEWS

These claims were of course quite startling to those who believed that such factors were important in determining how well-functioning the children would become. Since then a number of attempts have been made to reconcile the findings from twin and adoption studies with many studies pointing to dysfunctions in parenting and family dynamics as risk factors for later child maladjustment. (See Borkowski, Ramey, & Bristol-Power, 2002; Collins et al., 2000; Maccoby, 2000). For one thing, it is now clear that certain high-risk aspects of home environments can have different effects on different children in the same family, making them more different rather than more alike. Thus, family-wide environmental risks such as poverty or single-parent status can have clear effects, though they may not show up as shared environmental effects in quantitative genetic analysis. For our present purposes, the point to note is that for a time, the pendulum swung from the earlier unidirectional view of influence flowing from parent to child to an almost equally unidirectional view of children as the primary drivers of parent-child interaction.

Reciprocation

Nowadays, most students of family dynamics adopt a much more nuanced view of influence among family members. They see it as a set of reciprocal processes unfolding over time, with each family member adapting to the overall configuration of family roles and functions, as well as to each other family member individually. To illustrate, let us reconsider the matter of how a child's compliance or resistance influences a parent, and how a parent influences a child's compliance or resistiveness. In the study by Bugenthal and colleagues, the women being studied were interacting with an unfamiliar child who was pre-programmed to be either compliant or resistive to the adult's instructions. In this study, the direction of effects was clear. But let us consider an episode we might observe in a family's home. Suppose a parent demands something from a 4-year-old child, such as "I want you to turn off the TV now, and come to dinner". Suppose the child resists and perhaps becomes angry, and the parent then becomes increasingly coercive. Or, perhaps the parent backs off, and does not insist. Are these examples of the child driving the parent-child interaction? At the moment, they would certainly seem to be. However we must consider the history of the relationship between these two: Perhaps the underlying dynamic is that the child resisted because of a history in which the parent had been unresponsive to the child's needs or states of readiness; or, the parent had given in to child coercion (or both!). Was the child's noncompliance, then, an example of a parent effect? Probably yes. Was the parent's increased coercion, or backing off when the child resisted, an example of a child effect? Probably yes. And both were undoubtedly embedded in the relationship between them that had developed over time. As Kochanska's longitudinal studies (1997a) have shown us, children's readiness to cooperate with their parents' agendas rests on a history of parental responsiveness and shared positive affect from infancy onward, as well as on parental firmness as appropriately geared to a child's temperament (Kochanska, 1997b). The problem of assigning influence differentially to the parent or the child now becomes difficult indeed. We cannot know who started the cascade of mutual influences, or when particular defining events occurred (if any did) that set the long series of events in motion. What we have to work with is an existing dyad with a long history, whose interactions may have become mutually cooperative or coercive, or characterized by vacillation between these modes. The pair may have become either well connected and communicative, or alienated and avoidant. Whichever direction the parent-child relationship has taken, however, each participant almost of necessity has influenced the other, with the ebb and flow of influence changing over time.

Of course, the individual characteristics of each member of a dyad has an impact on how their dyadic relationship will develop. Deater-Deckard and O'Connor (2000) studied a dyadic property of the parent-child dyad, namely *mutuality*, defined to include mutual responsiveness, shared positive affect, and parent-child cooperation. Using data from both twin and adoption studies, they found a substantial contribution of the child's genetics to the degree of mutuality displayed by mother-child pairs when the child was three years old. Presumably, the mother's genetics and other individual characteristics were making a contribution too, though her contribution was not assessed. (Indeed, the contribution of a parent's genetics to parent-child interaction has almost never been studied.) But an example of how both partners in a dyad contribute to a joint outcome comes from the work of Coie and colleagues (1999) with pairs of male peers. They analyzed the probability of a fight occurring between two boys whose aggressive predispositions were known. They found that this probability depended in part, as might have been predicted, on the aggressiveness of each boy. Maccoby and colleagues (see below) have also found contributions of the gender of both parent and child to aspects of their dyadic interaction. The first point, then, is that characteristics of both members of a dyad feed into the nature of their interaction. But there is something more.

Emergent Properties of Dyad

If we are to take the study of relationships seriously, we must be aware that dyads (or for that matter larger social groups) have emergent properties that individuals cannot or do not have. This idea is familiar to biologists, who are accustomed to thinking of the emergent systemic properties of different levels of biological organization (e.g., cells, organs, whole animals), and in recent years have been thinking in terms of the self-organizing properties of the collective behavior of groups of individuals (e.g., hives of bees, flocks of birds, schools of fish; see Camazine et al., 2001). A number of developmental psychologists have been conceptualizing families as self-organizing and self-regulating systems that include dyadic subsystems which have their own distinctive properties. (See Parke & Buriel, 1998, for a summary of family systems approaches.) With respect to the parent-child subsystem, we can point to characteristics, such as parent-child closeness or mutuality, that are properties of their joint relationship, not of either partner alone. In the study by Coie and colleagues cited above, the probability of a fight between two boys depended not only on the aggressiveness of each boy, but also on the unique properties of the dyad. Thus a fight did not erupt with equal probability between any pair of aggressive boys. Its occurrence depended on an unspecified dyadic relationship property, perhaps something such as their relative rank on a dominance hierarchy, or a previous encounter that left a residue of mutual hostility between two particular boys.

New work on family dynamics by Cook (2001) has taken the emphasis on unique properties of dyads and larger groups to a new level. Cook has worked with four-person families in which each member—mother, father, college-age older sibling, adolescent younger sibling—provides an assessment of how much each individual can (and does) influence each other family member. Cook, following the Social Relations Model (Kenney & LaVoie, 1984), posits that person A's ability to influence person B will be affected by four factors: person A's actor effects; person B's partner effects; the unique relationship of person A to person B; and a family effect. In Cook's analysis, partner effects were generally stronger than actor effects. This means that parents' influence depends more on the child's characteristics than on the parents' own traits. This supports the central importance of child effects on parents. Conversely, however, a child's ability to influence a parent depends more on the parent's characteristics than the child's own, underlining the central importance of parents' effects on children. But these distinctive actor and partner effects are not all that is going on. *Relationship* effects proved to be stronger than actor effects for all family dyads, and more important than partner effects for most of the dyads. Moreover, relationship effects were usually reciprocal. That is, a parent who was able to influence a child was usually also open to being influenced by that child. And for mothers, relationships were remarkably unique to specific dyads; thus if a mother had a relationship of positive reciprocal influence with one child, she would not necessarily have the same kind of reciprocal relationship with another of her children.

When it comes to assessing the influence of parents and children on each other, what the above work implies is that in any pair or larger group, there will be elements in their interaction that cannot be attributed to the influence of any one member of the dyad or group, taken individually. They are properties of the dyad or group taken jointly, and the dyad or group becomes the proper unit of analysis. Why is this important for our efforts to understand the effects of children on their parents? Because, I would argue, certain emergent properties of the parent-child relationship cannot be labeled as either an effect of the child on the parent or an effect of the parent on the child, so that we cannot say that either member of the pair is "driving" this emergent aspect of the interaction.

GENDER IN PARENT AND CHILD

Early Emphasis on Gender Similarity

Let us turn now to the way in which a child's sex, and the sex of the parent, are involved in interactions and relationships within the family. In our 1974 book, *The Psychology of Sex Differences*, Carol Jacklin and I concluded that differences in the psychological development of boys and girls had previously been greatly exaggerated. In fact, we claimed that distributions for the two sexes on almost any psychological dimension of interest overlapped greatly, and that basically boys and girls were much alike, especially in the years up to about age 6, the age-range that had been studied in most of the research then available. This was surprising, considering that many developmentalists believed that parents socialized children of the two sexes in different ways befitting their sex roles. But we claimed that there was actually no inconsistency, since our review of the differential socialization research available at that time indicated that parents treated boys and girls much alike, a conclusion basically supported by the work of Lytton and Romney (1991) some 15 years later.

Current Work: Differential Socialization

However, all this seemed more than a little simplistic, as it does today. Even at that time, there were a number of intriguing phenomena where the gender of either the child or the parent was clearly involved, but that did not quite fit a picture of a simple sex difference. There are two current scholarly, comprehensive reviews (Leaper, in press; McHale, Crouter, & Whiteman, in press; see also Maccoby, 1998) that are clearly pointing to some differential treatment of sons and daughters by their parents. These differences, however, are shown to depend greatly on such things as the nature of the activity the actors are engaged in, certain aspects of the parents' work lives, parents' sex role attitudes and behavior, and their relationships with each other. Thus the focus of the earlier reviews on broad socialization dimensions such as warmth or restrictiveness, without regard to the context in which such parent attributes might or might not be manifested, probably served to obscure differential treatment of boys and girls that are found primarily in specific contexts (see McHale, Crouter, & Whiteman, in press).

An example of these kinds of complexities comes from the work of Brody (1999) who reports that nontraditional families may influence children's emotional development, but differently for boys and girls. She found that when fathers were highly involved in the lives of their children, their sons expressed more warmth as well as more fear, while their daughters were *less* likely to express fear and sadness than the daughters of more traditional families. These findings run counter to the trend in traditional families, in which parents, especially fathers, are shown to discourage expression of fear or sadness in their sons more than in their daughters. Obviously, merging these two kinds of families in an analysis—which has usually been done—would produce relatively weak overall findings.

Let us focus now on a few of the reliable findings that emerge in these recent reviews concerning the ways in which the gender of parent or child affect the socialization process. Studies continue to show that parental behavior depends much more on the sex of the parent than on the sex of the child. First and foremost, mothers are usually more involved than fathers in day-to-day interactions with children, particularly when the children are quite young. Mothers talk more to young children than fathers do, and there is some evidence that they more often adapt what they say to what the child had just said, and adjust their speech to a level appropriate to what the child can understand. This means that in teaching something to a child, a mother is more likely than a father to provide "scaffolding" for the child's learning, staying more within what Vygotsky called the child's zone of proximal development.

But within this general picture of greater maternal involvement with young children, there are some patterns of parent-child interaction that do appear to depend on the sex of the child. Mothers, for example, talk more to young daughters than young sons, and fathers may do so as well, though the evidence for this is not conclusive. Mothers' speech to daughters includes a substantial element of talk about emotions—more so than with sons, except that they do talk more with sons about anger and aggression. Both parents offer masculine toys such as cars or trucks or balls mainly to their sons, and dolls and items for playing house—such as toy tea sets—to their little daughters. Parents, especially fathers, react more negatively to crying or fearfulness or signs of weakness in a son than in a daughter. And, both parents play more roughly with boys.

Gender of Both Parent and Child

As McHale and colleagues note, some of the most robust gender findings emerge when one takes into account the genders of the parent and the child jointly. They report that both mothers and fathers spend relatively more time with a child whose sex is the same as their own. Furthermore, while mothers typically know more than fathers do about the daily activities of both sons and daughters, they know relatively more about their daughters' lives than their sons', while fathers know relatively more about their sons' activities – their skills, preferences, friends, schedules, etc.—than they know about their daughters'.

As part of the longitudinal study of gender development undertaken at Stanford University in the late 1970s and 1980s, one cohort of our longitudinal subjects were studied at age 45 months. We went to the family home, bringing a bag of assorted toys that included some male-type, some female-type, and some gender-neutral toys. Using whichever of these toys the parent and the child preferred, each parent played for 15 minutes with the child while the other parent was being interviewed in a different room. Every 6 seconds, an observer recorded the kind of interaction that was occurring—which toys were being used, whether the play was rough and active or quiet, and what themes were being enacted when the pair took roles in an imaginary episode.

Figure 14.1 shows that a father-son pair typically engaged in nearly three times as much rough-and-tumble play as a mother-daughter pair, and both parent and child were contributing to this effect (Jacklin, DiPietro, & Maccoby, 1984). Here is what the records showed with respect to rough-and-tumble play:

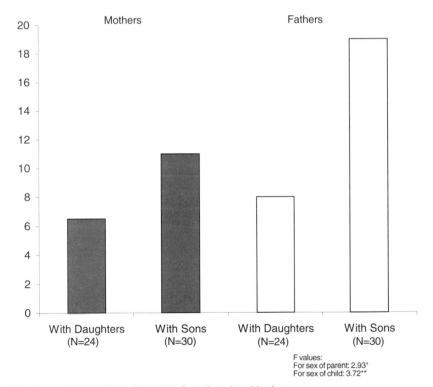

FIG. 14.1.   Mean number of intervals of rough and tumble play.

A notable strength of mother-daughter dyads appeared in the observations of a group of six-year-olds ($N = 54$) interacting separately with each parent in a game of referential communication[1]. The "sender" selected one from a set of ambiguous drawings, and described it to the "receiver", who had a matching set of drawings—the objective was for the sender to describe the target picture well enough so that the receiver could pick out the drawing the sender had intended, from an array of fairly similar pictures. (See Dickson, 1979, for a description of this method.) For the parent-child pair to get a good score, skill was required on the part of both the sender and the receiver. Halfway through the series, the parent and child switched roles, so that each served part of the time as sender and part of the time as receiver. In this situation, mothers were more skillful than fathers at describing the pictures so that the child would understand what was meant, or at decoding the child's message, or both. Additionally, 6-year-old girls were more skillful than boys. Once again, both members of the pair contributed to the effect, and the result was that mother-daughter pairs communicated with each other most successfully, while father-son pairs were the least successful.

Direction of Effects

We have now summarized a number of respects in which the interaction between a parent and a child varies depending on the sex of the child, the sex of the parent, or both. Now it's time to raise the question that is the major concern of this volume: Can we identify ways in which something about the child's sex drives the interaction? A first likely possibility is that under some conditions, children of the two sexes may typically behave differently enough to elicit different parental responses. A study of 12-month-old infants playing in the presence of their fathers provides a reasonably clear example (Snow, Jacklin, & Maccoby, 1983). Each father-infant pair was observed in a playroom that had been set up with a number of opportunities for mischief. In this situation, fathers issued almost twice as many prohibitions to their young sons as to their daughters. But it was also true that the boys approached the trouble-prone objects about twice as often as the girls, and multiple regression showed that the sex difference in father prohibitions was entirely accounted for by boys more often beginning to get into mischief and thus calling for paternal control.

Clearly, we have a child-effect here, based on a difference between boys and girls in their readiness to get into mischief in the experimental situation we provided. This difference might very well have a genetic component. It is possible, of course, that this male behavior was also partly a result of something parents had previously done to make boys more mischievous. We don't know, but for the moment let us accept this as an instance of a clear child effect, in which the parents' differential behavior was elicited by the differential behavior of the 12-month-old boys and girls.

[1] These findings are previously unpublished.

But there is a second, possibly more interesting way for a child's sex to affect parent-child interaction. Parents may treat boys and girls differently because of stereotypes they hold about what is appropriate behavior for a child of a given sex, or because they have different aspirations for what they want the child to become. We have traditionally seen this as a parent effect, not a child effect. However some of the parents' stereotypes may have been previously confirmed and strengthened by their observations of how their own sons and daughters actually behave, while other stereotypes may have been weakened or discarded because their real-life experience with children of the two sexes did not support them. So, when parents act on the basis of their stereotypes, is this a case of influence of child on parent, or of parent on child? I would argue that it is both, and thus is another case of a causal chain involving both child and parent influences. Our interpretation depends on how far back in the causal chain we choose to go.

In a similar vein, the fact that parents offer trucks and balls to boys and dolls to girls can reflect either the fact that parents are applying sex-typing pressure to shape their children toward playing with sex-appropriate toys, or that children of the two sexes have conveyed clear preferences for such toys to their parents, or both. Additionally, the fact that parents—especially mothers—typically talk more to girls than they do to boys can mean either that parents feel that chatting with a child is more appropriate for girls than boys, or that girls develop language skills somewhat earlier than boys so that girls can usually participate in rudimentary conversations sooner than boys can, and are judged by parents to be better able to understand what is said to them. If the primary reason is the latter, it can still be the case that parental conversations with daughters provide additional support for their more rapid verbal development. In other words, interpretations of most of the findings about differential treatment of the two sexes are shot through with issues about the direction of effects, and these issues remain largely unresolved. The best that most analysts can do is to suggest that influence must flow in both directions, and that often the parent's response serves to amplify the child's initial sex-linked predisposition.

Same-sex Parent-Child Dyads

The fact that parents spend relatively more time with a same-sex child, and are more intimately involved in a same-sex child's life, certainly deserves comment. My own hypothesis would be that this stems to some degree from the earlier childhood experiences of mothers and fathers. Fathers were once little boys and have probably participated in rough play during their childhood even though they seldom do so as adults (except perhaps vicariously through watching football or wrestling). Playing with a young son puts them back in the frame of reference of how males play together. And there are other aspects of male culture that a father can share with a son (e.g., taking him to sports events). Fathers' greater concern about a son's being weak, effeminate, or fearful undoubtedly also reflects their knowledge of the demands of male peer culture for a boy to be tough, able to defend himself, not be a "wimp". Fathers know that their sons will be judged by other boys in these terms.

Most mothers, for their part, grew up with girl friends with whom they engaged in "girl talk" (Eckert, 1990) that was not only more frequent but qualitatively different from talk among boys. They find it natural to talk in this way with a daughter, particularly if they find that the daughter is receptive to it. Students of interaction in workplaces, where people typically choose to spend their lunch times and other discretionary time with others of their own sex, have referred to the "comfort factor" that seems to motivate these choices (summarized in Maccoby, 2002). What I am suggesting is that parents of both sexes often find a comfort factor in being with a child of their own sex, despite the fact that there will also be sex-linked sources of conflict in these same-sex parent-child dyads. However, being in some way more comfortable with a same-sex child does not necessarily imply favoritism or preferential affection for that child.

I have been speaking rather glibly about boys having certain tendencies and girls others, and about the differences between mothers and fathers. It is well to remind ourselves at this point that some of these sex differences are not large, and there are many exceptions to the patterns I have been describing. Some sex differences are fairly robust, however, and deserve our analysis of what they may mean for the mutual influences between parent and child.

The Child's Genetic Sex

When we do find child effects that are linked to a child's sex, it is natural to ask: can we trace this to the child's genetic sex—that is, to a child's having either the XX or the XY configuration on the 23rd chromosome? We might think of turning to twin and adoption studies for insights, but will quickly find that they cannot provide an answer because there are no instances of identical cross-sex pairs of twins with whom to compare fraternal cross-sex twins. Furthermore, comparisons of adoptees with other-sex members of their adopted or biological families confound the effects of genetic sex with differential socialization effects.

A recent quantitative genetic study illustrates what can and cannot be revealed about the role of genetic sex in studies of children's development. Jacobson and Rowe (1999) used detailed interviews with exceptionally large samples of adolescents, assessing their depressed mood, their family relatedness, and their school relatedness. Their sample included MZ twins, DZ twins (including male pairs, female pairs, and mixed-sex pairs), full siblings, half siblings, and biologically unrelated siblings. The study design was therefore much richer than traditional twin studies in terms of the degrees of genetic relatedness that could be examined. Jacobson and Rowe found that genetic factors played a considerably stronger role in several outcomes for female than male adolescents, while the effects of shared environment were stronger for males. We see from this sophisticated study that it is possible to use quantitative genetic data to examine whether a characteristic is more heritable in one sex than the other. However, the study does not tell us something we would really like to know: how much difference does genetic sex (i.e., having the XX or the XY chromosomal pattern) make in the mean levels of depressed mood, family relatedness or school relatedness?

The study does show us that in comparisons within each of the groups in the genetic cascade, same-sex pairs resemble one another more than do mixed-sex pairs. Is this because same-sex pairs share the same configuration on the 23rd chromosome? Or because they have been treated "appropriately" for their sex from the day they were born? We cannot tell. There is no way that a statistical analysis can answer the question.

Let us turn for a moment to molecular genetics to see whether an answer is to be found there. As we all know, boys receive a Y chromosome from their fathers and an X from their mothers, while girls receive an X from both. We can easily see a mechanism whereby a trait could be directly passed from fathers to sons but never to daughters, creating an exclusively male, father-son genetic tie for any trait carried on the Y chromosome. It is not so clear how any trait could be transmitted only to girls, since there is no exclusive genetic transmission from mother to daughter. But a possible mechanism has emerged from some of the recent work on imprinting of genes. (See a popular exposition of this process in Ridley, 1999.) We now know that certain genes carry an imprint which specifies which parent it came from. Certain genes are received only by girls: namely, those carried on the X chromosome received from the father. If the matching gene received from the mother (which would go to both her daughters and her sons) is silenced, then we have a case of possible transmission of a trait to females only. In a fascinating experiment with mice (LeFebvre et al., 1998) this mechanism appears to have been operating: When a given gene (the Mest gene) is knocked out in female mice, they are able to engage in normal reproductive behavior and give birth normally. The pups, however, are somewhat smaller than normal. The maternal animals neglect and/or abandon the young once they are born. We do not know whether this is a reaction to the small size of the pups, or reflects some deeper deficit in maternal functioning. The effective gene in this case is imprinted as being inherited from the father—the mother's matching gene remains silent. We are only at the very beginning of work that can tell us about this kind of sex-specific inheritance in females, but further work will surely bring us evidence that is directly pertinent to behavioral sex differences.

Bi-directional Processes

Whatever this future research turns up, and whatever biological factors are detected that predispose boys and girls to elicit different responses from their parents, I want to urge that we do not let ourselves be drawn toward any assumption that when such child effects are strong, parent effects must be weak. Parental behavior is determined by many things other than the child's evocative behavior, including the parents' own genes and the stressfulness of the daily living context in which family interactions are embedded. There is a growing body of solid evidence concerning robust parenting effects, emerging from intervention studies in which groups of parents have been trained to improve their parenting skills – in some cases with random assignment to training and control groups (Cowan & Cowan, 2002; Forehand & Long, 1988; Henggeler et al., 1997; Martinez & Forgatch, 2001; Webster-Stratton, 1984, 1992; Wolchick et al., 1993). It has been demonstrated through such training that parents can change with professional guidance, and that their children's behavior also changes subsequently, in ways that are linked to the parental change. Such studies provide strong evidence, if any were needed, that many things about how parents treat their children, and about the kinds of household environments they provide, can and do influence children.

But let us return to the realm of child and parent effects related to gender. We have seen that boys and girls do elicit different parental responses under some circumstances. But it is also true that the elicited parental behavior has its own reciprocal effects, and indeed in some cases different effects for children of the two sexes. A recent example comes from a large-scale longitudinal study of the development of conduct problems from age 5 to young adulthood. (See description of study design in Dodge, Bates, & Pettit, 1990.) Dodge (2002) reported that in response to a kindergarten-aged child's misbehavior, parents were observed to become more controlling and to increase the coerciveness of their behavior toward the child—something we might have expected on the basis of Bugenthal's experiment reported earlier. Such parental responses were found to decrease girls' conduct problems over time, but to have the opposite effect on boys: for them there were increases in antisocial behavior over time in the families where parents had responded coercively to misbehavior. There is no question that child effects are at work here, in that it was child misbehavior that triggered the parents' early coerciveness, but effects of these parental responses are strongly indicated too. The fact that parent-child coercive cycles are then augmented in boys but not girls is a joint effect of characteristics of both parent and child. It serves to remind us that a child's gender matters. The way this will be manifested depends not only on the biological predispositions that children of the two sexes bring to the socialization arena, but also on the history of interactions with parents and other significant persons and events as the child grows up. This being so, it is extraordinarily difficult, when watching interaction among family members, to determine who is influencing whom. What we can be sure of is that influence will always be reciprocal in some way. I would urge that the most promising research domain now lies in studying reciprocity.

ACKNOWLEDGMENTS

The author thanks Wm. Cook and David Reiss for providing information about new as-yet unpublished studies and for guiding me to pertinent published studies. Carol N. Jacklin's close collaboration was indispensable in carrying out the longitudinal study of gender development from which data have been drawn for the present paper.

REFERENCES

Baldwin, A. (1955). *Behavior and development in childhood*. New York: Dryden Press.

Bell, R. Q. (1968). A reinterpretation of the direction of effects in studies of socialization. *Psychological Review, 75*, 81–95.

Borkowski, J. G., Ramey, S. L., & Bristol-Power, M. (2002) *Parenting and the child's world : Influences on academic, intellectual and social-emotional development*, Mahwah, NJ: Lawrence Erlbaum Associates.

Brody, L. R. (1999). *Gender, emotion and the family*. Cambridge, MA: Harvard University Press.

Bugenthal, D. B., Caporeal, L., & Shennum, W. A. (1980). Experimentally produced child uncontrolability: Effects on the potency of adult communication patterns. *Child Development, 51*, 520–528.

Camazine, S., Deneubourg, J. L., Franks, N. R., Sneyd, J., Theraulaz, G., & Bonabeau, E. (2001). *Self-organization in biological systems*. Princeton, NJ: Princeton University Press.

Coie, J. D., Dodge, K. A., Schwartz, D., Cillessen, A. H., Hubbard, J. A., & Lemerise, E. A. (1999). It takes two to fight: A test of relational factors, and a method for assessing aggressive dyads. *Developmental Psychology, 36*, 1179–1188.

Collins, W. A., Maccoby, E. E., Steinberg, L., Hetherington, E. M., & Bornstein, M. (2000). Contemporary research on parenting: the case for nature *and* nurture. *American Psychologist, 55*, 218–232.

Cook, W. L. (2001). Interpersonal influence in family systems: A social relations model analysis. *Child Development, 72*, 1179–1197.

Cowan, P. A., & Cowan, C. P. (2002). What an intervention design reveals about how parents affect their children's academic achievement and behavior problems. In J. G. Borkowski, S. L. Ramey, & M. Bristol-Power (Eds.), *Parenting and the child's world*. Mahwah, NJ: Lawrence Erlbaum Associates.

Deater-Deckard, K., & O'Connor, T. G. (2000). Parent-child mutuality in early childhood: Two behavioral genetic studies. *Developmental Psychology, 36*, 561–570.

Dickson, W. P. (1979). Referential communication performance from age 4 to 8: Effects of referent type, context, and target position. *Developmental Psychology, 15,* 470–471.

Dodge, K. A. 2002. Mediation, moderation and mechanisms in how parenting affects children's aggressive behavior. In J. G. Borkowski, S. L. Ramey, & M. Bristol-Power (Eds.), *Parenting and the child's world: Influences on academic, intellectual and social-emotional development.* Mahwah, NJ: Lawrence Erlbaum Associates.

Dodge, K. A., Bates, J. E., & Pettit, G. S. (1990). Mechanisms in the cycle of violence. *Science, 250,* 1678–1683.

Eckert, P. (1990). Cooperative competition in adolescent "girl talk". *Discourse Processes, 13,* 91–122.

Forehand, R., & Long, N. (1988). Outpatient treatment of the acting-out child: Procedures, long-term follow-up data, and clinical problems. *Advances in Behaviour Research and Therapy, 10,* 129–177.

Harris, J. R. (1998). *The nurture assumption: Why children turn out the way they do.* New York: Free Press.

Henggeler, S. W., Melton, G. B., Smith, L. A., Schoenwald, S. K., & Hanley, J. H. (1997). Multi-systemic therapy with chronic and violent juvenile offenders and their families: The role of treatment fidelity in successful dissemination. *Journal of Consulting and Clinical Psychology, 65,* 821–833.

Jacklin, C. N., DiPietro, J. A., & Maccoby, E. E. (1984). Sex-typing behavior and sex-typing pressure in child/parent interaction. *Archives of Sexual Behavior, 13,* 413–425.

Jacobson, K. C., & Rowe, D. C. (1999). Genetic and environmental influences on the relationships between family connectedness, school connectedness, and adolescent depressed mood. *Developmental Psychology, 35,* 926–939.

Kenny, D. A., & La Voie, L. (1984). The social relations model. In L. Berkowitz (Ed.), *Advances in experimental social psychology* (Vol. 18, pp. 142-182). Orlando: Academic.

Kochanska, G. (1997a). Mutually responsive orientation between mothers and their young children: Implications for early socialization. *Child Development, 68,* 908–923.

Kochanska, G. (1997b). Multiple pathways to conscience for children with different temperaments: From toddlerhood to age 5. *Developmental Psychology, 33,* 228–240.

Leaper, C. (2002). Parenting boys and girls. In M. Bornstein (Ed.), *Handbook of parenting, Vol. 1: Children and parenting* (2nd ed., pp. 189–225). Mahwah, NJ: Lawrence Erlbaum Associates.

LeFebvre, L., Viville, S., Barton, S. C., Ishino, F., Kaverne, E. B., & Surani, M. A. (1998). Abnormal maternal behavior and growth retardation with loss of the imprinted gene Mast. *Nature Genetics, 20,* 163–169.

Lytton, H., & Romney, D. M. (1991). Parents' differential socialization of boys and girls: A meta-analysis. *Psychological Bulletin, 109,* 267–296.

Maccoby, E. E. (1998). *The two sexes: Growing up apart, coming together.* Cambridge, MA: Harvard University Press.

Maccoby, E. E. (2000). Parenting and its effects on children: On reading and misreading behavior genetics. *Annual Review of Psychology, 51,* 1–27.

Maccoby, E. E. (2002). Gender and social exchange: a developmental perspective. In W. Graziano & B. Laursen (Eds.), *Social exchange in development* (pp. 87–106). New directions for child and adolescent development, No. 95. San Francisco: Jossey-Bass.

Maccoby, E. E., & Jacklin, C. N. (1974) *The psychology of sex differences.* Stanford, CA: Stanford University Press.

Martinez, C. R., Jr. & Forgatch, M. (2001). Parenting problems with boys' non-compliance: Effects of a parent training intervention for divorcing mothers. *Journal of Consulting and Clinical Psychology, 69,* 416–428.

McHale, S. M., Crouter, A. C., & Whiteman, S. D. (in press). The family contexts of gender development in childhood and adolescence. *Social Development.*

Parke, R. D., & Buriel, R. (1998). Socialization in the family. Ethnic and ecological perspectives. In W. Damon & N. Eisenberg (Eds.), *Handbook of child psychology, 5th edition, vol. 3: Social, emotional and personality development.* New York: Wiley.

Plomin, R., & Daniels, D. (1987) Why are children in the same family so different from one another? *Brain and Behavioral Sciences, 10,* 1–16.

Ridley, M. (1999). *Genome.* New York: HarperCollins.

Snow, M. E., Jacklin, C. N., & Maccoby, E. E. (1983). Sex-of-child differences in father-child interaction at 12 months of age. *Child Development, 54,* 227–232.

Webster-Stratton, C. (1984). Randomized trial of two parent-training programs for families with conduct-disordered children. *Journal of Consulting and Clinical Psychology, 52,* 666–678.

Webster-Stratton, C. (1992). Individually administered videotape parent training: Who benefits? *Cognitive Therapy and Research, 16,* 31–35.

Wolchick, S. S., West, S. G., Westover, D., Sandler, I. N., Martin, A., Lustig, J., Tein, J.-Y., & Fisher, J. (1993). The children of divorce parenting intervention: Outcome evaluation of an empirically based program. *American Journal of Community Psychology, 21,* 293–330.

15

How Do Children Exert an Impact on Family Life?

Susan M. McHale
Ann C. Crouter
The Pennsylvania State University

Maccoby's description of children's and parents' roles in the gender dynamics of families paints a broad and yet nuanced picture of how children develop in families; the paper integrates concepts and observations from a range of perspectives, giving us an even-handed account of the significance of child effects on families. In her analyses of child influence processes, Maccoby emphasized the systemic properties of parent-child dyads. She argued that the emergent properties of dyads and social groups mean that, with respect to social behavior, causality might be better understood as being located within social relationships rather than within the behaviors or attributes of a single social partner.

What does this systemic focus mean for the study of child effects? Does it show that we are directing our research efforts toward the wrong question in trying to isolate child effects on parent child relationships or family dynamics? Such a conclusion seems at odds with the richly detailed empirical observations Maccoby provided throughout her paper on the differing ways in which children have an impact on how their parents treat them and on how their families work. Indeed, these pictures of how children influence family relationships were a central theme of the paper. As such, the point we draw from Maccoby's analysis and will consider in this chapter is that answering "how much" questions about children's versus parents' relative importance, or even questions about the causal ordering of child versus parent effects, may be less useful scientific pursuits than delineating the array of processes or mechanisms through which children can exert an impact on family life. Targeting issues of gender, Maccoby described several quite different ways in which child effects may operate in families; this focus is in accord with Ge's (this volume) call for attention to the question of "how" children influence their families' lives. Toward the goal of delineating some of the mechanisms of child effects, we discuss two of Maccoby's ideas about how child effects operate highlighting processes of relevance to family gender dynamics, and we describe one additional mechanism that has become evident to us in our research on families.

CHILDREN AS BUILDING BLOCKS OF THE
FAMILY'S STRUCTURE

How do children affect their parent-child relationships and family life? One way children make a difference for family life is by helping to define the structure of their families. In social systems like families, Maccoby tells us, the whole is different from the sum of its parts. Properties of dyads and groups are emergent, not reducible to the characteristics or behaviors of any individual member. This means that family groups that are differentially constructed—and our interest here is the sex constellation of the family—provide quite different opportunities for the enactment of family roles and activities and for the formation of dyadic relationships or coalitions. Prior to the time that their family includes children, for example, the most non-traditional of couples have no opportunity to enact egalitarian parental roles.

Consistent with this argument are findings from the Penn State Family Relationship Project, our ongoing study of gender socialization in the family. Our analyses have shown that when the family structure includes a child of each sex, i.e., both a sister and a brother, parents are more likely to display sex-typed treatment toward their children (e.g., Crouter, Helms-Erikson, Updegraff, & McHale, 1999; McHale, Crouter, & Tucker, 1999). Using daily diary data from nightly telephone interviews, we find, for example, that *when they have the opportunity to do so* (because the family structure includes a mother and father and a mixed sex sibling dyad), parents spend relatively more time with a same-sex child (see Figure 15.1). These data are based on a longitudinal study of two cohorts of families: one cohort included a firstborn and second-born sibling in middle childhood (who averaged about 10 and 8 years of age, respectively, in the first year of the study), and the second cohort included families with a firstborn and second-born sibling in adolescence (who averaged about 15 and 13 years of age, respectively). All were two-parent families with intact marriages in Year 1 of the study (see McHale, Updegraff, Jackson-Newsom, Tucker, & Crouter, 2000, for more details about the samples and methods).

Figure 15.1 shows data from a series of seven structured phone calls that were conducted annually across the three years of the study to find out how children and parents spent their time during the day of each call. The findings reflect a 3-way interaction (sex of parent X sex of firstborn X sex of second-born) effect on children's time with parents. Important differences pertain, first, to how much time mothers spend with their children relative to fathers: in sister-sister families, where mothers spend more time with offspring than fathers do, children may derive a different notion about gender and parenting than do children from brother-brother families where fathers spend slightly more time with their offspring than do mothers. Differences also have to do with how much time girls spend with a parent relative to boys: in mixed-sex dyads there are greater discrepancies

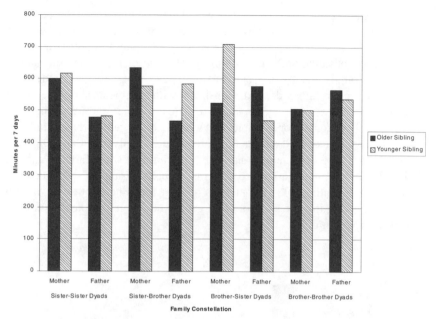

FIG. 15.1. Siblings' time with parents (in minutes across 7 days) as a function of the sex constellation of the sibling dyad (*N* = 388 families).

between the older and the younger siblings' time with a particular parent than are found in same-sex dyads. Importantly, these latter effects describe differences in the experiences of *individuals within the same family.* A methodological sub-text to our commentary about understanding child effects on family dynamics is the utility of making *within-family comparisons* of the experiences of wives versus husbands and sisters versus brothers (see also J. McHale, this volume). Conclusions about the significance of child and parent gender for family dynamics that are based on within-family comparisons will often differ from those derived from between-family comparisons of women versus men or girls versus boys from different families.

When we examined the amount of time children and adolescents spent on household chores we again found evidence of the importance of children's contribution to the family structure in the form of significant effects for the sex constellation of the sibling dyad (see Figure 15.2). In our sample, firstborn siblings are, on average, about 3 years older than their sisters or brothers, and it is typical for older siblings to spend more time on chores relative to younger ones. The effects of the sibling sex constellation are evident, however, when we examine families with mixed-sex sibling dyads: the discrepancy between siblings' time in household tasks is greatest for older sisters with younger brothers, and older brother-younger sister pairs are the only dyads in which the younger sibling is more involved in housework than the older one. Some of these differences may appear small—only a half our or so. These data were based on only seven days of phone calls, however. If we multiply these differences across weeks, months, or years, we get a sense that family life may be experienced quite differently depending upon the sex constellation of the sibling dyad—one of the important building blocks of the family. Importantly, our work has shown that these gendered activity patterns vary across family context. Consistent with arguments about the moderating role of context made by Crockenberg (this volume) and Menaghan (this volume), we have found, for example, that when fathers' gender role attitudes are more traditional, sex-typed patterns in parent-child involvement and children's household tasks are even more pronounced; in contrast, when fathers' attitudes are less traditional, these sex-typed patterns virtually disappear (McHale et al., 1999). The moderating role of context is not our focus here, but we would be remiss in implying that the story of child gender effects in families is simple or universal across families.

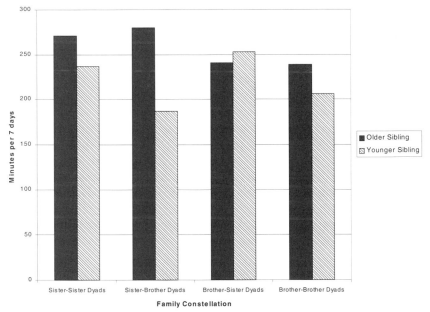

FIG. 15.2.   Siblings' total time in housework (in minutes 7 days) as a function of the sex constellation of the sibling dyad (*N* = 388 families).

What about parents? Does the sex of their children make a difference for parents' everyday activities? In the case of time spent with children we saw that it did, and we also found evidence of the importance of child sex—specifically the sex of the firstborn child—when we examined parents' involvement in stereotypically feminine and masculine household tasks (see Figure 15.3). These findings show that both mothers and fathers spent less time on stereotypically feminine tasks like washing dishes or doing the laundry when they had firstborn daughters (as compared to firstborn sons), and that fathers spent less time on stereotypically masculine tasks like taking out the garbage or doing home repairs when they had firstborn sons (as compared to firstborn daughters).

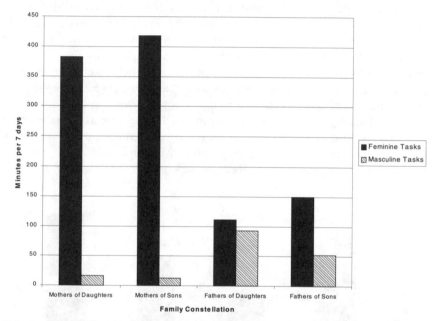

FIG. 15.3. Parents' household tasks (in minutes across 7 days) as a function of sex of the firstborn child ($N = 187$ families).

Importantly, in each of these examples of everyday family activities, we are unable to ascertain the extent to which *children* play the active role in family dynamics, such as by inviting their parents to join in their activities or choosing to cook dinner instead of shovel the driveway, versus the extent to which *parents* play the active role by choosing to participate in their children's activities or by assigning them sex-typed household tasks. The point that Maccoby made and that we are reinforcing is that children have an impact on family dynamics *because they are part of the family's structure*: their very presence affords opportunities for particular family patterns.

Just like their children, mothers and fathers develop during their child-rearing years, and the family structure in which they carry out their parenting roles serves as a context for adult development. Are parents affected by the experience of rearing daughters versus sons? We have suggestive evidence of potential long-term effects of offspring's sex on parents' attitudes and values. In the case of gender role attitudes, for example, our data indicate that fathers' attitudes vary as a function of the sex constellation of the sibling dyad. We collected data on parents' gender role attitudes using the Attitudes Toward Women's Roles Questionnaire (Spence & Helmreich, 1972) in the home interviews described earlier. Analyses revealed that fathers of sister-brother dyads reported less traditional gender role attitudes, particularly compared to fathers of brother-brother dyads (see Figure 15.4). (We found no effects for mothers; overall, their attitudes were less traditional than their husbands', and there may be a floor effect with respect to women's attitudes on this measure.) The significant findings for fathers may be grounded in social norms about equal treatment of siblings that sensitize fathers to gender role norms operating in the larger society and their potential implications for their daughters' lives. In the case of the older sister-younger brother dyad, in particular, fathers' attitudes also may be grounded in their social comparisons of their more mature, competent, and often better-behaved daughters versus their relatively inept younger sons: watching their own children grow up may jar even the most traditional fathers' ideas about the superiority of males versus females.

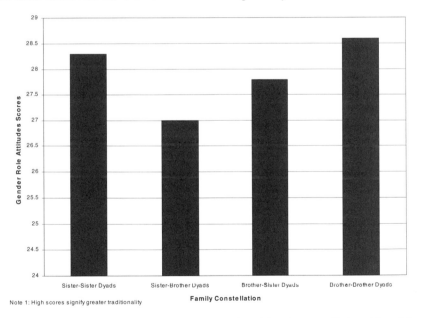

FIG. 15.4.   Fathers' gender role attitudes[1] as a function of the sex constellation of the sibling dyad (N = 388 families).

Our data on parents' sex-typed leisure interests also made us wonder whether parents' experiences with a *firstborn* child play a special role in parents' development. During the home interviews, we asked mothers and fathers to rate their level of interest in about 30 different free- time activities, many of which were gendered (see McHale et al., 1999 for details about this measure). Analyses revealed that when their firstborn offspring were 10 or 15 years old, parents' leisure time interests varied as a function of the firstborn's sex (i.e., a significant parent sex X firstborn sex interaction): mothers' interests were less stereotypically feminine when they had firstborn sons and fathers' interests were less stereotypically masculine when they had firstborn daughters. In other words, parents with firstborns of the opposite sex were less traditional in their leisure interests (see Figure 15.5). It makes sense that parents' interests would evolve this way: a father may develop at least a moderate interest in dance when his daughter stars in *The Nutcracker*; a mother who has never been interested in sports may become an avid fan once her son becomes a pitcher on his Little League team. These effects are probably culturally and historically bound, but in an era in U.S. society that highlights child-oriented parenting, it would not be surprising for parents to develop interests in the activities that their children like to do.

Indeed, we would conclude that the most parsimonious explanation for our findings of links between child sex and both parent attitudes and interests is that the causal direction involves child's sex causing parents' values rather than the other way around.

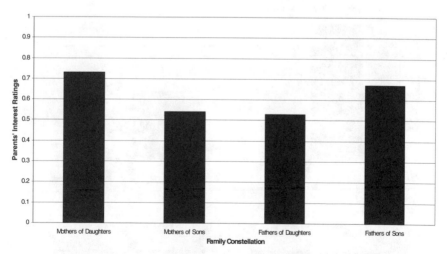

Note 1: High scores signify more stereotypical interests (greater feminine than masculine interests for mothers, greater masculine than feminine interests for fathers)

FIG. 15.5.   Parents' gender-stereotypical leisure interests[1] as a function of sex of the firstborn child (*N* = 388 families).

CHILDREN'S CHARACTERISTICS MODERATE THE EFFECTS OF FAMILY PROCESSES

A second mechanism for child effects that Maccoby identified pertains to child characteristics as moderators of the effects of family dynamics. The idea here is that what are measurably the same family experiences can have quite different outcomes depending on the characteristics of the individual child. In an ecological framework, this phenomenon is referred to as a person X process interaction (Bronfenbrenner & Crouter, 1983). Maccoby provides empirical examples of such effects from work by Brody (1999) and Dodge (2002), and these are the kinds of effects described by Udry (this volume) as being problematic for behavior genetics analyses: in such analyses, a family dynamic that is shared in the sense that it can be objectively observed as similar for two siblings is read as a non-shared effect because it has different implications for the two siblings' outcomes.

Findings from the Penn State Family Relationships Project suggest that child sex is an important moderator of the effects of family experiences (see Figure 15.6; these findings are described in detail in McHale et al., 1999). In this example we examined fathers' gender role attitudes (using the Attitudes Toward Women's Roles Scale) and the gendered personality qualities of girls and boys as measured by the Antill Trait Questionnaire (Antill, Russell, Goodnow, & Cotton, 1993).

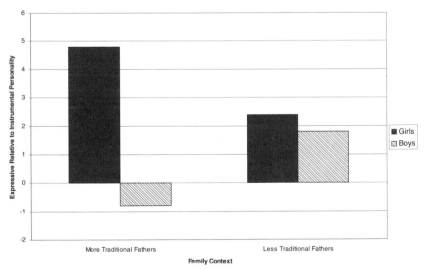

Note 1: High scores signify greater expressive (stereotypical feminine) relative to instrumental (stereotypically masculine) personality qualities.
Note 2: Findings reported in McHale. Crouter, and Tucker (1999).

FIG. 15.6.   Girls' and boys' gender stereotypical personality qualities[1] as a function of fathers' gender role attitudes (N = 97 families with same sex sibling dyads).[2]

Our findings showed in families with more traditional fathers, fathers' attitudes were linked in opposite ways to the personalities of girls and boys: girls displayed more traditionally feminine (expressive relative to instrumental) personality qualities and boys displayed more traditionally masculine (more instrumental than expressive) qualities. In contrast, when fathers were less traditional, girls and boys were more similar: girls were less stereotypically feminine than other girls and boys were less stereotypically masculine than other boys. In other words, the link between fathers' attitudes and children's personality qualities was moderated by the sex of the child. In this way, children, by virtue of their own characteristics, help to shape their own development. To the extent to which they help to shape their own personalities, children also influence the course of family interactions and family relationships.

SIBLINGS AS SOURCES FOR SOCIAL COMPARISONS

A third and final mechanism of child effects of interest here begins with a focus on parents' differential treatment (PDT) of their children. PDT is a family-level dynamic, one that cannot be reduced to the experiences of a single individual or even a single dyad. As several of the contributors to this volume have documented in empirical studies, the social comparisons children make regarding their own relative to their siblings' treatment by parents and parents' corresponding efforts to be equitable in their treatment of offspring are central facets of family life (e.g., Brody, Stoneman, & McCoy, 1992; Bryant & Crockenberg, 1981; Hetherington, Reiss, & Plomin, 1994).

In the face of a substantial body of work on PDT, we know very little from parents' points of view of what it is like to rear more than one child. We would argue, however, that analyses of similarities and differences in parents' roles, relationships, and activities with their different offspring may be a window into child effects on parents. According to folklore on families, parents believe in the effects their own socialization influence when they rear their firstborn child, but come to appreciate the role of biological influences—i.e., what the child herself brings to the situation—once they have a second child.

In the Penn State Family Relationships Project, we have been curious about how parents experience rearing more than one child. We found that when asked, most parents described their children as different from each other (see Figure 15.7). These data came from home interviews and involved mothers and fathers independently rating the extent to which their two oldest children are similar or different in four areas: conduct, academic performance, extracurricular activities, and sociability. Parents have an opportunity to compare their children in these ways on an everyday basis, and their understanding of what each of their children is like may arise as much from how a child compares to a sibling, e.g., "he's the studious one," "she's the athlete in the family," as from how that child scores, in an absolute sense, on a given dimension of behavior or development.

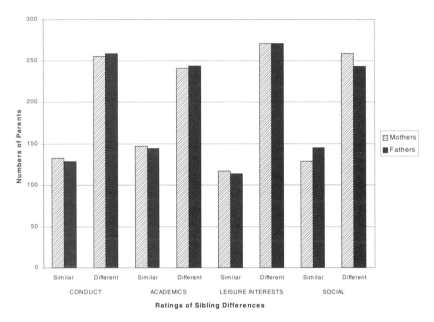

FIG. 15.7. Numbers of mothers and fathers who report that their first-and second-born children are similar or different in four domains (N = 388 families).

Even in the face of social norms that promote equal treatment of their children, at least in the predominately White middle- and working-class families which have thus far been the focus of research on PDT, parents often report that they treat their children differently. Figure 15.8 shows an example of parents' ratings of their differential treatment in three specific domains: affection, discipline, and the allocation of privileges (see Tucker, McHale, & Crouter, in press, for details about this measure). Only in the case of affection are parents inclined toward equal treatment, but even here, almost half report treating their first- and second-borns differently. In the case of discipline and privileges, differential treatment is clearly the norm. And, when we asked them why they treated their children differently, most parents highlighted *child effects* as their reason. Figure 15.9 illustrates significant within-person comparisons indicating that both mothers and fathers were more likely to say that they treated their children differently because of what their children were like than because of circumstantial or even parent-child relationship reasons.

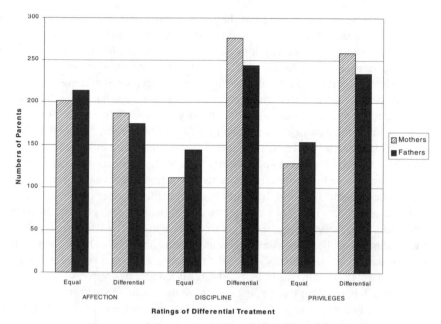

FIG. 15.8.   Numbers of mothers and fathers who report that they treat their two children equally vs. differentially in three domains ($N = 388$ families).

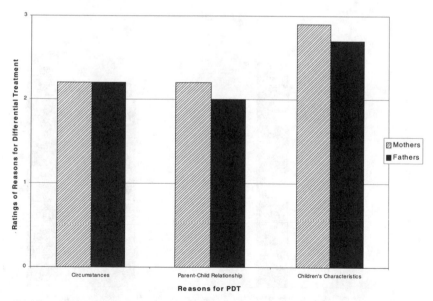

Note 1: Reasons rated on a five point scale; high scores signify more common reasons for differential treatment

FIG. 15.9.   Mothers' and fathers' rating of the reasons for their differential treatment of siblings[1] ($N = 187$ families).

Siblings vary in how different they are. Having both a daughter and a son means that parents have an objective and clearly identifiable difference around which to organize their perceptions and experiences of sibling differences. Do such experiences affect parents' views of themselves and their parental role? During the home interviews, we asked mothers and fathers about parental influences on child development. Specifically, parents responded to the question: "All things considered, do you think that parents are mostly responsible for the kinds of adults their children become or does it have more to do with what the child is like?" using a 5-point rating scale, with 1 defined as, "parents more influential than children," 3 defined as, "parents and children are similar in influence," and 5 defined as, "children more influential than parents." Our findings revealed that although virtually all parents believed that parents wielded the stronger influence, parents who had both a daughter and a son reported significantly stronger beliefs in child effects than did those with same-sex offspring (see Figure 15.10). This figure also shows that their offspring's developmental status had implications for parents' beliefs: parents of adolescents reported significantly stronger beliefs in child effects than did those with children in middle childhood. These effects are small and based on a 1-item rating from a single point in time with no attention to potential moderating factors. Nevertheless, we see this as suggestive evidence of child effects, specifically, sibling sex constellation effects on parents' beliefs, and a case where the causal arrow is not likely to point in the other direction.

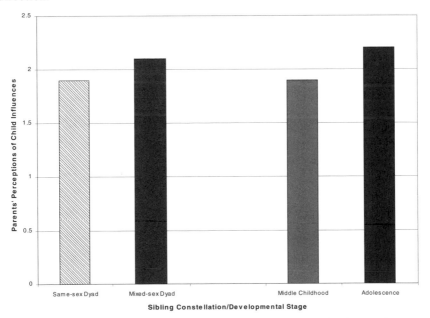

FIG. 15.10.   Parents' perceptions of children's influences on their own development[1] as a function of the sex constellation of the sibling dyad (N = 388 families).

SUMMARY AND CONCLUSIONS

In summary, we have highlighted three main points derived from Maccoby's thought-provoking paper. First, like Maccoby, we suggest that the *sex constellation of the family* is a wellspring of family dynamics. The examples we have provided based on the Penn State Family Relationships Project are drawn from families that differ in the sex constellation only of one sibling dyad. Family sex constellation, including the presence of a female and male parental figure and the constellation of the sibship, is highly variable, however, and such structural variation affords different opportunities for individuals to display their preferences and predilections about family roles, activities, and relationships. A second point worth further consideration is that *within-family comparisons* of the experiences of mothers versus fathers and sisters versus brothers are likely to provide the sharpest images of these kinds of family dynamics. Finally, our research suggests that an understanding of children's effects on their parents and on family dynamics will be enhanced by research that conceptualizes and studies parents as developing individuals in their own right, whose values, attitudes, and behaviors may change as a function of their experiences with their children. In conclusion, we suggest that although thinking about which comes first—parent or child effects—is an engaging intellectual enterprise, delineating the array of *processes through which* children and parents influence the course of family dynamics and the development of family members is the more likely path toward understanding how families work.

ACKNOWLEDGMENTS

We thank Matt Bumpus, Heather Helms-Erikson, Julia Jackson-Newsom, Mary Maguire, Corinna Tucker, and Kimberly Updegraff for their help in conducting this research, and Shawn Whiteman for his assistance in preparing this manuscript. This research was funded by grants from the National Institute of Child Health and Human Development RO1-HD32336-02 and RO1-HD29409.

REFERENCES

Antill, J., Russell, G., Goodnow, J., & Cotton, S. (1993). Measures of children's sex-typing in middle childhood. *Australian Journal of Psychology, 45,* 25–33.

Brody, G., Stoneman, Z., & McCoy, J. K. (1992). Parental differential treatment of siblings and sibling differences in negative emotionality. *Journal of Marriage and the Family, 54,* 643–651.

Brody, L. (1999) *Gender, emotion and the family*. Cambridge, MA: Harvard University Press.

Bronfenbrenner, U., & Crouter, A. C. (1983). The evolution of environmental models in developmental research. In P. H. Mussen & W. Kessen (Eds.), *Handbook of child psychology: History, theory, and methods* (Vol. 1, pp. 357–414). New York: Wiley.

Bryant, N., & Crockenberg, S. (1980). Correlates and dimensions of prosocial behavior: A study of female siblings with their mothers. *Child Development, 51*, 529–544.

Crouter, A. C., Helms-Erikson, H. H., Updegraff, K., & McHale, S. M. (1999). Conditions underlying parents' knowledge about children's daily lives in middle childhood: Between- and within-family comparisons. *Child Development, 70*, 246–259.

Dodge, K. (2002). Mediation, moderation, and mechanisms in how parenting affects children's aggressive behavior. In J. G. Borkowski, S. Ramey, & M. Bristol-Power (Eds.), *Parenting and the child's world: Influences on academic, intellectual and emotional development*. Mahwah, NJ: Lawrence Erlbaum Associates.

Hetherington, E. M., Reiss, D., & Plomin, R. (1994). (Eds.). *Separate social worlds of siblings: Importance of nonshared environment on development*. Hillsdale, NJ: Lawrence Erlbaum Associates.

McHale, S. M., Crouter, A. C., & Tucker, C. J. (1999). Family context and gender role socialization in middle childhood: Comparing girls to boys and sisters to brothers. *Child Development, 70*, 990–104.

McHale, S. M., Updegraff, K. A., Jackson-Newsom, J., Tucker, C. J., & Crouter, A. C. (2000). When does parents' differential treatment have negative implications for siblings? *Social Development, 9*, 149–172.

Spence, J. T., & Helmreich, R. L. (1972). The Attitudes Toward Women Scale: An objective instrument to measure attitudes toward the rights and roles of women in contemporary society. *JSAS Catalog of Selected Documents in Psychology, 2*, 153.

Tucker, C. J., McHale, S. M., & Crouter, A. C. (in press). Dimensions of mothers' and fathers' differential treatment of siblings. *Family Relations*.

16

Eleanor E. Maccoby on the Active Child: Gender Differences and Family Interactions

Håkan Stattin
Margaret Kerr
Örebro University

In her chapter, Dr. Maccoby raises two key questions: Who is affecting whom in family interactions, and how does gender enter the picture? She concludes that concurrent interactions between parents and children cannot reveal whether effects are child-to-parent or parent-to-child, because one cannot bypass the previous history of parent-child interactions. Furthermore, when it comes to gender effects, understanding how boys differ from girls is essentially a matter of understanding parent-child interactions from a dyadic point of view. Our commentary on Dr. Maccoby's chapter (this volume) will concentrate on two issues: bi-directionality and level of analysis on gender.

BI-DIRECTIONALITY

Eleanor Maccoby has firm knowledge of family research. Ten years ago, in a review of research in this field (Maccoby, 1992), she concluded that two major changes had occurred in family research. In the first, researchers who once viewed parents as the transmitters of the culture (the top-down look), moved toward a more interactive view of parent-child processes. The second change was a move toward understanding the complex mechanisms involved in parenting: moderating and mediating factors, multiple determination, and bidirectional and transactional processes.

The same conclusions are echoed in her present chapter. The first sentence in her chapter states forcefully, "That children do indeed influence family dynamics is no longer in doubt, if it ever was." Dr. Maccoby is probably right. There are few reasons to believe in a top-down model of parent-child interactions. However, Dr. Maccoby has probably overestimated the degree to which child characteristics have been taken into account in modern conceptualizations of parenting. Parenting research still deals mainly with parent-to-child issues. Conclusions are top-down, even today. In our presentation at this symposium, we cited the conclusions of one of the leading family researchers in his presidential address to the Society for Research on Adolescence (Steinberg, 2001): "We can stop asking what type of parenting most positively affects adolescent development. We know the answer to this question" (p. 13). What is pertinent for the present discussion is the next sentence in the presidential address: "The challenges ahead involve finding ways to educate adults with regard to how to be authoritative, and help those who are not authoritative to change." Thus, when it comes to drawing implications from research and spreading that information to the public, reference to child's active role is missing.

Dr. Maccoby says that from Bell (1968) onwards, we have generated much information about the ways children influence their parents. She says that these child effects are widely known. We agree that researchers have generated some knowledge about the child's active role in day-to-day interactions with parents. In our minds, however, that knowledge is less than Dr. Maccoby implies. It has not had much effect on the models we commonly use to study parent-child interaction, and it has not had much effect on the broad conclusions we normally draw. Indeed one can argue that research has shown that child-to-parent effects *can* happen. But even if, as Dr. Maccoby says, "nowadays, most students of family dynamics adopt a much more nuanced view of influence among family members… a reciprocal process unfolding over time," these views have not been transformed into much systematic adolescent research or had much affect on modern socialization and parenting models. They have not filtered into the broad conclusions about what parents should do and the practical advice given to them.

For example, in the parenting literature juvenile delinquency typically has been the *output* in most studies, and parenting has been the *input*. The child's active role in the types of parent-child interactions associated with juvenile delinquency has rarely been tapped. As we report in our chapter in this volume, the child's criminality can *lead to* changes in child-rearing methods. If we look at parenting only as input, we miss important information.

In summary, we agree with Dr. Maccoby that researchers realize that parent-child relationships are bi-directional, and that today there is a consensus among family researchers that family processes encompass issues of cooperation, coordination, and co-regulation operating between parents and children over time. Still, despite this strong prevailing systems view on family processes, much current empirical research proceeds from the assumption that parenting is something that parents do relative to their children. Measures of parenting still deal with determining which features of the parents are important, and research designs still treat child behavior as an outcome.

LEVEL OF ANALYSIS

Almost thirty years ago, Maccoby and Jacklin (1974) published their now classic book on sex differences. Their review revealed that there were fewer differences between the sexes than had previously been thought. Now, in view of that gender differences research, what conclusions should be drawn with respect to gender on the issue taken up in this volume—the active role of the child?

First, what are the robust findings on how the genders of parents and children affect the socialization process? In her present review, Dr. Maccoby argues that parental behavior depends more on the sex of the parents than on the sex of the child. For example, we consistently find more evidence of greater maternal than paternal involvement. Second, robust findings emerge when one combines the gender of the parent with the gender of the child. The literature, for example, seems to suggest that parents spend more time interacting with same-sex children—for good and bad.

What drives these results? Dr. Maccoby suggests a number of possible ways a child's sex can affect parent-child interactions. First, parents may have stereotypes about the appropriate gender-role behavior of the child. Moreover, parents may have differential aspirations. Dr. Maccoby asks whether this is a parent effect, or something previously confirmed in many daily interactions with the particular child. She argues that it is both a parent and a child effect: "Our interpretation depends on how far back in the causal chain we choose to go...The best that most analysts can do is to suggest that influence must flow in both directions" (p. 200, this volume). So, much of current interactions in a family are consequences and continuations of previous interactions, and should be interpreted, in part, in light of these earlier interactions. Hence, it is difficult to say who is influencing whom. The answer depends on how far back in the family history we are willing to go.

But, again, what drives the results when the gender of the parent is combined with the gender of the child? Dr. Maccoby offers different clues. She speculates that one reason fathers are more involved with their sons than their daughters may be the father's own childhood experiences, as well as his perceptions of demands of the male peer culture. The same might be true for mothers. Second, there might be a "comfort" factor. Parents find comfort interacting with a child of their own sex. Dr. Maccoby argues that each is a property of the parent-child dyad, not a property of either individual, representing the cumulative effect of shared experiences. In this way, Dr. Maccoby comes to the main point in her chapter, namely that, "...it is extraordinarily difficult, when watching interaction among family members, to determine who is influencing whom. What we can be sure of is that influence will always be reciprocal in some way" (p. 203).

The dyadic relationship apparently is a central issue in understanding gender differences. But what is a "dyadic relationship"? Is it something other than what children and their parents do and feel about each other? The intimate interaction of individual and context characteristics exists in all domains of psychology. We do not study "interactions" as something different from those who interact. Dr. Maccoby does not offer an operationalization of the concept of dyadic relationship.

Do we know more precisely who is driving the results when working with dyads? It does not seem so. In fact, the same critique that Dr. Maccoby raises regarding investigating everyday interaction episodes between children and parents, can also be applied to dyads. They are not more immune to the prior history of the family than are other features of the children or their parents.

The dyadic relationship is essential in Dr. Maccoby's account of gender differences. We also think attention to dyadic relationships is essential to the issue of sex differences. But is it the only way to understand sex differences and how the sex of the child influences parent-child interactions? Why not go the other way—to subordinate levels? One of Patterson's great contributions was his micro-level investigations of parent-child interactions (Patterson, Reid, & Dishion, 1992). Here, features that seemed to have long-term implications came to the fore and seemed to make sense. Other examples can be found in Crockenberg and Leerkes' chapter (this volume).

One can argue that studying parent-child interactions as a dyad (or triad) is just *another* level of investigation. At that level, other features come into play that were not seen when examining the picture from the point of view of the separate agents. But again, dyadic relationships are not independent of lower levels—of what parents and children feel, say, and do to each other in daily interactions. So, is the "dyadic" relationship level a more proper level, or just another level?

We also need to take into account the temporal perspective. Processes in systems at lower levels are generally characterized by shorter time perspectives than processes in systems at higher levels (Cairns & Cairns, 1985; Dowdney & Pickles, 1991; Weiner, 1989). We can talk about short-term interactions in terms of seconds and minutes and developmental interactions in terms of months and years. Cairns and Cairns (1985) proposed that social learning processes, which are central to short-term, current adaptations, might be reversed or overwhelmed in the long term by slower-acting maturational, biosocial processes. The exchange of behaviors and emotions between parents and children in specific situations analyzed on the micro level may not necessarily be reflected in analyses conducted at a more molar level. The study by Dowdney and Pickles (1991) on mothers' and children's expressions of negative affect in disciplinary situations is one example. In this study, the children responded to the behavior of their mothers in specific situations, whereas the mothers reacted more to the children's behaviors maintained over episodes.

As we see it, we need information from different temporal perspectives and different levels of analysis. None is better or worse. Parent-child interactions could be examined from subordinate or superordinate levels, but neither should be considered supreme. We agree with Dr. Maccoby that it is interesting in its own right to examine properties of dyads. Information at this level can be seen as a *pattern* or configuration that gives different information than that which exists in the separate parts—"the doctrine of epigenesis." But to study parent-child interactions at this level is not better or worse than studying it at another level.

In terms of measurement, what does Dr. Maccoby mean when she talks about "the dyad"? In her chapter, she uses the term in different ways: as an interaction effect; as a combination or a joint effect, where both members of the pair contribute; and as a pattern, system, or structure with its own properties.

So how should we assess and study dyads? Should we use relations among variables that reflect the ongoing, bi-directional process of interaction between the child and his/her parents, as is done with *variable oriented methods* (interactions and combinations)? Or, should we use the pattern or configuration of child and parent factors, as is done with *person oriented methods* (syndrome, typology)? Dr. Maccoby is unclear about this.

In summary, in her chapter Dr. Maccoby raises a number of important issues: the historical perspective on parenting; issues of bi-directionality and temporality; complications in understanding who is influencing whom; proper level of analysis; and how gender comes into the directionality picture. She is to be congratulated for offering new, fresh perspectives on how gender comes into play in understanding the active role of the child in parent-child interactions. But, at the same time we also wonder about alternatives. Why have these questions about problems with directionality not been turned around on the huge literature on parenting, which has located the main causal factors for children's functioning in parenting styles or parental monitoring? Suppose this was a symposium on "parent effects": would Dr. Maccoby have concluded that it is too complicated to know who is affecting whom in everyday interactions, and that we need to move over to a dyadic level?

We end our commentary with two questions. First, with regard to the proper level of analysis of parent-child interaction, why should we abandon investigations of parent-child interactions on subordinate levels and move to the dyadic? What empirical evidence shows that this is the supreme level of analysis? Second, concerning research strategies, how do we study dyads? Dr. Maccoby says *that* we should study dyads, *not how*. How should we operationalize the "dyadic relationship"?

REFERENCES

Bell, R. Q. (1968). A reinterpretation of the direction of effects in studies of socialization. *Psychological Review, 75*, 81–95.

Cairns, R. B., & Cairns, B. D. (1985). The developmental-interactional view of social behavior: Four issues of adolescent aggression. In D. Olweus, J. Block, & M. Radke-Tarrow (Eds.), *The development of antisocial and prosocial behavior* (pp. 315–342). New York: Academic Press.

Dowdney, L., & Pickles, A. R. (1991). Expression of negative affect with disciplinary encounters: Is there dyadic reciprocity? *Developmental Psychology, 27,* 606–617.

Maccoby, E. E. (1992). The role of parents in the socialization of children: An historical overview. *Developmental Psychology, 6,* 1006–1017.

Maccoby, E. E., & Jacklin, C. N. (1974). *The psychology of sex differences.* Stanford: Stanford University Press.

Patterson, G. R., Reid, J. B., & Dishion, T. J. (1992). *Antisocial boys: A social interactional approach.* Eugene, OR: Castalia.

Steinberg, L. (2001). We know some things: Parent-adolescent relationships in retrospect and prospect. *Journal of Research on Adolescence, 11,* 1–19.

Weiner, H. (1989). The dynamics of the organism: Implications of recent biological thought for psychosomatic theory and research. *Psychosomatic Medicine, 51,* 608–635.

17
Reply to Stattin-Kerr Critique

Eleanor E. Maccoby
Stanford University

I thank Drs. Stattin and Kerr for their scholarly critique. They are right: my thinking about the meaning of dyads, and various levels of analysis, needs to be clarified—in my own mind, as well as in my paper for this volume. First let me say that there was nothing in my paper that was meant to imply that we should no longer study the ways in which the actions and traits of each partner affect the kind of relationship that will develop in a parent-child pair. On the contrary. And of course, I do not (and did not in my paper) argue that there is anything wrong with studying the everyday interactions between parents and children. Such interactions provide the basic data from which we can identify the influence of each person (as actor and reactor, or agent and partner) on each other, but also the emergent properties of the relationship between the pair. In the work of Coie et al. (1999) and Cook (2001), for example, there is no thought of "abandoning the investigation of parent-child interaction on the subordinate level" (Stattin & Kerr, this volume) in order to "move over to the dyadic level". No "moving over" is involved. Instead, the role of each partner and that of their relationships are examined simultaneously. And the nature of the relationship will have a subsequent impact, at the individual level, on each person involved in it. Thus, the individual and dyadic levels are closely intertwined. Both dyadic and individual measures can be used as either antecedents or outcomes, and each can be examined without sacrificing the other. But I and others are claiming there is something to be gained by considering the nature of the relationships themselves, over and above the characteristics of the individuals who enter into them. Indeed, we claim that the relationships level has been neglected in favor of almost exclusive focus on the individual.

A "science of relationships" has grown up over the past 30 years or so—in developmental psychology, a landmark book with chapters on several aspects of relationships among family members appeared in 1986, edited by Hartup and Rubin. Since that time, there has been increasing interest in several ways of conceptualizing relationships within families, particularly those between parent and child. The idea of bi-directional causality is a key starting point for such theorizing. But as Maccoby (1999) and Kuczynsky and colleagues (1999) have noted, there is some difficulty in integrating the idea of reciprocity—which implies a significant degree of agency on the part of both parent and child—with the obvious differences between the two in power as usually defined. We are only at the beginning of understanding the dynamics of power as they work themselves out between a pair who interact so frequently and so intimately as a parent and child do. But relative power must be taken into account, and we should note that "power" or "hierarchy" are themselves intrinsically properties of dyads or larger groups, not of individuals.

When it comes to the gender of parent and child it has proved to be necessary to move to the dyadic level. This is true because with respect to some aspects of their interaction, what matters most is whether the genders of parent and child match or differ, not the gender of either actor considered regardless of parent gender. This "same/different" dyadic property has also proved to be of great importance for the social behavior of children interacting among themselves (Maccoby, 1999; Martin & Fabes, 2001). But this certainly does not imply that we would abandon analyses that look for individual gender effects.

Stattin and Kerr may well be right that I have underestimated how strong a grip the unidirectional concepts about parents' effects on children have on researchers and interpreters of parent-child relationships. Change in such deeply-held assumptions occurs slowly. I would only claim that it is happening.

REFERENCES

Coie et al. 1999—Coie, J. D., Cillessen, A. H. N., Dodge, K. A., Hubbard, J. A., Schwartz, D., Lemerise, E. A., & Bateman, H. (1999). It takes two to fight: A test of relational factors and a method for assessing aggressive dyads. *Developmental Psychology, 35*, 1179-1188.

Cook, W. L. (2001). Interpersonal influence in family systems: A social relations model analysis. *Child Development, 72*, 1179-1197.

Hartup, W. W., & Rubin, Z. (Eds.) (1986). *Relationships and development*. Hillsdale, NJ: Lawrence Erlbaum Associates.

Kuczynski, L., Harach, L., & Bernardini, S. C. (1999). Psychology's child meets sociology's child: Agency, power and influence in parent-child relations. In C. Shehan (Ed.), *Through the eyes of the child: Revisioning children as active agents of family life* (pp. 21–52). Stamford, CT: JAI Press.

Maccoby, E. E. (1999). The uniqueness of the parent-child relationship. In W. A. Collins & R. Laursen (Eds.), *Relationships as developmental contexts. The Minnesota Symposium on Child Psychology, 30*, 157–176.

Martin, C. L., & Fabes, R. A. (2001). The stability and consequences of young Children's same-sex peer interactions: A short-term longitudinal study of sex segregation. *Developmental Psychology, 37*, 431–446.

18

A Gender-Balanced Approach to the Study of Childhood Aggression and Reciprocal Family Influences

Nicki R. Crick

University of Minnesota, Twin-Cities Campus

Maccoby (this volume) offers a number of important new insights for those of us interested in the study of children and their families. So many, in fact, that I have limited my comments to a specific discussion of Maccoby's premise regarding the importance of considering gender in our investigations of reciprocal family influences. This is an extremely powerful and often neglected perspective. My goal is to take this idea and further illustrate its significance through discussion of research on the family relationships of aggressive children. This seems like an interesting and appropriate area for exploration, particularly given the recent focus in the childhood aggression literature on gender-balanced assessments of aggressive behavior and contributing factors.

PARENT-CHILD RELATIONSHIPS

Maccoby provides a cogent and exciting description of ways that children may influence parents and/or the parent-child relationship, and how these might depend on the gender of both parent and child. The importance of a focus on the gender composition of the parent-child dyad is extremely salient and timely for those of us who study aggressive children and their families. For many years, this particular literature targeted primarily mothers and their sons—fathers and daughters were often neglected. Additionally, forms of aggression most typical of boys were emphasized (e.g., physical aggression) and forms common among girls were overlooked (e.g., relational aggression; for a review see Crick et al., 1999). As a result, the role of gender in reciprocal family influences was nearly impossible to evaluate and, perhaps not surprisingly, was rarely considered.

Recently, a more gender-balanced approach has been taken to the study of childhood aggression by including male and female parents, male and female children, and types of aggressive behaviors that are salient for both males and females. Comparison of the findings resulting from this approach with those obtained using the more "gender-biased" approach provides an interesting illustration of the significance of Maccoby's arguments regarding gender. As an example, consider findings from our own longitudinal research on physical and relational aggression. Parents and their children were individually interviewed about parent-child interactions during the target child's 3rd grade in school (Time 1) and they were reassessed a year later when the child was in 4th grade (Time 2). Information about children's aggressive behavior was obtained from the school context during both time periods.

One of our goals for this study was to examine the association between parents' use of behavioral and psychological control and children's use of physical and relational aggression (Crick, Nelson, Casas, & Geiger, 2001). Based on research by a number of investigators (e.g., Barber, 1996; Nelson & Crick, 2002; Robinson, Mandleco, Olsen, & Hart, 1995; Steinberg, 1990), behavioral control was defined as parental behaviors that focus on controlling the child's behavior (e.g., punitiveness, unqualified power assertion), whereas psychological control was defined as parental behaviors that focus on controlling the child's psychological world (e.g., guilt induction, love withdrawal). Based on our own prior investigations, physical aggression was defined as behaviors that harm others through the use of physical damage or the threat of physical damage (e.g., threatening to beat someone up unless they comply with a demand) and relational aggression was defined as harming others through the use or threat of relationship damage (e.g., using social exclusion as a retaliatory strategy; threatening to end a friendship unless a peer complies with a demand) (for a review see Crick et al., 1999).

Both mothers ($N = 103$) and fathers ($N = 57$) took part in this research, as well as children of both sexes ($N = 106$ children). Associations between parental control strategies and child aggression were evaluated with correlation coefficients. Analyses were conducted separately for four dyad types that varied according to parent and child gender, namely, mother-son, mother-daughter, father-son, and father-daughter pairings.

In the first set of analyses, parental control strategies assessed during Time 1 (3rd grade) were used to predict children's use of aggression one year later at Time 2 (4th grade). Thus, these analyses were conducted to examine parent effects as a function of the gender composition of the parent-child dyad. Results for mother-son dyads revealed that mothers' use of control strategies, regardless of whether they were behavioral or psychological in nature, significantly predicted boys' future use of both physical and relational aggression. In contrast, results for mother-daughter dyads showed that mothers' use of behavioral control significantly predicted girls' future use of physical aggression. No other associations were significant for mothers and daughters.

The pattern of findings for fathers was quite different than that for mothers. Specifically, results for father-son dyads did not yield any significant findings at all for either type of control strategy or for either type of aggressive behavior. In contrast, results for father-daughter dyads revealed that fathers' use of behavioral control strategies significantly predicted girls' future use of physical aggression. Further, fathers' use of psychological control strategies predicted girls' use of relational aggression.

These findings provide evidence that the association between parental control and children's aggression varies significantly as a function of parent gender, child gender, and aggression type. If we had taken a more traditional approach to studying these issues, that is, focusing on mothers, boys, and physical aggression, we would have gleaned a much different and much less complex picture than that revealed here. That is, we would have concluded that parents' use of both behavioral and psychological control strategies significantly predicts children's future use of aggressive behavior. However, based on the current results, this conclusion is not applicable to mothers and daughters, fathers and sons, or fathers and daughters.

In the second set of analyses, children's use of aggression during time one (3rd grade) were used to predict parental control strategies one year later at time two (4th grade). Thus, these analyses were conducted to examine child effects as a function of the gender composition of the parent-child dyad. Results for the mother-son dyads indicated that boys' use of aggression, regardless of type, significantly predicted mothers' future use of control strategies, regardless of type (the association between relational aggression and psychological control was only marginally significant; $r = .25$, $p < .09$). Results for the mother-daughter dyads revealed that girls' use of physical aggression tended to negatively predict mothers' future use of psychological control ($r = -.23, p < .10$).

Results for the father-son dyads did not yield any significant findings. In contrast, results for father-daughter dyads revealed that girls' use of physical aggression tended to *negatively* predict fathers' future use of behavioral control ($r=-.39$, $p<.06$). Further, girls' use of relational aggression tended to positively predict fathers' future use of psychological control ($r = .36, p < .08$).

Similar to the first set of findings, these results also indicate that gender of parent and child and aggression type may play an important role in the association between parental control style and children's aggressive behavior. If we had taken the more traditional approach of targeting mothers and their sons, our conclusions from this second set of findings would have been that children's aggressive behavior predicts parents' future use of both behavioral and psychological control strategies. Based on our findings, this conclusion would not only have been inapplicable to the other three dyad types (mother-daughter, father-son, and father-daughter), but also would have been highly misleading regarding the dyads involving girls. Specifically, girls' aggression in this instance *negatively* predicted parents' future use of control strategies, in sharp contrast to our "conclusion" based on findings for mothers and sons in which *positive* associations were obtained.

These findings are certainly not conclusive and they do not *directly* assess gender differences. However, they provide at least a hint of how our conclusions may sometimes be incomplete or even biased if we do not take a more gender-balanced approach to the study of the reciprocal influences of family relationships. They also suggest the importance of, at minimum, explicitly indicating in our research the degree to which our findings are applicable to each gender (e.g., by avoiding use of the term "children" when the sample included boys only or use of the term "parent" when only mothers were assessed).

OTHER FAMILY RELATIONSHIPS

In addition to their impact on the parent-child dyad, children can also play a role in influencing other family relationships. Further, similar to parent-child relationships, the nature of this influence is likely to vary as a function of gender. Two examples of children's potential contributions to other family relationships are considered here—sibling relationships and interparental relationships.

Perhaps the most obvious family relationship to consider, beyond that of parent and child, is the sibling dyad. In contrast to those who study parent-child interactions, sibling researchers have long recognized the important role of gender composition for understanding the reciprocal influences of brothers and sisters (Buhrmester, 1990). For example, Bank (1997) demonstrated that older siblings may contribute in important ways to the antisocial tendencies of their younger siblings. However, this is particularly likely when the older sibling is male and the younger sibling is female. This might occur, for example, if older, antisocial brothers involve their sisters in their interactions and activities with deviant friends (e.g., the sister might start dating one of these friends and get pressured into early sexual activity, drug use, or other antisocial behaviors).

Children also may treat their siblings in aggressive ways that, if severe, are likely to impact the sibling by placing him or her at risk for social-psychological adjustment difficulties (e.g., depressive symptoms; Hofmann, 2001). Evidence shows that this treatment may vary depending on gender as well as birth position. For example, older siblings, regardless of gender, are more likely to use physical aggression with younger brothers than with younger sisters (e.g., Stoneman, Brody, & MacKinnon, 1984). In contrast, there is some evidence that older siblings are more likely to use relational aggression with younger sisters than with younger brothers (O'Brien, 1999). The reverse also appears to be true. That is, younger siblings are more likely to use physical aggression with older brothers and relational aggression with older sisters (O'Brien, 1999).

In addition to their direct impact on each other, siblings can also influence parent-child relationships. Findings from several studies of childhood aggression provide examples of the processes by which this influence might occur. Specifically, these studies indicate that children sometimes draw parents directly into their interactions with siblings in ways that may impact family dynamics. As an illustration, research has shown that younger siblings often seek assistance from parents when their older siblings are physically attacking them (Felson & Russo, 1988; Sutton-Smith & Rosenberg, 1968). Additionally, evidence from our own studies indicates that relationally aggressive acts between siblings often involve using the parents in a manipulative fashion to punish the brother or sister (for a review see Crick et al., 1999). This might involve, for example, lying to Dad about the misbehavior of a sister so that he will become angry with or sanction her in some way. If so, the child may negatively impact Dad's view of the sister and may contribute to more conflictual interactions between them.

Children, alone or in the context of the sibling dyad, may also influence the nature of the interactions between parents (i.e., in families where there are two caretakers). For example, a number of studies have examined the association between sibling relationship quality and features of the interparental relationship. In general, this body of research has demonstrated that poor sibling relationships are associated with conflictual and other negative characteristics of the interparental relationship (e.g., Brody, Stoneman, McCoy, & Forehand, 1992; Jenkins, 1992; McGuire, McHale, & Updegraff, 1996;). One limitation, however, is that most of these studies have been either correlational or have looked primarily at the impact of the parental dyad on the sibling dyad rather than the reverse. Thus, conclusions have generally been about how the parental relationship impacts children. It seems quite reasonable, however, given the evidence discussed in this symposium, to conclude that children may also impact the interparental relationship. For example, siblings who fight a great deal may create stressors that impinge on the quality of the parents' relationship. Or, siblings may directly manipulate the interparental relationship. For example, Danielle may attempt to get Dad to side with her against her sibling, Josie in a conflict, and, in turn, Josie may attempt to attract the sympathies of Mom. If Danielle and Josie are successful in these endeavors, problems between Mom and Dad may ensue.

Findings from our own research indicate that some children may attempt to more overtly impact interactions between parents. In this study we found that relationally aggressive children were more likely than their peers to play the role of peacemaker when their parents were fighting or engaging in conflictual interactions (Grotpeter, 1997). This type of intervention, if taken seriously by the parents, may significantly impinge on the nature of the interparental relationship. For example, it may reduce the severity and longevity of the parental conflict, thereby contributing to more harmonious parental feelings and interactions. Of course, it may also exact a negative toll on the intervening child.

Maccoby's discussion focused primarily on the salience of child and parent gender for understanding reciprocal influences within the parent-child relationship, however, it appears that her ideas also may serve as a useful guide for future research on reciprocal influence within other family relationships. Although the current research was limited to discussion of sibling relationships and interparental relationships, other family contexts also should be considered in future studies, such as grandparent-child relationships or parents' relationships with their own parents and siblings.

CONCLUSIONS AND DIRECTIONS FOR FUTURE RESEARCH

The focus in this paper has been the application of Maccoby's premise regarding gender-composition and family relationships to aggressive children. This was done for illustration purposes only. That is, it will be important in future investigations to apply this gender-balanced approach not only to aggressive children and their families but to the study of children and families of all types. Further, it will be essential (albeit amazingly complex) to consider reciprocal influences within family relationships. Both of these approaches seem crucial for generating an empirical understanding of children and families that is accurate and applicable to both males and females, and that properly identifies the etiology of particular behaviors, emotions, and cognitions of both individuals and dyads.

ACKNOWLEDGMENTS

Preparation of this paper was supported by grants from the National Institute of Mental Health (MH63684-01) and the National Science Foundation (BCS-0126521).

REFERENCES

Bank, L. (1997). *Younger sisters of antisocial brothers: Bad days at black rock.* Paper presented at the biennial meeting of the Society for Research on Child Development, Washington, DC.

Barber, B. K. (1996). Parental psychological control: Revisiting a neglected contruct. *Child Development, 67,* 3296–3329.

Brody, G. H., Stoneman, Z., McCoy, J. K., & Forehand, R. (1992). Associations of maternal and paternal direct and differential behavior with sibling relationships: Contemporaneous and longitudinal studies. *Child Development, 63,* 82–92.

Buhrmester, D. (1990). The developmental courses of sibling and peer relationships. In F. Boer & J. Dunn (Eds.), *Children's sibling relationships: Developmental and clinical issues* (pp. 19–39). Hillsdale, NJ: Lawrence Erlbaum Associates.

Crick, N. R., Nelson, D. A., Casas, J. F., & Geiger, T. (2001). *Parental psychological and behavioral control: Longitudinal associations with childhood relational and physical aggression.* Paper presented at the biennial meeting of the Society for Research in Child Development, Minneapolis, MN.

Crick, N. R., Werner, N. E., Casas, J. F., O'Brien, K. M., Nelson, D. A., Grotpeter, J. K., & Markon, K. (1999). Childhood aggression and gender: A new look at an old problem. In D. Bernstein (Ed.), *The 45th Nebraska Symposium on Motivation: Gender and motivation* (pp. 75–141). Lincoln, NE: Nebraska University Press.

Felson, R. B., & Russo, N. (1988). Children's evaluations of retaliatory aggression. *Child Development, 59*, 961–968.

Grotpeter, J. K. (1997). *Relational aggression, overt aggression, and family relationships*. Unpublished doctoral dissertation, University of Illinois at Urbana-Champaign.

Hofmann, I. C. (2001). *Sibling victimization and psychological adjustment*. Unpublished first-year paper, University of Minnesota, Twin Cities Campus.

Jenkins, J. (1992). Sibling relationships in disharmonious homes: Potential difficulties and protective factors. In F. Boer & J. Dunn (Eds.), *Children's sibling relationships: Developmental and clinical issues*. Hillsdale, NJ: Lawrence Erlbaum Associates.

McGuire, S., McHale, S. M., & Updegraff, K. A. (1996). Children's perceptions of the sibling relationship in middle childhood: Connections within and between family relationships. *Personal Relationships, 3*, 229–239.

Nelson, D. A., & Crick, N. R. (2002). Parental psychological control: Implications for childhood physical and relational aggression. In B. Barber (Ed.), *Intrusive parenting: How psychological control affects children and adolescents*. Washington, DC: American Psychological Association Books.

O'Brien, K. M. (1999). *Relational and physical aggression in aggressive and nonaggressive children's sibling relationships: Do gender, gender composition, and birth position influence aggressive behavior towards siblings?* Unpublished doctoral dissertation, University of Minnesota.

Robinson, C. C., Mandleco, B., Olsen, S. F., & Hart, C. H. (1995). Authoritative, authoritarian, and permissive parenting practices: Development of a new measure. *Psychological Reports, 77*, 819–830.

Steinberg, L. (1990). Autonomy, conflict, and harmony in the family relationship. In S. S. Feldman & G. R. Elliot (Eds.), *At the threshold: The developing adolescent* (pp. 255–276). Cambridge, MA: Harvard University Press.

Stoneman, Z., Brody, G. H., & MacKinnon, C. E. (1986). Same-sex and cross-sex siblings: Activity choices, roles, and behavior, and gender stereotypes. *Sex Roles, 15*, 495–511.

Sutton-Smith, B., & Rosenberg, B. (1968). Sibling consensus on power tactics. *Journal of Genetic Psychology, 112*, 63–72.

19
Child Effects as Family Process

Lilly Shanahan
Juliana M. Sobolewski
The Pennsylvania State University

INTRODUCTION

Child effects have intrigued behavioral scientists for decades, and for good reason. The concept of child effects has provided a generative twist on socialization theory: Not only do adults raise children, but children may, in turn, shape the attitudes and behaviors of adults (e.g., Bell & Chapman, 1986; Russell & Russell, 1992). For example, child effects can help explain why parents change throughout the course of the family cycle. Further, by employing the concept of child effects, researchers recognize that parents are not solely responsible for family interactions. Thus, child effects could partially account for why some parents of children with behavioral problems have particularly ineffective parenting strategies, or why some child behaviors remain resistant to parenting efforts (e.g., Anderson, Lytton, & Romney, 1986; Bugenthal, Caporeal, & Shennum, 1980; Patterson, 1981). Moreover, child effects are consistent with a constructivist perspective on human development, which views the child as an active agent who shapes his or her proximate setting (e.g., Lerner & Busch-Rossnagel, 1981).

Nevertheless, many of the papers in this volume seriously undermine the concept's current scientific utility. We begin with a brief review of how child effects have been conceptualized in past research and in this volume. We address weaknesses of traditional approaches to child effects and explain why they lead to research questions that run contrary to basic realities of close interpersonal relationships. As an alternative, we argue for a re-conceptualization of child effects that acknowledges the diverse behaviors the concept currently references. Moreover, in agreement with many contributions to this volume, we propose that future research should attend to mediating and moderating variables—such as pre-existing characteristics of children and their parents, relationship history, gender, age, neighborhood, school, work, and other contextual variables—that may reveal insights about the diverse nature of child effects and their mechanisms. In the second part of the chapter, we discuss the common misinterpretation of parenting measures, and uncertainty about the appropriate unit of analysis. Finally, we propose future directions for research that views child effects as part of the ongoing family process.

TRADITIONAL MODELS OF CHILD EFFECTS

Child effects are commonly defined as "reactions of parents or adults to child characteristics" (e.g., Bell & Chapman, 1986, p. 595) or "the influence that children have on parents" (Russell & Russell, 1992, p. 164). Consistent with these definitions, some studies have examined child effects with experimental designs that attempt to separate the influence of children on parents from the influence of parents on children, and to establish child characteristics as causal agents for change in adult behavior (e.g., Bugenthal, Caporeal, & Shennum, 1980; Brunk & Henggeler, 1984; Osofsky & O'Connell, 1972; Stevens-Long, 1973). As acknowledged in many of the contributions to this volume, a better understanding of families will undoubtedly be achieved by broadening the scope of inquiry beyond parents as sole influences on family dynamics. The concept of child effects is a step in this direction. Nevertheless, several criticisms of how child effects have been conceptualized and studied should be addressed in future research.

The Range of Meanings of "Child Effects"

First, the concept is vague, referring to an overly diverse set of phenomena. For example, a child effect could be exerted on a parent, an unrelated adult, a teacher, a sibling, or a whole family system. Furthermore, few studies indicate whether they consider child effects to be contemporaneous or lagged (e.g., Bell & Harper, 1977; Russell & Russell, 1992). In other words, a child effect could occur at one point in time or over a period of time, and could impact parents immediately or in a delayed manner. In addition, child effects can take place during different stages of the life-course. Accordingly, the construct could encompass infants influencing adults as well as adult-children influencing their elderly parents. Most child effect studies focus on children between infancy and adolescence, although characteristics of adult children may indeed influence their aging mothers' behaviors and well-being (e.g., Cicirelli, 2001; Fingerman, 1996). In sum, child effects encompass a highly heterogeneous class of phenomena, ranging from instantaneous subtle reactions to long-lasting developmental trajectories. Future research should thus distinguish among types of child effects—defined by who the child is interacting with, the ages of the child and adult, and the developmental features of the effect.

Diverse Mechanisms of Child Effects

A second flaw of traditional models is that, with the exception of parental cognitions (e.g., Russell & Russell, 1992), few underlying mechanisms have been empirically studied. In analytic terms, child effects could be direct, indirect (mediated), or moderated by child (or parent) characteristics. Thus, there are three possible types of child effects: The first type refers to main effects, such as gender effects or effects measured in experimental designs (Russell & Russell, 1992); the second refers to mediational processes, such as child behavior leading to parental cognitions, which, in turn, influence parenting behaviors; and the third highlights the importance of moderating factors that focus on differential susceptibility of children to parental behavior or vice versa.

Theories regarding mechanisms of child effects are diverse and offer numerous opportunities for future studies. For instance, "reverse socialization" studies of child effects maintain that child characteristics influence parents. Past research identified many factors that could trigger children's influence on parents, including physical characteristics of the child such as attractiveness (e.g., Elder, 1974), psychological and behavioral characteristics of the child such as delinquency (e.g., Anderson, Lytton, & Romney, 1986; Kerr & Stattin, this volume), the child's gender (Crick, this volume; Maccoby, this volume), and the gender-constellation of a sibling dyad (S. McHale & Crouter, this volume). The processes of how these factors influence parents, however, need to be explored further.

Traditional temperament researchers argue for the importance of studying the effects of constitutionally based characteristics of children (e.g., "difficult" temperament) on parents and on the family system more generally. Temperament is defined as relatively stable individual differences that have physiological correlates, such as arousal (e.g., Derryberry & Rothbart, 1984). For example, children with a "difficult" temperament could increase maternal negative reactions (Kelly, 1976) by way of decreased maternal well-being (Crockenberg & Leerkes, this volume).

Family researchers in behavioral genetics, such as Reiss (this volume), suggest that children with particular genetically based characteristics (e.g., irritability) elicit certain reactions from parents; in turn, these parental behaviors mediate the expression of the heritable characteristic of the child (the *parent effect evocative model*). Behaviors of children who are closely related are more likely to evoke similar behavioral reactions from parents in domains such as positivity, negativity, and monitoring and control than children who are not closely related (e.g., step-siblings). At present, few empirical studies provide clear support for this theory.

Darwinian behavioral scientists might argue that evolutionary theory offers a frame for all of these models. Accordingly, child and parent effects may have evolved to ensure survival and reproductive success by way of diverse mechanisms, such as socialization, temperament and genetics. Evolutionary models may also provide reasons for child and parent effects. For example, Trivers (1974) claimed that conflict between parents and children is foreseeable, because parents' and children's genes differ, on average, by 50%. Although genetic relatedness contributes to intense parental care, the diverging genotypes may ultimately contribute to parents' and children's conflicting interests, which may in turn be reflected in either parent or child effects. Whether socialization, temperament, and genetic mechanisms are indeed consistent with evolutionary theory (i.e., the maximization of reproductive fitness), however, remains to be seen.

The Implausibility of "Pure" Child Effects

A third limitation of the concept of child effects is the underlying assumption that the "pure" causal influence of two individuals on each other can be isolated. This assumption leads to misguided research questions, such as "how much" one person causally affects another person in a relationship or "who influences whom" (e.g., Belsky, Lerner, & Spanier, 1984; Ge, Donnellan, & Harper, this volume; Maccoby, this volume; McCartney, this volume; J. McHale, Kavanaugh, & Berkman, this volume; S. McHale & Crouter, this volume; Scarr & McCartney, 1983). Accordingly, researchers who adopt a "reverse socialization" perspective sometimes fail to consider how child characteristics may have emerged in the first place. For example, in Kerr and Stattin's study (this volume), little is known about whether and how parents contributed to children's delinquency, poor school adjustment, or their deviant peers prior to age 14.

Just as genes and the environment interact in producing outcomes, family members are linked in ongoing, reciprocal processes. That is, just as it is impossible to isolate "pure" nature from nurture effects, parent effects cannot be separated from child effects. Consequently, "how much" questions, which try to partition variance between parents and children or between nature and nurture, have been viewed with increasing skepticism (e.g., Anastasi, 1958; Ge et al., this volume; McCartney, this volume; Scarr & McCartney, 1983; Vreeke, 2000). Rather, questions about how parents and children (and nature and nurture) are intertwined need to be asked. As Maccoby asserts, "Our interpretation depends on how far back in the causal chain we choose to go." That is, because child and parent effects are ongoing family processes, one might find a parent or a child effect depending on how far back one goes in the causal chain. Thus, "reverse socialization" may be an artefact of a temporally limited perspective on parent-child relationships; "*reciprocal* socialization" would be a more accurate characterization.

In sum, the notion of child effects needs to undergo considerable refinement and reconceptualization to maximize the potential of research in this area. The study of mechanisms of child effects offers rich research opportunities and needs to be further explored. The following sections will be devoted to discussing possible expansions of child effects. We will first discuss how models of child influence need to consider both proximal and distal contexts as potential moderators and mediators of child effects. Next, we will argue that some instruments that are intended to measure individuals actually assess dyads, and that it is important to consider the dyad and larger units of analysis as the analytical level in the study of relationships. Finally, we will argue for refined research designs that will facilitate the study of relationship processes.

MEDIATING AND MODERATING PROCESSES
OF CHILD EFFECTS

Crockenberg and Leerkes (this volume) indicate that most associations between child characteristics and adult behavior are conditional on such factors as family characteristics (see also Crockenberg, 1986). For instance, the risk characteristics of parents (such as low SES) or the resources and skills of children (such as emotion regulation) can moderate links between child characteristics and parental well-being. Understanding relationship processes also requires more information about mediating factors. For instance, Brody's research (this volume) revealed that the link between child temperament and maternal monitoring was mediated by maternal psychological functioning and closeness of the mother-child relationship. Therefore, what could be seen as a child effect in simpler models may be one factor in a more complex interplay of parent and child behaviors and reactions. Consequently, as many of the contributors to this volume argue, models of children's influences on parents should consider the role of mediators and moderators, such as the history of relationships, pre-existing characteristics of participants of relationships, gender, age, and the broader extrafamilial context, including the neighborhood, school, and workplace (see also Belsky, Lerner, & Spanier, 1984).

Relationship History and Pre-existing Individual Characteristics

Parents form expectations about their children even before birth. As parents and children interact over time, they develop routines and expectations that influence subsequent interaction patterns (e.g., Bell & Chapman, 1986; Lytton, 1990; Maccoby, this volume). For example, mothers were found to have more negative reactions to their own (biological) conduct-disordered children than to unrelated conduct-disordered children with whom they did not have a history of interactions (Anderson, Lytton, & Romney, 1986). This "owness effect" is most likely based on a combination of past cumulative interactions, biological relatedness between parent and child, and intentions and responsibilities of adults for their own versus unrelated children (e.g., Anderson, Lytton, & Romney, 1986; Halverson & Waldrop, 1970; Maccoby, this volume; Reiss, Neiderhiser, Hetherington, & Plomin, 2000). Thus, parental reactions are not unique to a specific child behavior, but rather to a specific behavior displayed by a specific child with his or her unique (relationship) history with that particular parent. Consequently, the study of child effects needs to take into consideration the unfolding parent-child relationship over time (e.g., Kochanska, 1997; Maccoby, this volume).

When they establish a relationship together, individuals bring pre-existing characteristics and behavioral styles to a relationship. For example, Seifer and his colleagues (1994) report that pre-birth characteristics of the mother (i.e., high anxiety) were more predictive of her report of child temperament than the observed behaviors of her child. Thus, previous characteristics, especially of parents, need to also be considered in efforts to understand relationship dynamics (e.g., Crockenberg & Leerkes, this volume), because current interactions are rooted in situational factors, individuals' previous and current characteristics and behavior styles, and mutual expectations of behaviors that are based on a long-standing relationship.

Gender

Gender is a crucial moderating variable in parent-child relationships (Crick, this volume; Maccoby, this volume; S. McHale & Crouter, this volume; Menaghan, this volume). Girls and boys may elicit different responses from parents depending on the gender-composition of the parent-child dyad, as well as the gender-constellation of the family as a whole (e.g., Crick, this volume; Maccoby, this volume; J. McHale, et al., this volume; S. McHale & Crouter, this volume). Furthermore, mothers and fathers tend to parent differently: Mothers tend to be more involved in parenting on a day-to-day basis than fathers. Moreover, both mothers and fathers tend to play more roughly with young boys than with young girls, and mothers talk more to daughters than to sons (see Maccoby, this volume).

S. McHale and Crouter's findings (this volume) illustrate the importance of considering the gender-constellation of the family, because whether a family includes sons or daughters affords different opportunities for family roles, relationships, and activities. For example, parents are more likely to engage in sex-typed treatment of their children when sibling dyads are mixed rather than same-sex. Further, the gender composition of sibling dyads interacts with birth order, resulting in more discrepancy in how much time parents spend with older versus younger children in mixed-sex compared to same-sex sibling dyads (e.g., McHale, Crouter, & Tucker, 1999; see also McHale & Crouter, this volume).

In sum, parental responses to a child may be a function of the child's actual behavior, stereotypes about the child's gender that may or may not be reinforced by the child's behavior, the gender of the parent and siblings, or, most likely, a combination of these and other factors (e.g., Crick, this volume; Maccoby, this volume; S. McHale & Crouter, this volume). Children's responses to a parent, in turn, may also vary by their own gender, the gender of the parent and siblings, parents' stereotypes about their children's gender (and possible self-fulfilling prophecies), and gender-stereotypes of the children.

Age and Birth Order

Menaghan (this volume), Crick (this volume), and Brody (this volume), among others, point to the importance of the child's age when considering the influences that children and parents have on each other. This is best illustrated by the seemingly conflicting findings of Kerr and Stattin (this volume) and Brody (this volurne). Whereas Kerr and Stattin found evidence for a child effect on parents' knowledge of their offspring's daily experiences, Brody's analyses indicated a parent effect on a closely related construct—parental monitoring. This finding could be explained, in part, by the fact that youth from different cultures were studied using different measures. The authors also studied different age groups, however. Kerr and Stattin's sample was composed of Swedish adolescents who were 14 and 16 years old in the two waves of data collection, while Brody's sample consisted of economically disadvantaged young adolescents in rural Georgia, who were 11, 12, and 13 years old. Age differences may have played a role in the discrepant findings in that child effects may be more likely to occur in families with adolescents than in families with children (Russell & Russell, 1992; Udry, this volume). As Udry (this volume) argues, for example, as they get older, children increasingly select and influence their own environments based, in part, on their genetic predispositions (see also Scarr & McCartney, 1983). Child influences may be much more noticeable in this age-range than earlier in childhood when parents have more control over where, how, and with whom children spend their time. Moreover, the meaning and importance of parental and child behaviors may shift as child and parent age. For example, Brody (this volume) argues that some kinds of parental control techniques are neither effective nor necessary once children reach a certain age or stage of development.

In addition to the child's age, his or her birth order also plays an important role in family processes and outcomes as established in S. McHale and Crouter's research. This is further supported by Sulloway (1997), who proposed a model in which birth order interacts with context to predict children's behavioral strategies for eliciting resources from parents. Specifically, Sulloway argued that firstborns more often identify with parents in order to garner parental attention, whereas laterborns seek diverse unoccupied "niches" that reflect novel developmental pathways and openness to new experiences. Although tests of this model prove sensitive to measurement issues, there is some empirical support for this theory (e.g., Sulloway, 1997). From a methodological perspective, studies of age and birth order can be difficult to design, however, as the two variables are often confounded. Nevertheless, future designs need to include within-family components that can illuminate unique age and birth-order effects (e.g., S. McHale & Crouter, this volume).

School, Work, Neighborhood, and SES

Early in life, children enter school, where they are exposed to different people and new ideas. Further, children in school begin or continue peer relationships that can play a large role in their behavioral choices (e.g., Harris, 1995). Capaldi (this volume) notes that some risky behaviors are a product not only of parent and child interactions but also of the peer environment. Indeed, parental influences can be moderated by child peer behaviors (Steinberg, Darling, & Fletcher, 1995). Contributing to risk and the choice of peers is the particular school that children are attending, which, in part, reflects parental socioeconomic status. Thus, the school that children attend, the quality of care and education that they receive at school, children's own personal successes or difficulties in the school setting, and the friends they make at school can contribute to children's and their parents' family experiences (e.g., Menaghan, this volume).

Menaghan also points to the parents' (and sometimes adolescents') involvement and experiences in the labor force, which can place additional stress, or, alternatively, create a needed diversion for family members in ways that influence family dynamics. Related to work stressors are economic pressures that can exacerbate conflict or break down communication and warmth within the family (e.g., Elder, 1974). Socioeconomic status and work are, of course, not only individual concerns, but community ones as well. As several authors in this volume argue (e.g., Brody, this volume; Menaghan, this volume; Capaldi, this volume), individual and neighborhood socioeconomic status can be important factors contributing to opportunities for parents and children that influence harmony or disruption in family interactions and behavioral choices. Therefore, research that seeks to describe and explain the effects that parents and children have on each other also needs to consider forces external to the family as moderating or mediating factors that may be at work.

Culture and Historical Time

The interplay of child and parent influences also varies by historical time and culture. For example, children may have greater influences in post-industrial nations with low birthrates than children in the same nations centuries ago. As the birthrate and children's economic value for families decreased in the United States, for example, children gained sentimental value for parents (Zelizer, 1994). Perhaps this "emotionally priceless child" (p. 3) would wield a greater influence on parents' emotions and behaviors than a child who is first and foremost needed to contribute to the family's economy (Zelizer, 1994). In any event, childhood mortality has declined and the period of childhood has been prolonged in postindustrial nations. Therefore, by virtue of time alone, children may have greater influences on families. Accordingly, in cross-cultural studies, children in the postindustrial nations may have greater (or perhaps different) influences on their families compared to children growing up in developing countries.

In sum, the study of child influences should be expanded to include the study of possible mechanisms and moderators of family process. In addition to proximal variables pertaining to individuals and their relationships, more distal factors, such as the social milieu and historical time in which families are embedded, need to be taken into consideration.

METHODOLOGICAL CONSIDERATIONS

Interpretations of Measures and Constructs

The impossibility of separating "pure" parent and child effects (discussed above) is evident from the constructs used to measure them. Regardless of the data source, measures of parenting often reflect unknown mixes of parent and child influences. For example, Kerr and Stattin (this volume) emphasize the importance of child disclosure as a route to how much knowledge parents have about the child's activities and experiences. They argue that *parental knowledge* may be an indicator of a *child effect* via child disclosure. Yet other authors argue that parental knowledge indicates a *parent effect* via parental monitoring (Brody, this volume; Steinberg, Lamborn, Darling, Mounts, & Dornbusch, 1994). Actually, parental knowledge may plausibly reflect the interplay among parental efforts to learn about children's activities (such as tracking their child's whereabouts and spending time with the child), the maintenance of a home environment that encourages child disclosure, children's reactions to these efforts, and actual child disclosure (e.g., Capaldi, this volume).

The construct of *parental sensitivity* also reflects the interactive nature of the parent-child relationship (e.g., Cole, this volume; Crockenberg & Leerkes, this volume; J. McHale et al., this volume; Stifter, this volume). As J. McHale and his colleagues (this volume) observe, parental sensitivity cannot be accurately assessed unless child characteristics are taken into consideration. For example, a sensitive parent (i.e., a parent who "is attuned to needs of the individual child, whatever these may be", Mangelsdorf & Frosch, 2000, p. 198) of a behaviorally inhibited child may differ from a sensitive parent of a child who is not behaviorally inhibited on dimensions such as intrusiveness and warmth (e.g., Park, Belsky, Putnam, & Crnic, 1997). Steps toward a dyadic measurement of parental sensitivity (and responsivenss) have been taken and should be expanded in the future (e.g., van den Boom, 1994).

Parental control represents an additional construct that illustrates the inseparability of parent and child effects. As several of the authors in this volume suggested, parental control may be differentially important and take various forms at different stages of child development (e.g., Brody, this volume; Crick, this volume; Menaghan, this volume). A deeper understanding of control is needed, however, in order to appreciate its role in the parent-child relationship. For instance, researchers should ascertain the motivation behind parental control as being child-centered versus parent-centered (Gough & Reavey, 1997). In other words, are parents attempting control for the sake of the safety and well-being of their child, or does parental control reflect power-struggles between parent and child? While such data are difficult to obtain, understanding different forms of control at different developmental stages may facilitate the understanding of parent and child influences.

Parenting styles themselves may reflect the close interplay between parents and children. Different parenting styles (e.g., Baumrind, 1968) are usually defined and interpreted as reflecting parental attitudes and behaviors. Again, however, parents also react to children's behaviors. That is, parenting styles not only reflect parental attitudes and behaviors but also child behavior, varying degrees of freedom a child has in the parent-child relationship, and the adaptations of parents to child behaviors. For example, authoritarian parenting may reflect adaptations of parents to children who are difficult to control. Alternatively, authoritarian parents may have a child who does not want to actively participate in determining family rules. Perhaps a permissive parenting style represents a large child effect as either an adaptation to an extremely mature child or capitulation to an uncontrollable child. Indeed, some empirical studies support the idea that child characteristics influence parenting styles, which, in turn, impact child behavior (e.g., Rubin, Nelson, Hastings & Asendorpf, 1999).

In sum, parent and child influences are inseparable, as illustrated by the measures of parental knowledge, parental sensitivity, and parental control, and constructs describing parenting styles. Constructs and their measures often refer to dyadic properties that reflect transactive and interactive qualities of the parent-child relationship, rather than individual characteristics. As Hinde and Stevenson-Hinde (1987) noted for observational measures, because "interactions and relationships depend on both participants, data obtained from observation of interactions cannot be ascribed solely to the characteristics of one or the other participant" (p. 2). The same is also true for pencil-and-paper questionnaire data. Thus, rather than trying to capture individuals, measures and constructs pertaining to individuals in relationships should be understood as reflecting all participants of a relationship.

Unit of Analysis

A closely connected methodological issue is posed by the question of which unit of analysis to study. Should child influences be assessed at the individual, the dyadic, or the family level? Capaldi, Brody, and Kerr and Stattin (all this volume) model individual effects of parents and children, even though they each approach the issue somewhat differently. Maccoby, Cole, Crick, and Stifter (all this volume) argue for modeling such interactions at the dyadic level. Crockenberg and Leerkes, J. McHale and colleagues, and S. McHale and Crouter (all this volume) emphasize the study of family relationships at the family level, considering the parent-child dyad in a larger family setting.

Whereas Crockenberg and Leerkes (this volume), Maccoby (this volume), and others recommend the dyad or even larger, more inclusive, units as the preferred level of analysis, Stattin and Kerr (this volume) question whether either individual or dyadic levels of analysis are better choices or simply choices. Specifically, they argue that the dyadic level of analysis is another level rather than the better level. As suggested by our analysis of parenting measures, however, the individual as the unit of analysis may not capture people in an ecologically sensitive manner. By using the dyad or more as the unit of analysis, researchers can capture the goodness-of-fit between individuals and within the family (e.g., Lerner, Baker, & Lerner, 1985; Thomas & Chess, 1977). Further, as Maccoby (this volume), explains, dyads have properties that individuals do not have, and dyadic characteristics may "amplify and channel" characteristics that may otherwise be weak in the individual. So, if an individual's social behavior alone is measured, without simultaneously considering the social relationships in which he or she is nested, incomplete or even incorrect conclusions could be reached.

FURTHER DIRECTIONS FOR FUTURE STUDIES OF CHILD EFFECTS AS FAMILY PROCESS

McCartney (this volume) provides an excellent overview of state-of-the-art developmental methods. She concludes that although current models and methods are becoming more advanced and sophisticated, they do not reflect the reciprocity of parent-child interactions. How can the study of the reciprocal influences between children and parents be improved?

First, because analyzing dyads and larger units over time poses unique challenges (e.g., Maguire, 1999; Thompson & Walker, 1982), the field needs to turn its attention to developing instruments and methods that capture dyads and family systems rather than only individual characteristics and experiences. Many new developments in research methods have focused on drawing inferences about individuals; these tools may not be appropriate, however, for the study of dyads and family systems. As a first step, the development of research tools that describe individuals in context needs to be enhanced. Descriptive methods may, in fact, be the greatest tool yet for capturing social processes and should thus be given appropriate attention. Although correlational, cluster-analytic, configurational, and multilevel analyses techniques already offer statistically sophisticated ways to examine dyads or constellations of people, even greater emphasis on basic description and measurement is needed.

Second, research designs need to facilitate the study of process. Research on smaller, intensely studied samples of families could illuminate processes underlying findings from larger-scale studies. Furthermore, qualitative data from small studies could provide ideas for interpretations of extant studies (e.g., Crockenberg & Leerkes, this volume). In future research designs all members of the family should be assessed, and an individual's development should be examined in the context of other individuals, or of other subsystems in the family (e.g., Reiss et al., 2000). In addition, the different subsystems within the family could be examined in light of one another (e.g., links between marital relationship and sibling relationships).

Further, although this poses well-known methodological problems of attrition, learning effects, and measurement equivalence, future designs need to assess families more frequently. Data collected annually may not provide enough detail to study family processes and the mechanisms of child effects. That is, although yearly data allow one to model change and constancy over long periods of time, they may not provide an understanding of how observed patterns come about. As Cole (this volume), Crockenberg and Leerkes (this volume), J. McHale et al. (this volume), and Stifter (this volume) point out, only microanalytic techniques that involve second-to-second analysis of observations may in fact be fine-grained enough to capture processes in infancy. To facilitate the study of process, more studies beyond infancy should consider using observational methods. Observational methods may be one reason, for example, why studies in infancy seem better informed about processes than do studies in later periods of the lifespan. Observational studies may be a less valid representation of what life is like in middle childhood and adolescence, however (see Reiss et al., 2000, for observations of individuals and family subsystems in adolescence, however).

Third, the different approaches to the study of the family and child influences need to cross-inform, and, ideally, cross-foster designs (see Crockenberg & Leerkes, this volume; Reiss, this volume). Genetic, socialization, temperamental, and other models, such as evolutionary models, may all inform the study of child influences. After all, children and parents are subject to all of these influences in concert. For example, as Crockenberg and Leerkes (this volume) point out: "even before 6 months, the physiological assessment of temperament reflects the interplay of genetic and environmental factors." If these respective theories render hypotheses about how parents and children influence each other, studies need to examine these mechanisms one at a time, as well as in combination, in order to best understand family processes. Furthermore, the different theories have common issues that they all need to address. For example, scientists attached to socialization, temperament, or genetic theories all state that their models need to move beyond additivity to include interactions (e.g., Crockenberg & Leerkes, this volume; Ge et al., this volume; Maccoby, this volume; Reiss, this volume). Finally, research on different parts of the lifespan cannot be segregated; rather, these studies need to inform each other both in theoretical and methodological terms. For example, researchers beyond infancy could learn from observational methods used in infancy, including microanalytic techniques such as second-to-second analysis. Researchers from infancy through adolescence also may learn from each other about how extreme characteristics of children influence parents at different points in the life-course (e.g., Stifter, this volume).

CONCLUSION

The construct of child effects is a useful tool for the development of new ideas in the study of children and their parents. Yet, "there are some surprising complexities in arriving at an answer concerning who is 'driving' the interaction" (Maccoby & Martin, 1983, p. 30). Consequently, researchers need to revise their studies and methods toward an understanding of individuals in the context of long-standing "nested sets of relationships" (J. McHale et al., this volume) and the associated "cascade of mutual influence" over time (Maccoby, this volume).

Future research on child effects should consider several refinements. First, future research should explore the value of a typology that reflects the great diversity of meanings of "child effects." Such a typology would probably be defined, in part, by the participants of an interaction, their age, and the developmental qualities of the child effect. Second, studies should include mediators and moderators, such as the history of relationships, and pre-existing characteristics of participants of relationships, gender, age, and the broader context (i.e., neighborhood, school, and work). Third, researchers need to take a hard look at their constructs and measures and consider whether they do indeed capture individuals, dyads, or families. Finally, future studies need to develop descriptive methods that capture dyads and larger units of analysis. Future research should also design studies in ways that facilitate the investigation of processes and different mechanisms that are involved in reciprocal parent-child relationships (e.g., smaller intervals, extensive measurements of individuals and their families, genetically informed studies).

Children not only react to parental behaviors and choices, but also actively contribute to family dynamics, creating new contexts and responding to other family members in their own ways. Parents react to children, and children react to parents. The questions of "who came first" or "how much" variance is explained by the child or by the parent run contrary to the realities of family relationships. Rather, attitudes, behaviors, and relationships are part of an ongoing process, and "parental and child characteristics converge in the genesis" of behavior (Lytton, 1990, p. 693). Individuals in relationships are characterized by bi-directionality and transactive influences over time. Above all, influences of individuals on each other need to be viewed as more than the sum of their parts (e.g., Maccoby, this volume).

ACKNOWLEDGMENTS

The authors thank Alan Booth, Ann C. Crouter, Susan M. McHale, and Michael J. Shanahan for helpful comments.

REFERENCES

Anastasi, A. (1958). Heredity, environment, and the question "how"? *Psychological Review, 65,* 197–208.

Anderson, K. E., Lytton, H., & Romney, D. M. (1986). Mothers' interactions with normal and conduct-disordered boys: Who affects whom? *Developmental Psychology, 22,* 604–609.

Baumrind, D. (1968). Authoritarian vs. authoritative parental control. *Adolescence, 3,* 255–272.

Bell, R. Q., & Chapman, M. (1986). Child effects in studies using experimental or brief longitudinal approaches to socialization. *Developmental Psychology, 22,* 595–603.

Bell, R. Q., & Harper, L. V. (1977). *Child effects on adults.* Hillsdale, NJ: Lawrence Erlbaum Associates.

Belsky, J., Lerner, R. M., & Spanier, G. B. (1984). *The child in the family.* Reading, MA: Addison-Wesley.

Bugenthal, D. B., Caporeal, L., & Shennum, W. A. (1980). Experimentally produced child uncontrollability: Effects on the potency of adult communication patterns. *Child Development, 51,* 520–528.

Brunk, M. A., & Henggeler, S. W. (1984). Child influences on adult controls: An experimental investigation. *Developmental Psychology, 20,* 1074–1081.

Cicirelli, V. G. (2001). Intergenerational decision making by mother and adult child: Effects of adult child gender and age of dyad. *Gerontologist, 41,* 12.

Crockenberg, S. (1986). Are temperamental differences in babies associated with predictable differences in caregiving? In J. V. Lerner & R. M. Lerner (Eds.), *New directions for child development: No. 31. Temperament and social interactions in infants and children* (pp. 53–73). San Francisco: Jossey-Bass.

Derryberry, D., & Rothbart, M. K. (1984). Emotion, attention, and temperament. In C. E. Izard, J. Kagan, & R. B. Zajonc (Eds.), *Emotion, cognition, and behavior* (pp. 132–166). Cambridge, England: Cambridge University Press.

Elder, G. H. Jr. (1974). *Children of the great depression.* Chicago: University of Chicago Press.

Fingerman, K. L. (1996). Sources of tension in aging mothers and adult daughter relationships. *Psychology and Aging, 11,* 591–606.

Gough, B., & Reavey, P. (1997). Parental accounts regarding the physical punishment of children: Discourses of dis/empowerment. *Child Abuse and Neglect, 21,* 417–430.

Halverson, C. F., & Waldrop, M. F. (1970). Maternal behavior toward own and other preschool children: The problem of "ownness". *Child Development, 41,* 839–845.

Harris, J. R. (1995). Where is the child's environment? A group socialization theory of development. *Psychological Review, 102,* 458–489.

Hinde, R. A., & Stevenson-Hinde, J. (1987). Interpersonal relationships and child development. *Developmental Review, 7,* 1–21.

Kelly, P. (1976). The relation of infant's temperament and mother's psychopathology to interactions in early infancy. In K. F. Riegel & J. A. Meacham (Eds.), *The developing individual in a changing world* (Vol. 2, pp. 23–34). Chicago: Aldine.

Kochanska, G. (1997). Mutually responsive orientation between mothers and their young children: Implications in early socialization. *Child Development, 68,* 908–923.

Lerner, J. V., Baker, N., & Lerner, R. M. (1985). A person-context "goodness of fit" model of psychosocial adaptation: Assessment and optimization issues. In P. C. Kendall (Ed.), *Advances in cognitive-behavioral research and therapy* (Vol. 4, pp. 111–136). New York: Academic Press.

Lerner, R. M., & Busch-Rossnagel, N. (Eds.) (1981). *Individuals as producers of their development.* New York: Academic Press.

Lytton, H. (1990). Child and parent effects in boys' conduct disorder: A reinterpretation. *Developmental Psychology, 26,* 683–697.

Maccoby, E. E., & Martin, J. A. (1983). Socialization in the context of the family: Parent-child interaction. In P. H. Mussen & E. M. Hetherington (Eds.), *Handbook of child psychology: Socialization, personality, and social development* (4th ed., pp. 1–101). New York: Wiley.

Maguire, M. (1999). Treating the dyad as the unit of analysis: A primer on three analytic approaches. *Journal of Marriage and the Family, 61,* 213–223.

Mangelsdorf, S. C., & Frosch, C. A. (2000). Temperament and attachment: One construct or two? In H. W. Reese (Ed.), *Advances in child development and behavior* (Vol. 27, pp. 181–220). San Diego, CA: Academic Press.

McHale, S. M., Crouter, A. C., & Tucker, C. J. (1999). Family context and gender role socialization in middle childhood: Comparing girls to boys and sisters to brothers. *Child Development, 70,* 990–1004.

Osofsky, J. D., & O'Connell, E. J. (1972). Parent-child interactions: Daughters' effects upon mothers' and fathers' behavior. *Developmental Psychology, 7,* 157–168.

Park, S., Belsky, J., Putnam, S., & Crnic, K. (1997). Infant emotionality, parenting, and 3-year inhibition: Exploring stability and lawful discontinuity in a male sample. *Developmental Psychology, 33,* 218–227.

Patterson, G. R. (1981). Mothers: The unacknowledged victims. *Monographs of the Society for Research in Child Development, 45.* Chicago: University of Chicago Press.

Reiss, D., Neiderhiser, J. M., Hetherington, E. M., & Plomin, R. (2000). *The relationship code: Deciphering genetic and social influences on adolescent development.* Cambridge, MA: Harvard University Press.

Rubin, K. H., Nelson, L. J., Hastings, P., & Asendorpf, J. (1999). The transaction between parents' perceptions of their children's shyness and their parenting styles. *International Journal of Behavioral Development, 23,* 937–958.

Russell, A., & Russell, G. (1992). Child effects in socialization research: Some conceptual and data analysis issues. *Social Development, 1,* 163–184.

Scarr, S., & McCartney, K. (1983). How people make their own environments: A theory of genotype à environment effects. *Child Development, 54,* 424–435.

Seifer, R., Sameroff, A. J., Barrett, L. C., & Krafchuk, E. (1994). Infant temperament measured by multiple observations and mother report. *Child Development, 65,* 1478–1490.

Steinberg, L., Darling, N., & Fletcher, A. C. (1995). Authoritative parenting and adolescent adjustment: An ecological journey. In P. Moen, G. H. Elder, Jr., & K. Luscher (Eds.), *Examining lives in context: Perspectives on the ecology of human development* (pp. 423–466). Washington, DC: American Psychological Association.

Steinberg, L., Lamborn, S. D., Darling, N., Mounts, N. S., & Dornbusch, S. M. (1994). Over-time changes in adjustment and competence among families from authoritative, authoritarian, indulgent, and neglectful families. *Child Development, 65,* 754–770.

Stevens-Long, J. (1973). The effect of behavioral context on some aspects of adult disciplinary practices and affect. *Child Development, 44,* 476–484.

Sulloway, F. J. (1997). *Born to rebel.* New York: Vintage Books.

Thomas, A., & Chess, S. (1977). *Temperament and development.* New York: Brunner/Mazel.

Thompson, L., & Walker, A. J. (1982). The dyad as the unit of analysis: Conceptual and methodological issues. *Journal of Marriage and the Family, 44,* 889–900.

Trivers, R. L. (1974). Parent-offspring conflict. *American Zoologist, 14,* 249–264.

van den Boom, D. C. (1994). The influence of temperament and mothering on attachment and exploration: An experimental manipulation of sensitive responsiveness among lower-class mothers with irritable infants. *Child Development, 65,* 1457–1477.

Vreeke, G. J. (2000). Nature, nurture and the future of the analysis of variance. *Human Development, 43,* 32–45.

Zelizer, V. A. (1994). *Pricing the priceless child: The changing social value of children.* Princeton, NJ: Princeton University Press.

Author Index

Laub, J. H., 123, *150*
Lauretti, A., 99, *107*
LaVoie, 195, *205*
Leaper, C., 196, *206*
Leavitt, L. A., 100, *105*
LeDoux, J. E., 58, 59, 76
Leerkes, E., 70, *75*, 79, 81, 82, 84, 87, 88,
    91, 92, 93, 95, 96, 99, 100, 103,
    110, 111, 113, 115, 153, 226,
    241, 243, 244, 247, 248, 249, 250
Leerkes, E. M., 58, 60, 63, 64, 65, 69, *75*,
    76, 96, *106*
LeFebvre, L., 202, *206*
Lemerise, E. A., 194, 195, *204*, 229, *230*
Lemery, K. S., 12, *22*, 59, *76*
Lerner, J. V., 249, *253*
Lerner, R. M., 239, 242, 243, 249, *252, 253*
Lesh, K. P., 19, *21*
Lester, B., 92, 93, 94, 100, *106*
Levander, S., 134, *146*
Leve, L., 39, *47*
Lewis, C., 124, 125, 142, 143, *149*
Li, F., 122, *147*
Lichtenstein, E., 171, *179*
Lichtenstein, P., 11, 12, 12, 14, *23, 24*
Lickliter, R., 29, 30, 33, 34, *35*
Lieberman, M. A., 158, *161*
Linnoila, M., 19, *21*
Litman, C., 67, *75*
Loeber, R., 122, *149*
Loehlin, C. C., 29, 30, *36*
Loehlin, J. C., 5, *23*, 41, *47*
Long, J., 19, *21*
Long, N., 203, *205*
Lorenz, F. O., 158, *160*
Lorenz, J., 19, *21*
Lower, R. J., 60, 69, 78, 96, *108*
Lustig, J., 203, *207*
Lytton, H., 9, 19, *21, 23*, 42, 43, 45, *47*,
    100, *104*, 111, 112, *118*, 144,
    146, 149, 196, *206*, 239, 241,
    243, 251, *252, 253*

M

Maarala, M., 18, *25*
Maccoby, E. E., 28, 29, 31, *35*, 67, *76*, 95,
    100, *104*, 144, *149*, 158, *161*,
    193, 194, 196, 198, 199, 201,
    204, 205, 206, 209, 210, 213,
    216, 221, 223, 224, 225, 226,

    227, *228*, 229, 230, *230*, 231,
    235, 236, 241, 242, 243, 244,
    248, 249, 250, 251, *253*
MacDermid, S. M., 122, *147*
MacKinnon, C. E., 234, *237*
Madden, P. A., 51, *54*
Magnus, P., 39, 41, *46, 48*
Maguire, M., 249, *253*
Mandleco, B., 232, *237*
Mangelsdorf, S., 63, 67, *77*
Mangelsdorf, S. C., 247, *253*
Markon, K., 231, 232, 235, *237*
Martin, A., 203, *207*
Martin, C. L., 230, *230*
Martin, J. A., 144, *149*, 251, *253*
Martin, N. G., 51, *54*
Martin, R. P., 165, *169*
Martin, S. E., 60, *77*
Martinetti, M. G., 95, *107*
Martinez, C. R., Jr., 176, *179*, 203, *206*
Martinez-Fuentes, M. T., 94, *104*
Maughan, B., 43, *47*
McCall, R., 79, *88*
McCartney, K., 29, 32, *35, 36*, 172, *179*,
    242, 245, 249, *254*
McClearn, G. E., 5, 7, 11, 12, 14, 19, *23, 24*
McConnell, M., 99, *107*
McCord, J., 123, *149*
McCoy, J. K., 217, *221*, 235, 236
McGrath, M., 100, *106*
McGue, M., 7, *21*
McGuire, S., 31, *36*, 235, *237*
McHale, J., 70, *75*, 98, 99, 101, *107, 108*
McHale, J. P., 96, 97, 101, 103, *104, 107*,
    112, 211, 242, 244, 247, 248,
    250, 251
McHale, S. M., 112, 122, *147*, 196, 197,
    206, 210, 212, 215, 216, *216f*,
    218, *222*, 235, *237*, 241, 242,
    244, 245, 248, *253*
McLoyd. V. C., 158, *161*
McMahon, R., 122, *147*
McMahon, R. J., 164, *169*, 171, 173, *178*,
    179, 182, *187*
McNally, S., 144, *149*
Melton, G. B., 203, *205*
Menaghan, E. G., 158, 159, *160, 161*, 212,
    244, 246, 247
Metzler, C. W., 123, *149*
Meyer, J., 43, *47*
Michel, M. K., 112, *118*

Subject Index

Family research
  critical to behavioral genetics, 15–16
  developmental methodologies in,
      30–32, 34–35, 72–74,
      249–251
  transactional models for, 71–74, 71*f,*
      112–117, 251
  see also research designs, child and fam-
      ily
Family systems, 145, 176
  child effects on, 98–103, 189–254
  gender roles in, 210–215, 244
  household chores in, 211–213, 212*f,*
      213*f*
  process in, 15–16, 239–254
  siblings in, 210–212, 211*f,* 212*f,* 214,
      214*f,* 234–235
  social context of, 157–160, 191–192
Father-child relationships
  antisocial behavior and, 15, 54
  emotional warmth and, 16, 122, 197
  household chores and, 213, 213*f*
  infants in, 58, 61*f,* 66, 68–71, 73–74,
      102, 103, 199
  middle childhood aggression and, 232,
      233
  toughening sons through, 102, 200–201
Fathers, 60, 61*f,* 99
  child's gender and, 197–201, 198*f,*
      210–215, 216–217, 216*f*
  emotional well-being of, and infant irri-
      tability, 68–70, 101, 102
  leisure interests of, and firstborn child,
      215, 215*f*
  monitoring by, 127, 232, 233
  siblings and, 210, 211*f,* 214, 214*f*
Fear, 58–59, 92, 100
  gender differences and, 67, 197
FinnTwin16 data, 41
Foster care, delinquency intervention and,
      176
Frustration
  brain physiology and, 58–59
  maternal, and child behavior, 116–117
  preschooler, and parental scaffolding,
      112–114
  trials of, and developmental predic-
      tions, 115–116

G

G • E correlations. *See* gene • environment
      correlations
G × E interactions. *See* gene × environ-
      ment interactions
Gender, 156
  aggression and, 231–237
  child effects and, 199–202, 209, 244
  child personality by, 216–217, 216*f*
  child's, and family issues, xi–xii,
      67–68, 191–254
  differential treatment of, 100–101,
      196–200, 198*f,* 218, 219*f*
  roles in family systems, 83, 210–215,
      244
  sex-typical behavior by, 53, 200, 215,
      215*f,* 231–232
  socialization and, 196–197
Gene • environment correlations, 11–13,
      31, 32, 37–40, 94, 192
  definitions, 11, 29
  G × E interactions and, 17, 19
  passive, 12, 16, 17
Gene × environment interactions, 17–19,
      31, 40–42, 50–54, 74, 191, 242
  adolescence and, 51–52
  adoption studies and, 44–45, 50
  definitions, 17, 29, 41
  G • E correlations and, 17, 19
  molecular genetics and, 32, 51
Genes
  behavioral differences due to, 3–16, 27,
      241, ix
  environment and, 43–44, 98 (*see also*
      gene • environment correla-
      tions; gene × environment in-
      teractions)
  primacy of, and isolation assumption,
      37, 45
  sex, of child, 201–202
Genetic cascade, 14
  definition, 4
  equal environments assumption in, 4–5,
      6, 30, 38–40
Genetics. *see* behavioral genetics; molecu-
      lar genetics

H

Household chores, family systems and,
      211–213, 212*f,* 213*f*

I

Date D